WORLD
RUGS & CARPETS

WORLD RUGS & CARPETS

Edited by DAVID BLACK

COUNTRY LIFE
BOOKS

Published by Country Life Books, an imprint of Newnes Books,
a division of The Hamlyn Publishing Group Limited,
84–88 The Centre, Feltham, Middlesex, England
and distributed for them by
Hamlyn Distribution Services Limited,
Sanders Lodge Estate, Rushden, Northants, England

ISBN 0 600 35896 8

**Conceived, designed and produced by
Robert Adkinson Limited, London**

Editorial Director Clare Howell
Editor Lucy Trench
Art Director Christine Simmonds
Designer Ken Williamson
Illustrator Gerald Larn
Cartographer Rosalind Caldecott

Phototypesetting by
Tradespools, Frome, Somerset

Colour and black-and-white illustration
origination by La Cromolito, Milan

Printed and bound in Italy by New Interlitho, S.p.A.

Key to maps

★ Towns or villages associated with carpet production

Contents

*A nomad weaving a kilim in a
clearing among Roman
sarcophagi in Southern
Turkey.*

Foreword

I was lucky enough to live in Persia (or Iran as it is now officially called) for a number of years before the troubled events of 1978–79 which led to the overthrow of the Shah. It was there that my own interest in carpets was first stimulated. I became a modest collector and have since derived enormous pleasure from my carpets and kilims, whose lively colours and beautiful designs brighten even the dullest of winter days; they also revive happy memories of the circumstances in which I bought them – often after hard bargaining – some from a favourite dealer in Teheran (who now flourishes in London's West End), some from nomads and villagers in remote corners of the country or in the crowded covered bazaars of Meshed, Isfahan, and Shiraz.

Since then I have appreciated as never before the magnificent carpets displayed in museums in England and abroad, as well as in a number of splendid exhibitions staged in this country and North America in recent years. These, together with the great increase in travel to the Middle East, Central Asia, and China have, I believe, created a wide public interest in hand-woven carpets.

A great many books have, over the years, been published about rugs and carpets. As far as I am aware none has the scope of this new volume. As the title suggests, it ranges worldwide – from Turkey, across Persia and Central Asia to China, then to Europe and Morocco, and finally to North America with its domestic and Navajo weaving. The book provides, together with its excellent illustrations, a wealth of information on carpet production, design, history, purchase, and care.

As education, industrialization, mechanization, and higher standards of living become more universal I fear for the survival of the traditional skills and patience required for carpet weaving. The Industrial Revolution destroyed our own handicrafts. Those of the Middle East are fast disappearing; so, too, the nomadic way of life. Soon carpet weaving may only be carried on in workshops and factories run by the State, as in the Soviet Union today. Gone forever then will be the individualism and spontaneity that characterizes yesterday's and many of today's rugs.

This volume is a worthy testimonial for the great art of carpet weaving that has brought beauty into the homes of both rich and poor during the past two millennia.

DENIS WRIGHT

Sir Denis Wright served as a diplomat in Turkey as well as Iran, where he was British Ambassador from 1963 to 1971.

8

Introduction

First seen adorning the thrones of virgins and the tables of princes, later trodden to rags and cut up for upholstery, now hung on walls and revered as works of art, the carpet has suffered many changes of fortune in the West. Now it is enjoying great popularity: it takes pride of place in many houses, carpet prices have soared, and exhibitions and conferences are held all over the world.

The first serious studies on carpets appeared early in this century and since then this small trickle of work has gathered force and become a veritable river. As the subject becomes more vast and our knowledge more diverse a clear introduction to carpets becomes essential. This book is intended to be both an authoritative guide to the layman and a helpful companion to the specialist. Its principal aim is to illustrate the vast range of carpets produced throughout the world, relating them through design and structure to their place of origin. This is done in the form of a Gazetteer with the aid of detailed maps.

Before embarking on the Gazetteer, however, it is necessary to establish a background to a study of carpets, hence the two introductory sections of the book – 'Carpet Production and Design' and the 'History of Carpets'.

The form and appearance of carpets is subject not only to their place of origin but also to the way in which they were made. This may be in a nomad camp on a makeshift loom, or in a highly organized commercial workshop; it may involve a pile or flat weaving technique, or a combination of various methods. The dyes too are important, for they often determine the quality of the carpet and may also provide valuable evidence of its age.

There are two aspects of oriental carpets that are often particularly mystifying to Western observers: the design and the symbolism. All over the orient carpets are composed of designs and motifs whose roots may lie deep in the past. In analyzing and identifying carpets it is necessary to recognize these, however distant they may be from their original prototypes. Although much debate surrounds the symbolism of carpets, it is clear that some of the great carpets of the past carry carefully formulated religious and philosophical messages; in less sophisticated weavings it is unwise to seek such complex symbolism, but it does seem that many motifs have totemic, tribal, or religious significance.

The oldest surviving carpet, the celebrated Pazyryk carpet, is over two thousand years old and its quality suggests that carpet weaving was already a highly developed art. The subsequent development of carpets is obscure and most of the earliest pieces date only from the fourteenth century. Major developments in design and technique then took place in the Middle East between the fourteenth and seventeenth centuries and later carpets reproduce, even today, the designs of earlier periods, albeit in a highly stylized form.

The main part of the book consists then of the Gazetteer, which is illustrated mainly with nineteenth and early twentieth-century carpets, since these are most accessible to today's buyer yet have usually escaped the ravages of poor chemical dyes. The illustrations have been chosen with particular care, not only to show the characteristics of the region, but also as prime examples of their kind. Each carpet-producing area of the orient is examined in detail – Turkey, the Caucasus, Persia, East Turkestan, Tibet, China, and India – and where possible the major centres of production are identified. But carpet production is not confined to the orient: in Europe, carpets were initially based on Eastern models but later displayed their own forms and styles; in America, the domestic weavings have a delightfully individual character and the Navajo work is justly famous for its dynamic, abstract designs.

In any discussion of oriental carpets certain problems arise, especially as research, though developing rapidly, has not yet been able to resolve many important questions. The first is that of attribution. Traditionally many carpets have been given certain names which relate them to a particular area or town. While many of these names remain useful as a means of identifying types of design, we can no longer claim with confidence that they all describe accurately the provenance of the carpet. For instance Turkoman carpets were formerly known as 'Bokhara', after the town from which they were exported to the West, but now, after intensive research into the designs and structure of these weavings, it is possible to assign them to specific tribes.

The second major problem is that of dating, and while many people would like to know the precise age of their carpets it is rarely possible to establish this. The scientific methods of dating textiles have many limitations and stylistic yardsticks are difficult to establish, since many areas continue to weave old, even archaic, designs long after they have fallen from use elsewhere. Carpet experts tend to be somewhat subjective in their approach to dating and may differ considerably in their opinion.

However fascinating the history and social background of carpets may be, and however tantalizing the questions posed by modern research, the heart of the subject lies in the beauty of the carpets themselves. We hope that this book will communicate our delight in carpets and our belief that they fully deserve to be seen as works of art – folk art, ethnographic art, decorative art, or abstract art.

A carpet woven in Bidjar, Persia around 1860. The brilliant madder red of the ground is enhanced by the tightly woven, dense pile. 3.45m × 2.13m, 11'4" × 7'.

Carpet Manufacture

a. Left *A camp in Afghanistan. Weaving provides many essential household goods for these nomads – bedding, storage bags, and carpets. It is believed that carpet weaving first developed among the Central Asian pastoral tribes.*

Even to an unpractised eye it is clear that oriental carpets vary greatly not only in design but also in feeling. Some are refined, balanced, and sophisticated; others are irregular, powerful, and even 'primitive'. Yet they are all made in the same fashion and sometimes in the same country, so how can this variety be explained? The reason lies in the circumstances in which the carpets are made. In the orient carpets are an integral part of daily life at every level of society, as well as being important trading items in both the domestic and export markets. The wide social and economic role that they play means that they are produced in very different circumstances, and in fact four distinct carpet-making environments can be identified: the tribal milieu, the village industry, the commercial workshops, and – somewhat outside this mainstream – the court ateliers. In each of these the final purpose of the carpet, the methods of working, the materials, and the designs all differ. A knowledge, therefore, of carpet manufacture is an essential key to understanding carpets.

The black tents of the nomads are still to be seen in the grasslands and deserts of Turkey, Persia, and Central Asia, and it is probably among these pastoral tribes that carpet making first developed over two thousand years ago. For such tent dwellers weaving is an essential skill and provides many of their domestic needs. They use their own wool, which is often of the highest quality, and reserve cotton and silk, obtainable only through trade, for special details. In the past the yarn was coloured with those vegetable dyes that were available in the locality, though indigo was bought in a prepared form, but these have now been superseded by chemical dyes. The weaving takes place on a simple horizontal loom which can be easily dismantled and transported.

Although tribal weavers do sell some surplus goods for cash, this is not their prime object and the demands of the market exert little influence over their work. Instead, in these slowly changing communities, both the form and the pattern of the textiles are dictated by tradition. A wide variety of woven articles is made – rectangular carpets which fit the tents to provide protection against the stony ground, large and small storage bags to hold household goods or food, and decorative hangings for tents and animals. Sometimes the shape of these weavings will be askew if the beams of the loom are crooked or set up badly in the encampment.

With no cartoon, or pattern, to follow the weavers work from memory, combining in geometric repeating designs the well-known motifs handed down from generation to generation. Many of these are of great antiquity and have particular significance to the weaver or tribe, even though the precise meaning of the symbolism may be lost. The skill in such weaving should not be underestimated, for although each motif may be simple, it is not easy to remember and plot a design that develops satisfactorily as the carpet progresses. The best tribal carpets, woven with an unerring sense of colour, pattern, and design, are a considerable artistic achievement.

It is tragic that this great tradition has almost come to an end. Owing to the social and political pressures of the twentieth century, the purity of tribal weaving has now been debased by commercial constraints, changing life-styles, and poor chemical dyes.

As nomadic people settle in villages – a process that has been going on for hundreds of years and continues today – they continue to weave in the tribal manner. But eventually weaving becomes less of an environmental necessity and more a means of earning an additional income. So, in effect, a village or cottage industry develops, a form of carpet production that has a long history and is perfectly exemplified by nineteenth-century Caucasian weaving. The materials remain the same as those of tribal weavers, and the carpets are still restricted in size by the simple loom and the space available for weaving, so they rarely exceed $2\frac{1}{2}$ metres (8 feet) in width. Other domestic weavings such as bags are not needed in the market place and will only be made for use at home.

No longer bound by tribal convention the weavers become more adventurous and inventive, seeking to please buyers who are looking for new designs. Inspiration for these is found in other carpets, which may have been woven in distant cities, and other textiles, possibly even European imports. Sometimes the weaver will buy a rough pattern for a corner of the carpet, or she will combine elements from a number of sources. In either case, she will have to interpret and carry through the design and this departure from the familiar brings many problems. She may miscalculate the repeat of the border pattern and have to make a clumsy adjustment at the corners, or limited by her coarse knotting and lack of cartoon, she may be unable to reproduce the finely graduated curves of the model so her interpretation will have a geometric, perhaps uneven, quality. These 'faults' increase rather than lessen the charm of the carpet, giving it a sense of vitality lacking in more perfect renderings.

Some village weavers obtain their own materials, and design and market their own products. Others become involved in a highly organized commercial operation under the control of a local merchant. He will provide them with looms and materials, requiring them to work to his designs

a. Above *A nineteenth-century Caucasian prayer rug. The irregular, angular forms of this carpet show that it was woven without a cartoon. The weaver has selected a wide range of motifs and arranged them in a lively manner.*

and standards. Here village weaving overlaps with workshop production, and indeed some workshops employ weavers both on the premises and in their own home.

In the workshop system the weavers no longer use their ingenuity in developing their own designs. Instead, they become more like technicians as they execute the designs of an artist, following a full-scale squared and coloured pattern which enables them to reproduce fine curves and complex designs in a wide range of colours. These designs may be eclectic in inspiration and commercial in nature, often aimed at the foreign market. The carpets may be very

a. Left *Carpet weaving on an upright loom. The pattern is written out in a code known as a 'talim'. This is the usual practice in India, but in other countries the pattern is transferred, in the form of coloured squares, to a sheet of paper or cartoon.*

large as the upright workshop looms can be enormously wide and impose no limits on the length of the carpets. The materials also become more varied as both cotton and silk are readily available. Cotton may be seen in the warp and weft because it is cheap and strong, and silk is used in the more expensive carpets for its fineness and strength which allows very close knotting. The success of carpets woven in such workshops depends less on the skill of the weaver, though that may be considerable, than on that of the designer. The carpets no longer have the direct appeal of folk art, which derives from the intense personal involvement of their creator, and they should be judged instead by the standards of factory-produced decorative objects, and as such may be excellent.

Commercial workshops really only developed on a large scale in the late nineteenth century, but a similar system of production had been seen from the sixteenth century in the court ateliers of the Ottoman, Safavid, and Mughal rulers. These princes were all of pastoral descent and remained attached to the traditions of their ancestors, so carpets were central to the decoration of their tents and palaces. Court artists, who also worked in other media and transferred

motifs from one to another, conceived the sophisticated and complex designs, which again were woven from a cartoon. These carpets used the richest materials, including silk and gleaming metal thread, and an extensive range of colours.

The splendour of these court carpets has somewhat unbalanced our response to oriental carpets. Judging them by Western aesthetic and art-historical standards we have tended to see them as the peak of the carpet-making tradition, just as Renaissance painting may be considered the apogee of the Western painting tradition. But in fact oriental carpets do not fit into such a linear pattern, and influences pass in all directions – the most exquisite products of the court developing out of the work of nomads and, in reverse, court designs influencing village and workshop weavers.

A knowledge of the circumstances in which carpets are made is helpful in judging individual carpets and developing our own taste, whether it is for the refined products of a workshop or the more direct village and tribal weavings. Each have their own merits, none are inherently inferior or superior to others, and any one can be a masterpiece.

Materials and Weaving Techniques

A handwoven carpet is a unique object. To fully appreciate its individuality and craftsmanship it is important to gain an understanding of the basic principles of carpet weaving, which in itself can add a new intimacy to our love of carpets.

Despite the wide distribution of carpets throughout the world, the weaving techniques involved are remarkably consistent. In some areas, particularly in the East, the same techniques are used to make other handwoven textiles, such as storage bags and animal trappings which are essential household items in a nomadic life. These, and carpets, are primarily practical objects which require a substantial fabric, resistant to wear both from handling and surface abrasion; at the same time they are highly decorative and on occasion quite sumptuous.

Within the limitation of relatively few and simple techniques are created an endless variety of designs and patterns. But certain restrictions may be imposed by different techniques, for instance it is easier for a weaver to create curvilinear designs using a fine pile weave than a slit-tapestry technique which lends itself to more geometric patterns.

Materials

The yarns used in carpet making vary both in type and quality. They include the spun threads of wool (usually sheep, goat, or camel), silk, cotton, linen, hemp, and jute; of these, the most important and widely used is wool in its various forms. The prevalence of wool is partly due to its strength, versatility, and ability to retain warmth. For many nomadic weavers it is also the cheapest and most readily available material. Many carpets are made entirely of wool, or it may be used only for the pile.

When using wool the weaver must first select and sort the fleece, parts of which vary in length and quality producing, when spun, different types of yarn. Handfuls of fleece are then either carded or combed to prepare the fibre for spinning. Carded wool is pulled by hand between two rectangular wooden implements, set with rows of metal teeth, called wool cards. By holding one in each hand, placing a small amount of wool on one card and dragging the other over it several times, the wool is cleaned and untangled to form slivers, or long rolls of wool, ready for spinning. The fibres lie in different directions, so yarn spun from carded wool is softer and more 'hairy' than that spun from combed wool. It is more often used for making warmth-retaining textiles such as clothing and blankets. Combed wool results in the fibres lying parallel to each other and, when spun, produces a yarn that is hard, smooth, lustrous, and strong. These qualities make it a perfect yarn for both pile and flat-woven carpets.

The art of spinning lies in knowing the correct amount of fibre to release from the roll of prepared wool, and the degree of spin required from the spindle to achieve a yarn of uniform thickness and twist. Anyone who has practised spinning, whether from a drop spindle or a wheel, knows that is easy to produce a slubbed yarn but very difficult to get fibre and motion working to one rhythm to make a smooth thread. Once mastered it can be done automatically, without thinking, and is indeed done by women while engaged in other activities such as tending sheep or walking along the road (see 14a and b).

Silk is the next most important yarn in carpet making. It is secreted as a viscous fluid by two glands in the larva of the caterpillar, *Bombyx mori*, commonly known as the silk worm. The continuous filament is processed and spun to form a usable thread. The smooth uninterrupted surface of the fibre enables silk to reflect light; in contrast, wool absorbs light and appears dull because microscopically it is made up of tiny, overlapping scales. Silk is very strong in relation to its thickness and is used for exceptionally fine, high quality carpets. In such carpets, for example seventeenth-century Persian silk kilims and 'Polonaise' carpets, metal thread may also be found. This is made by winding a flat strip of gold or silver around a silk core to form a thread. Being less flexible, the metal thread is often woven over and under groups of warps, rather than individual ones, or it is woven only though the top layer of a depressed weave, so forming a flat-woven area within a pile rug.

The other yarn used in carpets is cotton, a cellulose fibre obtained from the seed hair of plants of the *Gossypium* genus. Cotton is most often used for the warp and weft, though some Indian carpets have a pile entirely of cotton. In other carpets it is used sparingly in the pile to highlight details, providing a strong contrast which is unobtainable with the duller whites of silk and wool. Turkoman weavers used the brilliant white of cotton with great skill, allowing tiny details to sparkle against the woollen pile.

The loom

The loom is essentially a frame for holding, under tension, the warp threads upon which the whole fabric is woven. It may be made simply of two horizontal wooden bars, lying parallel to each other. The bars are long enough, and sufficiently far apart, for the finished size of the carpet. Nomadic tribes use this sort of horizontal loom (see 15a) because it can be easily dismantled and the weaving rolled up when moving from camp to camp. When it is set up the bars are lodged apart by stakes driven into the ground. It is common for the warp to lie very close to the ground and for the weaver, or weavers, to sit on top of the weaving as it grows along the length of the warp.

Another type of loom (see 12a) is vertical, or upright, one beam being raised on two side supports. Where a permanent workshop is established, as in a village or town, the vertical loom is the most practical as its increased weight and rigidity enables the weavers to make carpets of almost unlimited size. The weaver sits in front of the loom and, while working, either raises the seating platform or winds the finished part of the carpet onto the lower beam, so releasing fresh warp from the upper. In this way very long carpets, or carpets in series, can be woven on one warp.

On both types of loom the alternate warp threads are connected by loops of yarn to a third bar which is positioned in front of the warp. This facilitates the insertion of the weft and enables the weaving to proceed more easily. When this bar is raised, as with a horizontal loom, or the loops of yarn pulled, on the vertical loom, these

a. Above *A group of women spinning in Turkey.*

b. Left *The wool is lightly twisted, or roved, before being drawn onto the spindle. Malatya, Turkey.*

a. Above left *A nomad summer camp in the Engizek Mountains, Turkey. The women are weaving a bag on a rough but sturdy horizontal loom.*

b. Above right *On this vertical loom the warp is separated by loops of yarn attached to alternate warps. The pattern of the kilim is created by inserting the different colours of weft in separate blocks.*

alternate warps lie on a different plane and a space is created between the warps through which the weft can pass (see 15b). Other devices can also be added to make the weaving process more accurate. Two tools are essential – a heavy metal comb for beating down the rows of weft and, in the case of pile carpets, a sharp, curved knife or scissors for trimming the pile.

Pile weaves

Most carpets are woven with a pile, provided by the 'knots'. In such carpets, there is a foundation consisting of two sets of threads – the warp and the weft. The weft interlaces with the warp at right angles, passing over and under adjacent warp threads in a pattern that alternates in each successive row of weft. This foundation forms a fabric that is in itself cohesive, based on the simple pattern of a 'plain weave'. In addition, there are inserted extra rows of threads in the form of knots, which are known as the pile. The pile and the foundation weave are interdependent: the pile provides warmth and takes the wear; the foundation weave, protected and often obscured by the pile, holds the fabric together. As each knot can be of a different colour the pile also carries the pattern of the carpet, so the foundation acts as the 'paper' on which the design is 'drawn' or knotted; the difference being that the foundation and pile are built up together, and one is not applied on top of the other.

CARPET PRODUCTION AND DESIGN

The foundation

Although the rows of knots are introduced into the weaving at the same time as the weft, it is convenient to consider the foundation separately. The warp has to be extremely strong, with little stretch, so that the tension can be maintained throughout the weaving process, which might take several months or even years. It usually consists of two or three strands of undyed natural yarn plied together.

The preparation of the warp is time consuming and difficult. The yarn is attached at one end of the lower beam of the loom. It is then taken up and over the upper beam and back to the lower beam, in a continuous motion, until a sufficiently wide warp has been made. It must be correctly and evenly spaced, as well as under constant and even tension. Once started the warping must continue until finished, otherwise the rhythm and tension may be lost, which will result in distortions in the final cloth.

The thickness and spacing of the warp threads on the loom is the chief factor in determining the fineness of the weave. The threads can lie so close together that they will not stay all on one level, but fall into two layers once weaving starts. This can be seen at its most extreme in certain types of seventeenth-century Persian 'Vase' carpets and is often called the 'vase-carpet technique' (see 17a). Three rows of weft are placed after each row of knots. The first and last rows are pulled tight and lie practically straight, but the middle one is sinuous. This forces the warp to lie in two layers which are visible from the back of the rug, the depression of alternate warps giving it a ridged appearance. In some cases, one layer can completely conceal the other. It is important to observe this when taking a knot count, for the number of warps may be thought to be half the actual number.

The weft is generally of the same material as the warp, but it is more loosely spun and may be dyed. The type and thickness of the yarn used for both knots and weft, also the way in which they are arranged and beaten down, determines the fineness of the weave in the vertical direction.

The weaving is started by entering a number of rows of weft to set the spacing of the warp. When this is established, the first row of knots will be tied. This is followed by more weft – one, two, three 'shoots', or rows – to keep the knots in place. This pattern of knots followed by wefts continues until the carpet is completed. In a pile weave the weft is generally continuous from selvedge to selvedge, though it may be broken into overlapping lengths if a team of weavers are working side by side. As the carpet is woven the outermost warps are often grouped together to make a thicker cord, giving the carpet a firm edge.

Once the knots are introduced the warp may spread to accommodate them; so great care is taken in placing the subsequent rows of weft, which have to pull the warp together and keep the spacing even, as well as holding the knots in place and maintaining a straight edge at the selvedge. The insertion of the weft is the most difficult part of the process and occasionally, as in the Hereke workshops in Turkey, is done by an older, more experienced weaver if the carpet is exceptionally fine.

After the carpet is cut from the loom the warps form fringes which can be finished off in a variety of ways that prevent the weave from unravelling, as well as being decorative. Looping, braiding, twisting, and knotting, singly or in groups, are all methods used in both flat and pile weaves. Sometimes knotted carpets are finished with a band of plain weave at each end before the fringe. This may be adorned with stripes or brocaded patterns, greatly adding to the interest of the carpet, but unfortunately it is often totally worn away and the ends are reduced to the first and last row of knots.

The pile

The yarn which makes up the pile is more loosely spun than the warp, therefore more bulky, and may be made up of two or more strands. The pile is sometimes extremely short, almost showing the base of the knots, and sometimes quite long and lush. When inserting the knots, it is not necessary to tie them in strict order in the row. It is quicker instead, to tie all those of one colour before moving on to the next. The placing of each colour is extremely skilful, especially when the design is woven from memory rather than following a drawing or cartoon. The pile is formed from various types of knot, of which the 'symmetrical' and 'asymmetrical' are the most common.

Symmetrical knot

This is found in both antique and modern rugs from Turkey, the Caucasus, and Turkestan. It is also used in those Persian carpets made by tribes of Turkish or Kurdish descent, and it is this Turkish connection that gave it its former name, the 'Turkish' or 'Ghiordes' knot. English and other European carpets also employ this knot, and it is considered by many to be the easiest one to work. As seen from the right side of the rug, the pile yarn lies flat across each pair of warps, the cut ends passing behind one warp each to emerge between the pair, below the horizontal part of the thread (see 17b). Very occasionally the warp pairs are broken up in the areas where a smoother outline is required for the design.

Asymmetrical knot

This is also known as the 'Persian' or 'Senneh' knot and is found in Persia, India, Turkestan, Turkey, Egypt, and China. From the back of the rug it may look identical to the symmetrical knot. However, in the front the yarn only lies across and encircles one warp of the pair, rather than both. The cut ends are separated by the other warp and therefore emerge to either side of the two warps, and not between them (see 17c). Depending on which warp is encircled, the knot is described as being open to the left or the right. Carpets woven with the asymmetrical knot are often finer, containing more detail in the design, and the weave is tighter, resulting in a more hard-wearing fabric.

Jufti knot

Both symmetrical and asymmetrical knots can be tied around more than two warp threads (see 17d). Usually four are employed which makes the weaving faster, but the design becomes coarser and the fabric less strong.

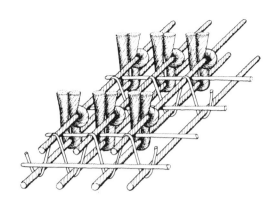

a. Left *The vase-carpet technique. Three shoots of weft lie between each row of knots, and when the outer ones are pulled tight the warp is forced to lie on two planes.*

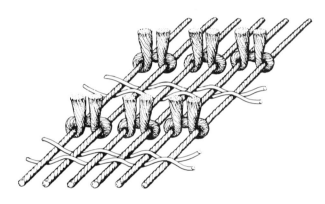

b. Left *The symmetrical knot, used principally in Turkey, the Caucasus, and Turkestan. The cut ends of the knot emerge in the middle of the two warps around which it has been tied.*

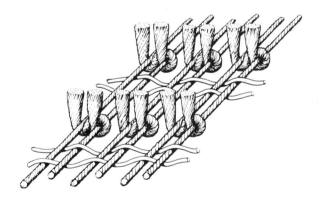

c. Left *The asymmetrical or Persian knot. This encircles only one of the warps, and depending on which is encircled, is described as being open to the left or the right. A finer weave can be achieved with this knot.*

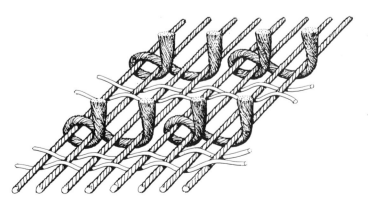

d. Left *The jufti knot. Both asymmetrical or symmetrical knots can be tied around more than two warps. This knot is quicker to work but makes a less strong fabric, so it is often considered to be an undesirable economy measure.*

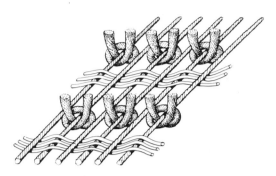

a. Left *The single-warp knot is found in Spanish carpets and is suitable for very fine designs. The knot is tied around one warp only, and this alternates from row to row.*

b. Left *The Tibetan knot, in which the yarn is passed around a gauge rod during the weaving. The yarn is later cut to form the knots.*

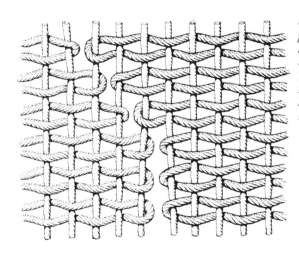

c. Left *In slit tapestry the pattern is created by the weft alone, and where the two colours join a slit is formed. The outlines of the colours are stepped, to keep the slits short and thereby maintain the strength of the weaving.*

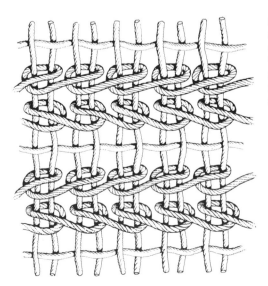

d. Left *Soumak may also be referred to as weft-wrapping or weft-float brocading. The weft is wrapped over and under two or four warps, making a raised and slightly oblique 'stitch'.*

Single-wrap knot

This is also known as the 'Spanish' knot and is found in most Spanish carpets, but is hardly used elsewhere. It is tied, or rather wrapped, around single, alternate warps (see 18a). The bare warp in the first row being wrapped in the second and so on. The yarn completely encircles the warp, the cut ends crossing at the back to emerge on the front at either side. It is easily distinguished from other types of knot.

Tibetan knot

The technique of knotting a Tibetan carpet is quite different and relies on the use of a gauge rod, the width of which determines the length of the pile. This is held in front of the warp and the yarn is passed from left to right, under and over two, or even three, warps at a time. The thread is brought back under two warps and looped around the rod, before proceeding forward again (see 18b). When the row is finished, the loops are cut with a knife to produce the tufts of pile. This may be trimmed more evenly once the whole carpet is complete. Single knots may also be included in the construction depending on the needs of the design.

Flat weaves

In flat-woven carpets the warp and weft alone make up the weave, without the addition of rows of knots. The surface is therefore flat. Generally speaking, in flat weaves the weft yarn is finer and more loosely spun than the warp, allowing the weft rows to be packed down close together. In this case the weft, entirely covering the warp, provides the pattern and the fabric is described as 'weft-faced'. A less common variation, to be seen in some modern carpets, is where the warp conceals the weft so the fabric is 'warp-faced'. Flat weaves are quicker to make and are usually intended for more everyday use. Sometimes both flat and pile weaving will be found in the same carpet.

Slit tapestry

A carpet made in this technique is called a 'kilim' (Turkish) or a 'gelim' (Persian). Here, in the main body of the carpet, the weft does not pass as a continuous thread from selvedge to selvedge. Instead the weft, and consequently the pattern, is built up in blocks of colour. A vertical gap, or slit, is formed in the fabric between the two warps where the boundary of the coloured areas runs parallel to the warp (see 18c). The slits are rarely more than 2½ centimetres (1 inch) long, otherwise the fabric would be rather vulnerable to wear since the slits are not sewn up on completion as in the making of European pictorial tapestry hangings. To keep the slits short, the boundary is moved to left or right, so creating the stepped and diagonal patterns characteristic of kilims. However, this boundary between the colours need not always result in a slit and there are various methods by which the yarns can be looped, interlocked, or dovetailed together over one or more shared warps.

Most kilims are double-sided and the ends of the threads are concealed. Occasionally yarn from one area, instead of being finished off, is carried up and over a short distance to the next section requiring that colour. The resulting surface thread, characteristic of some Anatolian and Kurdish kilims, is the only means of telling the front from the back.

Weft-wrapping or soumak

The term 'soumak' describes a flat-weave technique and not, as is sometimes assumed, a group of weavings from a geographical location. It can be referred to as 'weft-float brocading'. Soumak may constitute the entire fabric of a carpet, or be used to form decorative bands or individual motifs, adding interest and texture to kilims and the ends of pile carpets.

The weft is passed over two or four warps, then back under one or two before travelling forward again (see 18d). The result is a slightly raised oblique 'stitch', rows of which produce a distinctive pattern. The 'stitch' may slope up or down, and lines of opposite slope in alternate rows can resemble lines of embroidered chain stitch. When soumak constitutes the whole fabric it is necessary to weave in at frequent intervals a thinner foundation weft, which is then hidden by the surface weft. This maintains the strength of the fabric and prevents it from becoming too loose.

Analysis of carpet structure

The analysis of carpet weaves has become increasingly valuable to carpet studies. It takes us into the heart of the carpet, further than just visual appreciation, making us more aware of both the people and the process involved in its creation. A carpet is a product, the manufacture of which is influenced by a change in circumstances, either economic or social, by the availability of materials and dyes, and by contacts that might alter a traditional pattern or way of working. Data on known types of rugs will help to place them in a more exact social, geographical, and historical context, and may throw light on the more obscure pieces, helping the almost impossible task of dating. Structural analysis has shown, for example, that the 'S' spin for weft threads is not generally seen outside

Egypt, some North African countries, and Spain. It has also shown that in Central Asia silk was only used by those tribes who had contact with Merv, the most important silk-producing region in the area; therefore tribes, such as the Yomut, who were outside this territory did not use silk and it will not appear in their weavings.

Rug analysis does not necessarily mean laboratory tests or the use of a microscope. Although these methods can provide additional information, they are unfortunately somewhat destructive as they require small samples taken from the object. Instead, the normal procedure relies on the simple recognition, both visual and tactile, of various features of the carpet. For this a magnifying glass is essential, especially in the case of very fine weaves. The

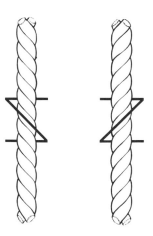

a. Left *Yarns are spun and plied in either an 'S' or a 'Z' direction.*

b. Below *Details of the front and back of a nineteenth-century Kazak rug, which is illustrated on page 113. Four shoots of cream weft can be seen between each row of knots.*

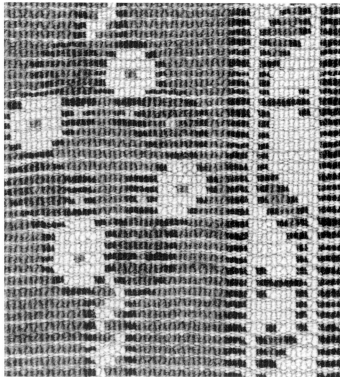

best type of hand-glass has a magnification of 7×, a built-in light, and a measurement gauge to make knot counting easier. It should be laid flat on the surface of the carpet.

To carry out a structural analysis, take the carpet and fold it gently over your fingers to separate the pile and expose the base of the knots. Note the following:

The type of knot and how many warps it uses. Be careful to check for depressed warps which may be hidden.

The knot count. This is done from the reverse side, both horizontally and vertically as it may differ. It is then multiplied for the number per square unit measure. This figure denotes the fineness of the weave and is likely to range from 186 to 6200 knots per square decimetre (12 to 400 per square inch). It is advisable to make several counts in different parts of the rug as the space taken up by the weft may vary.

The number of weft lines between each row of knots. This can vary in the same rug but it is usually constant.

Whether the wefts are of equal thickness and tension. This is easier to see in a damaged carpet as the transverse section of warp and knots can be seen.

The composition of the warp, weft, and pile yarns, usually cotton, silk, or wool.

The direction of twist of warp, weft, and pile yarns, together with the direction of spin and the number of individual strands which are plied together to make up each of these yarns. Each will be twisted in an 'S' or 'Z' direction (see 20a).

The dimensions; the finish of the selvedge; and the fringes.

The number of colours in the design and whether they are light or dark shades. Some rugs use an enormous palette, whereas in others there will be only three or four colours.

The subsequent information is written down in a form of shorthand which can be tabulated and mathematically coordinated into graphs if required. In this way certain characteristics within a group of weavings may be clearly observed.

A nineteenth-century Caucasian Kazak rug (see 20b, 113c) can be described as follows:

Warp: wool, undyed, pale brown and cream, Z3S.

Weft: wool, undyed, cream, 2S. 4 shoots.

Pile: wool, Sy. 8H × 8V = 992 knots per square decimetre, (64 knots per square inch).

Dimensions: (taken on the central axis), 2.20m × 1.60m, 7'2" × 5'3".

Warp ends: 1 – flat weave followed by plaited warp with no fringe; 2 – free warp, short, with possible loss of flat weave.

Selvedge: 6 outer warps, flat-woven in pairs, cream wool.

Colours: 9; bd (dark blue), bm (mid blue), gd (dark green), gl (light yellow/green), y (yellow), p (purple), r (red), w (white), bd (dark brown/black).

Abbreviations used for analysis

S	Direction of spin or twist, clockwise
Z	Direction of spin or twist, anti-clockwise
Z2S	The spin of the individual yarns is anti-clockwise; two of these strands are then twisted or plied together in a clockwise direction to form the yarn.
H	Horizontal
V	Vertical
As	Asymmetrical knot
Sy	Symmetrical knot
Wa	Warp
We	Weft
PW	Plain weave
L	Left
R	Right
WW	Weft wrapping
W	Wool
S	Silk
C	Cotton

Colours

B	Blue	Pk	Pink
Bl	Black	R	Red
Br	Brown	W	White
G	Green	Y	Yellow
I	Ivory	L	Light
O	Orange	M	Medium
P	Purple	D	Dark

Dyes

The beautiful colours of oriental rugs give great pleasure to carpet collectors, as they did to their creators for whom colour was often a rare and hard-won delight. But these colours are also the source of many myths and preconceptions, usually based on the belief that 'natural' dyes are better than 'synthetic' ones. Unfortunately there is no such simple distinction between natural and synthetic dyes. More usefully, dyes can be classified by the methods used to apply them, which affect their appearance not only when new but also after the vicissitudes of prolonged use. These different types of dye may also establish both the age and value of a carpet, which is why no serious collector can afford to ignore them.

Vat dyes

The only vat dye used in oriental carpets is indigo, traditionally obtained from the indigo plant but also made synthetically since about 1890. Indigo is an insoluble pigment which is dissolved in an alkaline vat by chemical reduction, for example through fermentation. The fibre is soaked in this vat and then exposed to the air, whereupon the dye turns blue by a process of re-oxidation and is fixed to the fibre. Indigo is stable to acids and alkalis, and does not fade or 'run'.

Mordant dyes

These are acidic compounds which are fixed on the fibre with a 'mordant', in which the yarn is first soaked. The mordant itself is a metal hydroxide, usually obtained from an iron salt or a solution of alum. The colours include the reds, usually obtained from madder (the roots of a plant), or cochineal and lac, the insect dyes. There are also a great number of yellows, including weld (which was sometimes grown for the purpose), wild plants, and many residues from food crops. Chemically, these are either flavonols, found for example in vine leaves or onion skins, or flavones found in millet husks or weld. The colours of these dyes are affected by the mordant; thus madder, which is red or orange-red with an aluminium mordant, is bluish violet with iron, and a variety of maroon and purple shades with mixtures.

Black is obtained with tannins, often derived from oak galls, and iron. This combination sensitizes the fibre to light and corrodes it, so even if the piece is only twenty years old, the black areas may be worn down.

Mordant dyes are easily decomposed by acids, sometimes even the weak acids present in wine or fruit juice. If the acid is neutralized before washing, perhaps by bicarbonate of soda, the colour will be restored; but washing alone will remove both mordant and dye. (Mild alkalis such as urine are less dangerous and can be washed away.) Light decomposes most mordant dyes, the flavonols reacting faster than the flavones, madder, and cochineal. Museums keep their carpets in very dim light to prevent this, and although their caution may be considered extreme, certainly no good carpet should be placed in direct sunlight.

a. Left *Dyeing in a home-based industry in Tunisia. The wool is being wrung out after dying.*

b. Right *In this early seventeenth-century Persian carpet fragment the red was dyed with lac, the yellow with weld, and the orange with a mixture of madder and weld. The blue is indigo.*
0.71m × 0.53m, 2'4" × 1'9". Victoria and Albert Museum, London

Direct dyes

These are usually synthetic and work only on protein fibres like wool and silk. As the name suggests, the dyer simply dips the fibre in the dyebath and washes out the excess dye. The notorious 'aniline' dyes are *basic direct dyes* which are applied to the fibre in an alkaline solution. The earliest of these was fuschine, a brilliant magenta dye invented in 1858. Violet, blue, and green dyes of similar chemical structure followed. All these dyes share the same fault of fading easily in light, or in the presence of alkalis such as washing soda and some soaps. Often the carpets, thought too bright in the West, have been deliberately faded giving a pile which is beige at the ends but still magenta at the roots. This is intended to give the carpet a more antique appearance, and may be brought about by 'chemical washing'. Aniline dyes do not 'bleed' into neighbouring fibres but the other main group of direct dyes, the *acidic dyes*, often do.

The earliest acidic dye was indigo-disulphic acid, known as 'extract of indigo' and obtained from indigo and concentrated sulphuric acid. It is first mentioned in France in 1740, but may have been known earlier. It gives a somewhat greenish blue, often used with yellow to make green, and both runs and fades readily, but despite this it was used by William Morris and his followers who disapproved of the aniline dyes. Whether regarded as natural or synthetic, it is inferior to true indigo.

Azo-dyes are the most important acid direct dyes, and are often confused with the early aniline dyes like fuchsine. Usually yellow, orange, red or violet red, they were introduced from 1875 to about 1890. Certain types, for

example Congo Red, can be used as direct dyes not only on protein fibres but also on cotton and linen. As a group, azo-dyes show good fastness to light and resistance to acids and alkalis. Some run, spoiling adjacent areas of the carpet, on treatment with detergents or even plain water; this tendency varies from dye to dye, and even from one dye batch to another, according to the skill of the dyer. Like the basic direct dyes they are often 'tip-faded', the ends of the pile being more or less bleached. Often the colours of the azo-dyes are purer, therefore harder, than madder and can be distinguished by eye; but one, amaranth, is remarkably similar to cochineal and is usually fast to washing, so it may well pass as a natural dye to most people.

The *chrome dyes* are a special group of azo-dyes which interact with a non-traditional mordant, chromic oxide, and are then firmly bound to the fibre, resisting acids, alkalis, and light. As they often have quieter colours than most azo-dyes, they may also appear to be natural. However, they were only introduced in this century and are unlikely to be associated with early designs. Used widely in India, China, and Afghanistan, they are not cheap (which is why the simple azo-dyes continue to be widely used) but they certainly are good.

Before the wide colour range of synthetic dyes became available, some colours were obtained by using mixtures of the few natural dyes. Thus, orange was usually made by mixing madder and a yellow dye in the same dye-bath, and adding alum-mordanted wool. Green required two separate operations, mordant dyeing with yellow and vat dyeing with indigo. As the flavonol yellows tend to be very fugitive, some greens fade over the years, leaving only the blue. Purple can be similarly obtained from madder and indigo, but this rarely occurs in oriental carpets. Subtle alterations of shade may result from minor constituents in the dye-bath, not easily detectable by the chemist.

Sometimes dye identification can tell us where and when a carpet was made. Madder and indigo, plus undyed light and dark wool, have been used for centuries in many areas so provide no clues; nor do yellows when they have been destroyed by light, faded to cream, and cannot be detected. But the insect dyes, indistiguishable to the eye, are useful in dating textiles. Kermes was used in Europe and lac, from India, in Egypt and Persia, until the Spaniards brought back cochineal from Central America. Being cheaper than the other insect dyes, it gradually took their place, and became dominant in Europe from about 1550, Egypt from about 1600, and Persia around 1800; though lac held out in India into this century. Cochineal was not actually produced in Europe until 1820 or 1850, and appears in many types of rug only after this time. Indigodisulphonic acid arrived in Anatolia and eastern Persia before 1850, and fuchsine reached there and East Turkestan after 1860. The use of particular dyes can be plotted by early carpets with woven dates or purchase records – thus, a Kazak dated 1886 containing Ponceau 2R (a red azo-dye) tells us when this dye reached the Caucasus. My favourite weavers, the Turkoman, missed the first two synthetic dyes almost completely but welcomed the arrival of the azo-dyes.

Much discussion of dyes in standard rug books is misleading. Naturally- dyed carpets are favourably com-

pared with synthetically-dyed ones, the assumption being that synthetic dyes were cheaper and of inferior quality. In fact, many carpets exist in which most of the wool is naturally dyed but important details, perhaps one to ten per cent of the whole, contain brighter synthetic dyes. These must have been used for aesthetic reasons as they were probably more expensive than natural dyes. In one Turkoman flat-weave bag-face (see 24b), probably made in Afghanistan between 1890 and 1920, the ground is dyed with madder, while the brocading features dark and light wool, indigo blue, yellow, and green (the latter a combination of indigo and yellow). The yellow is the direct azo-dye, Orange IV, discovered in London in 1875, a good dye which neither runs nor fades. I once compared this with a similar piece having the same design and colours, except that the yellow had faded to cream and the green to blue. No doubt the yellow had been dyed with *isparuk* (*Delphinium sulphureum*), a favourite natural dye in this area but one which fades easily. Much of the merit of the design in the second piece was lost. Had the superior natural dye, weld (*Luteola tinctoria*), been used, it would have continued to look as good as its synthetically-dyed equivalent.

Yet synthetic dyes continue to have a bad name because of their sometimes harsh colours, the unpleasant consequences of the fading of fuchsine, and the 'running' of some of the acid direct dyes. Also the belief persists that older carpets are superior in design to newer ones – it should be remembered though that rug experts use this belief in attributing ages! A generally sceptical attitude about all this is useful. Nevertheless, a rug collector usually wants early examples for they do tend to be better drawn. Therefore the pieces which are entirely naturally-dyed are generally preferable to the many mixed-dye pieces referred to above. Carpets made entirely with synthetic dyes are usually crude, when tribal, or in the case of the commercially produced carpets of the average rug-shop, are intended merely as furnishing articles.

b. Left *A Turkoman flat-weave bag-face. The yellow details are dyed with a direct azo-dye that neither runs nor fades and is therefore superior to the natural yellow used by these weavers. 1890–1920.* 1.16m × 1.77m, 3'10" × 5'10".

Oriental Carpet Design

The design of a work of art is influenced by many factors, economic, sociological, political, as well as cultural. This is never more true than in the Islamic world which is a complex blend of cultures and races, extending from Morocco to China, over which Islam is the dominant but by no means the exclusive religion. Carpets are highly regarded by all the peoples of the orient and so have been woven by Arabs, Persians, Turks, and Greeks; Christians, Jews, and Muslims. Whereas the majority of rugs display motifs relating to Islamic culture and religious symbolism, some show those of the minorities in these regions.

The function of the carpet

In the orient textiles play a far greater role in daily life, both religious and secular, than in the west. Apart from their usual domestic functions as floor and bed coverings and cushions, textiles have also served as animal trappings, garden and tomb furniture, and military paraphernalia. The prayer rug had a very specific function, which will be discussed in more detail below.

A glance at Islamic painting suffices to illustrate the importance of this tradition (see 25a). Royal personages throughout the Muslim world held court seated on a throne with a fitted carpet and cushions. If the reception took place outside, the princely khan would receive dignitaries seated on a rug placed directly on the ground, or on a throne protected from the sun by a canopy. He would depart on military campaigns with magnificent tents furnished with rugs and hangings.

The elaborate court ritual recorded in miniatures has of course disappeared today, but some of the rugs made for these occasions still survive. These include round rugs probably woven for use in tents, and octagonal rugs woven to fit inside thrones or for the kiosks which were an indispensable adjunct to the Islamic garden.

In less palatial Persian homes the host received his guests seated on a carpet placed horizontally at one end of the room. Three others were placed perpendicularly to it, the one in the centre wider and in a different design to the two runners in an identical design on either side. Occasionally the four were woven as one.

In societies which survive by sheep husbandry, woven goods still serve their traditional functions. Thus bags, cradles, tent decorations, and animal trappings are woven by tribal women all over the orient, from the Turkoman in Central Asia to the Berber in North Africa.

The development of Islamic design

The Arab conquest of the Near East by Mahomet and his followers began in 622 AD and was followed by a period of relative stability. This facilitated cultural and commercial exchange between the regions dominated first by the Umaiyad (661–750 AD) and later by the Abbasid (750–1258 AD) dynasties. Although political disintegration later ensued, the Islamic faith served as a powerful cohesive force in maintaining contact between rival or opposing powers. Artists, including rug weavers, were on more than

a. Above *A fifteenth-century Persian miniature showing a prince and his retinue entertained at night in a garden. Carpets are placed on the bare ground and the prince is sheltered by an embroidered canopy.*
British Museum, London

a. Above *A drawing of a Sassanian bas-relief in the Louvre, Paris. It shows two ibex on either side of the tree of life. This theme was adopted by many tribes as a heraldic device and is interpreted more naturalistically in modern rugs.*

b. Below *Mosaic decoration at the Dome of the Rock, Jerusalem, built by the Umaiyad dynasty in 687–691. This vase motif is in the Sassanian style, but it is also a recurrent theme in Islamic art.*

one occasion victims of political maneouvering, dispatched from one region to another either for diplomatic reasons or as prisoners of war. Islamic art in many media, from books to carpets, is therefore characterized by a certain stylistic unity which may be recognized even by the uninitiated.

The Umaiyad artists, searching for a suitable vocabulary, adopted and reinterpreted many of the motifs traditional in Mesopotamian art since the Sumerian period (2500–2000 BC), including the palmette, vine meander, vase, and tree of life (see 26a and b). No carpets survive from this early Muslim period but they are likely to have featured similar designs, which are found even to this day in the oriental rug repertoire. The influence of textiles from the Sassanian dynasty, which had preceded the Muslims in Mesopotamia and Persia, can be seen in the earliest known Islamic textiles with their roundels containing bird and animal motifs including the mythical bird, the simurgh.

In contrast, some of the motifs used by early Muslim artists are specifically Islamic. The art of calligraphy, particularly the angular arabic script known as 'Kufic', was extended to the decoration of buildings and objects (see 27a). By the tenth century scribes had abandoned it for more flowing forms of script, but Kufic continued to be used to decorate other art forms for centuries after it had ceased to be used in manuscripts. Artists also developed symmetrical arabesque, floral, and geometrical compositions based on grid forms. By overlapping and interlocking the motifs on one, two, or even three planes, varying degrees of density were achieved in the patterns.

Early carpet designs

As the square shape of the knots tends to lend itself naturally to rectilinear designs, it is logical to assume that the repertoire initially adopted in rug weaving was geometric. In fact, the earliest known pile-woven rug, the Pazyryk carpet, shows a mixture of geometric and curvilinear motifs (see 45c). Fourteen centuries separate this rug from the next oldest fragments and the vocabulary used during the intervening period must remain a matter of conjecture.

It is possible though that the design of very early carpets still survives in the work of tribal weavers, who are relatively isolated from the outside world and hand down their repertoire from one generation to the next. Their rugs tend to be characterized by geometric rather than curvilinear designs. One particular motif, the *gul* or tribal emblem, can be seen in fifteenth-century 'Memling' carpets (see 52a) and is interpreted in much the same form four hundred years later in tribal weavings from provenances as diverse as Central Asia, the Caucasus, and Anatolia. In village and urban weavings the influence of more rapidly evolving court models can be observed, as the settled lives of the inhabitants renders them more permeable to external influences.

At the beginning of the eleventh century, the Seljuk Turks of Central Asia moved westwards, seizing power in Persia and Mesopotamia and establishing themselves some decades later in Anatolia, then known as Rum (from Rome). According to early historians Mahmud of Kashgari and Rashid-al-Din the Turkoman tribes of Central Asia, from whom the Seljuks were descended, used heraldic

a. Left *Kufic script in a eleventh-century Koran copied in Iraq or Persia. The angular letters were elegantly adapted to architectural decoration and other works of art, including carpets.*
Keir Collection, Richmond, Surrey

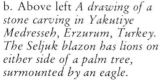

b. Above left *A drawing of a stone carving in Yakutiye Medresseh, Erzurum, Turkey. The Seljuk blazon has lions on either side of a palm tree, surmounted by an eagle.*

c. Above right *The blazon on the neck of this fourteenth-century Mamluk jar shows a* tamgha *or brand mark.*
Victoria and Albert Museum, London

devices derived from zoomorphic and totemic motifs, as well as the *tamgha* or brand mark employed by each tribe to identify their flocks. It is probable that many of the motifs which appear on more recent Turkoman rugs derive from this source, although little ancient Turkoman art has survived to prove this. Heraldic devices were however used in carpets and other media by the Seljuks, the Ottomans, and the Mamluks (see 27b and c).

In the wake of the Turkic invasions came the Mongol hordes, who established their domination over Persia as the Ilkhan dynasty (1206–1353) and with the sack of Baghdad in 1258 extended their rule to Mesopotamia and Eastern

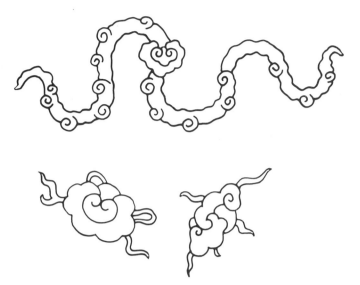

Anatolia. Later they were succeeded by Timur, of mixed Turkic and Mongol descent, who established the Timurid dynasty (1369–1500). In spite of his legendary cruelty and rapacity, Timur was an extraordinary patron of the arts and contemporary miniatures show many carpets. The designs are mostly geometric, but towards the end of the fifteenth century the first floral designs appeared. A number of motifs of Chinese origin were also introduced. These included cloud bands in ribbon form and of the rolled-up variety known as *chi* (see 29a), the infinite knot, naturalistic floral forms such as peonies and sprays of prunus, mythical beasts such as the *chi'lin*, and finally the combat of the dragon and phoenix. Emblem of the Mongol dynasty which reigned over China, this dragon-and-phoenix combat appears on a fifteenth-century Anatolian rug (see 50b) and survives in later Caucasian rugs until the nineteenth century.

The subsequent dynasties of the Safavids in Persia (1502–1736) and Mughals in India (1526–1857) interpreted these floral and animal designs to the heights of perfection.

European influences

Oriental rugs first became highly prized possessions in Europe during the Middle Ages, when they were probably brought back by the crusaders. They later became the object of intensive trading – and copying.

It is somewhat surprising that the influence was so unilateral. Although it is true that European herbals inspired the realistic plant motifs found in seventeenth-century Mughal rugs, in general Western influence on the oriental rug is rare before the beginning of the eighteenth century. From then on, diplomatic relations between the Ottomans and the European powers were increased. This was not without influence on Turkish art and architecture and some of the naturalistic flower arrangements found in Turkish rugs of the period were influenced by the baroque.

Industrialization and the corresponding rise in income of the middle classes led to an increased demand for oriental rugs in the nineteenth century. Greater numbers of rugs in the classical style were produced and floral designs in more muted shades were woven from cartoons sent from Europe

and America. The widespread diffusion of printed publications, including the first rug books with coloured illustrations, also gave weavers access to a wider selection of designs than hitherto available.

Types of designs

The vast majority of rugs are rectangular in format and most of them obey certain rules of composition. With the exception of runners, they tend to be half as long again as they are wide, with a field design framed by a border encased by one or several narrower bands, called guard stripes (see 29b). It is rare to find an undecorated field, although this does happen, notably in Talish rugs. Occasionally one encounters rugs with no borders, which are generally those which have been subjected to European influence.

The field pattern may be organized in several different ways. It can be directional, with a design that is intended to be seen from one direction only, as in the case of prayer rugs. Or it may be non-directional, when the design may be viewed from any angle. A third type is the centralized design, in which the motifs are disposed in such a way as to set off the central motif, usually a medallion. Finally, the pattern may be arranged as an endless repeat, in which rows of motifs, frequently offset, are cut in an arbitrary fashion at the upper and lower borders in the manner of a textile design.

The form of the borders, the style, width, and number, is often a helpful guide to the rug's provenance, as a weaver who adopts a new field design may remain faithful to an older border repertoire. Sometimes borders bear a design known as 'kufesque', derived from the arabic Kufic script. This is to be seen in Mongol, Timurid, and early Anatolian carpets, and it survives, almost unrecognizable, in numerous nineteenth century rugs from the Caucasus (see 121b).

Occasionally real inscriptions are to be found, particularly in the borders. The Ardebil carpet in the Victoria and Albert Museum has an inscription in Persian indicating the name of the weaver and the date.

Other languages used on rugs include Armenian and Hebrew. Curiously, those on Ottoman court rugs of the eighteenth and nineteenth century are generally in Persian, due to the fact that Safavid rugs served as models and odes by Persian poets were in vogue. Occasionally inscriptions are woven back to front, mirror-fashion. This occurs when an illiterate weaver copies the design from an existing rug, taking it from the back of the rug where it is clearer.

Unlike the script, Islamic numerals are read from left to right:

Turkish	· ۱ ۲ ۳ ٤ ٥ ٦ ۷ ۸ ۹
Persian	· ۱ ۲ ۳ ۴ ۵ ۶ ۷ ۸ ۹
	0 1 2 3 4 5 6 7 8 9

The Islamic era starts with the Hegira, that is with Mahomet's flight from Mecca in 622 AD, and the shorter lunar calendar is used. As the lunar system gains one year

a. Opposite *The Mongols introduced cloud bands into Islamic art. They are either in ribbon form or of the rolled-up variety known as* chi.

b. Right *The layout of a medallion rug with the terminology used to describe details of the design.*

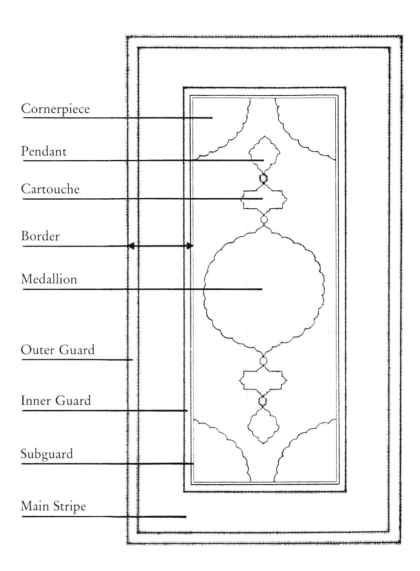

Cornerpiece

Pendant

Cartouche

Border

Medallion

Outer Guard

Inner Guard

Subguard

Main Stripe

every 33.7 years over the solar calendar, a date – say 1258 AD – may be calculated thus:

$$\frac{1258}{33.7} = 37$$

$$1258 + 622 - 37 = 1843 \text{ AD}$$

Caution should be exercised in reading dates, as these may have been altered to make the rug appear older than it in fact is. One should also remember that in recent years the Persians have adopted the solar calendar.

Prayer rugs

The Koran prescribes that a practising Muslim must pray five times a day in a clean place, after a ritual ablution. Prayer may be performed anywhere, as long as the suppli-cant faces Mecca. Rush mats are used by the poorer classes to protect themselves from the dirty ground. The more fortunate use either the small-format prostration rugs known as *sejjade*, or *namazlik*, rugs with a design of the niche in the mosque wall which serves to orient the faithful towards the holy city. Other motifs such as the mosque lamp, symbol of Allah, the water basin symbolic of ritual ablution, or even the sacred stone, the *Kaaba* in Mecca, may also be represented (see 30a).

Prayer rugs are woven all over the Muslim world but particularly in Anatolia. Sixteenth-century Ottoman prayer rugs served as models for generations of rugs woven in provenances from Anatolia to Morocco, and motifs of Turkish origin can also be detected in certain nineteenth-century Tabriz prayer rugs.

Medallion designs

Used in every conceivable shape, the medallion is perhaps the most popular single element in the oriental rug reper-toire. The oldest Turkish rugs display octagons, hexagons, lozenges, stars, and other small-format polygons, some-what reminiscent of later Turkoman work. The medallions in fifteenth and early sixteenth-century Turkish and Mam-luk rugs tend to be of larger format, probably due to the influence of manuscript illumination and bookbinding, which was exquisitely developed by this period. Similar compositions, with the medallions featuring singly, or in groups of two, three or more, and even in a 2:1:2 arrange-

a. Left *A Turkish prayer rug of the Bellini type. The motifs in the field include the lamp (heavily restored) which is the symbol of Allah. Within the mihrab is a niche which may represent a basin for ritual ablution or a stylized mountain to symbolically elevate the worshipper. Late fifteenth or early sixteenth century.*
1.70m × 1.24m, 5'6" × 4'.
Museum für Islamische Kunst, Staatliche Museen Preussischer Kulturbesitz, Berlin (West)

ment survive in many of the nineteenth-century tribal weavings from Anatolia and the Caucasus.

Ottoman and Safavid court rugs benefited from the refined knotting techniques developed in the sixteenth century, which enabled the weaving of graceful circular and ogee medallions. In the centralized compositions favoured by Persian designers, the medallion is often set off by identical quarter-medallions placed in the corners. Ottoman designers on the other hand tended to prefer rows of offset medallions in an endless repeat.

Cartouche designs

The cartouche, decorated with arabesques and often a superimposed inscription, is a frequent motif in manuscript illumination from the fourteenth century onwards. Either plain or polylobed, linked by small circles or stars, cartouches are used to frame a text or as decorative bands above and below it (see 31a). Both compositions are found in rugs. The Mamluks used it as a border motif, as did the Ottomans in seventeenth-century 'Transylvanian' rugs and later 'Salting' carpets. In Ottoman prayer rugs, the niche is similarly encased above and below by decorative bands. The Safavids not only used the cartouche as a border motif, but adapted it to the field in the so-called compartment rugs. An effective means of framing a *gul*, the cartouche is also a frequent border design in Turkoman rugs.

Pictorial designs

It is a popular misconception that the Koran forbids the representation of living creatures, and thus human and animal figures do not appear in Islamic art. The prohibition is not in fact mentioned in the Koran but in the *Hadith*, the sayings of Mahomet which were compiled by his followers after his death. On the contrary, human figures abound in certain domains of Islamic art, particularly in miniatures. The ban is however respected for objects intended for religious use and it is rare, but not unknown, to find living forms represented on articles made for use in mosques.

Hunting scenes and those depicting exploits related in popular Persian epics such as the *Shahnameh*, or *Book of Kings*, first appear in sixteenth-century court rugs. The figures – hunters and their prey, mythical beasts, and occasionally scenes from love stories such as Leila and Majnoun – are either disposed in a directional design or grouped gracefully around a central medallion. The cartoons for these textiles were probably designed by the same artists who created the miniatures. Similar themes are found on Mughal rugs, generally with a directional design (see 81a). The Sunni Ottomans, more orthodox than the Persian Shiites, rarely depicted living creatures in any form other than in their miniatures.

In response to Western demand, Turkish centres in Hereke and Kum Kapou started weaving classical hunting scenes at the turn of this century, and similar designs are still woven in Isfahan and Qum. The tradition of book illustration continued as a design source, but was replaced in the nineteenth century by printed publications. Scenes copied from both Persian and European books were used by weavers in Kerman, Tabriz, and Meshed in Persia, and at the Hereke workshops in Turkey. Photographs were also occasionally used.

a. Above *A binding from a fifteenth-century Mamluk Koran, with a cartouche border containing a Kufic inscription.*
Victoria and Albert Museum, London

CARPET PRODUCTION AND DESIGN

Floral designs

In regions of the world where water is a precious commodity, it is perhaps not surprising that the garden, with an abundance of flora and fauna, is the Muslim symbol of paradise. Perhaps in no other type of composition does the Muslim artist so successfully give rein to his imagination. Floral designs are limitless, in directional, non-directional, centralized, and endless-repeat designs. They are, of course, particularly appropriate for use in mosques and in the Ardebil carpet (see 37d) the dome of the mosque and its pendant lamps are superimposed over a floral ground.

Some of the motifs, such as the cypress and prunus blossom represented in Ottoman and Safavid rugs of the first half of the sixteenth century, are drawn naturalistically. This is specially true of Mughal weavings, in which beautifully observed flowers, including lilies, irises, and bluebells are often represented three or five to a plant as in a herbaceous border. The Ottomans developed the so-called *quatre fleurs* style, composed of tulips, hyacinths, and carnations, with a fourth flower interpreted variously as a rose or a peony.

Most floral forms used in rugs are, however, represented in a highly stylized manner. A curious motif, probably of Indian origin, is the pear-shaped leaf known as the *boteh*, best known in the West for its use on Kashmir shawls. Absent from classical rugs, it is found as both a field and border motif in many nineteenth-century rugs, particularly those from Senneh and the South Caucasus (see 127c). In tribal rugs, it appears in the form of a *gul*.

Perhaps the most ubiquitous floral form is the palmette, which probably takes its name from the palm frond which it initially resembled in Assyrian times. In Islamic art, the term 'palmette' covers a wide range of floral motifs. It may resemble a sliced artichoke, a vine leaf, or a stiffly drawn lotus blossom (see 32). The Ottomans developed a particular style of their own, called *hatayi* (from Cathay), in which lotus blossoms are drawn in a delicate, feathery manner with overlapping lanceolate leaves, called *saz*.

The floral forms known as palmettes are mostly derived from the lotus or peony, combined with leaf forms.
a. Above left The artichoke palmette.
b. Above right The flaming halo palmette.
2. Below left The lotus palmette.
d. Below right The leaf palmette.

In-and-out palmette designs

A particularly graceful composition is the 'in-and-out palmette' design, so-called because the tips of two pairs of leaf palmettes alternately face inwards and outwards at the intersections of scrolling arabesques. Secondary palmettes, or blossoms and cloud bands, fill the lozenge-shaped area formed by the latter. Sixteenth-century designers first used the pattern on rugs of the 'Herat' type and it was subsequently adopted by Indian weavers (see 33a). By the eighteenth century the design had evolved in North Persia and the Caucasus into the 'Harshang' design. By this time the scrolling arabesques and cloud bands had disappeared, leaving groups of palmettes of the 'flaming halo' variety attached to the tips of the lozenge in an endless repeat composition. An ogee form with two pairs of forked leaves projecting from the ends to face each other fills the spaces once occupied by feathery leaves.

The design survives in recent rugs as the stiffly drawn, small-scale 'Herati' motif, popularly known as the fish pattern, due to the shape of the lanceolate leaves placed around the lozenge. It is found today in rugs made all over Persia, including Sarouk, Ferahan, Bijar, Tabriz, and Yazd.

Another descendant from the sixteenth-century prototype is the so-called 'Afshan' design, also common in eighteenth-century North Persian and Caucasian rugs. Here too, the arabesques have disappeared. The palmettes have been replaced by large rosettes and the cloud bands by octofoils in a stiffly drawn endless repeat. The secondary palmettes remain, however, with pairs of forked leaves issuing from their tips to meet in a quadrifoil arrangement in the centre (see 78a). The Afshan design is perpetuated in many recent rugs as a trellis composition known as the *mina khani* design. It is found mostly in rugs from North Persia and particularly in Kurdish, Hamadan, and Veramin weaves (see 139b).

Arabesque designs

Although the design itself is entirely based on floral motifs, the underlying pattern of the arabesque takes the form of a grid. Based on the antique scroll, it first appears as sculptural decoration on the walls of the Umaiyad palace at Mshatta, built in the eighth century. In one version scrolling vines, decorated with buds and leaflets, unfurl and

a. Right *A sixteenth-century Persian carpet of the Herat type. The in-and-out-palmette design includes scrolling arabesques, primary and secondary palmettes, cloud bands, and feathery leaves.* 3.45m × 1.77m, 11′4″ × 5′10″. *Thyssen-Bornemisza Collection, Lugano*

a. Above *A detail of the Persian carpet illustrated on page 68. The arabesque of the field takes the form of scrolling vines decorated with buds and leaflets which unfurl and intersect in rows.*
Museu Calouste Gulbenkian, Lisbon

intersect in rows (see 34a). Alternatively, new shoots may fork off in an axial stem arrangement, covering the surface with a symmetrical pattern (see 35a). Occasionally the arabesque is found in a lattice design.

Rug weavers were slow to adopt the arabesque, probably because of their difficulties in weaving the finely graduated curves, but this design was eventually introduced in the Safavid and Ottoman periods. Delicately interlaced scrolling arabesques form the background to a fifteenth-century medallion rug in New York, and in some Ottoman rugs four diagonally arranged arabesques cross to form a lozenge motif in an extensible repeat pattern.

Arabesque designs are still widely woven, particularly in Persian rugs. Somewhat stiffly drawn, the arabesque rugs of Bidjar and Heriz contrast with the looser style of those from Kerman. Scrolling arabesque designs are still interpreted in a traditional manner in rugs from Qum and Nain.

Garden rugs

Floor coverings with garden designs were already being woven in the Sassanian period. A floral carpet woven with jewels, so remarkable that it was named the 'Spring of Khusrau' after its royal owner, was found in the palace of Ctesiphon was near Baghdad when it was captured by the Arabs in 637 AD.

Later Islamic rugs probably differ little in design, as they represent the grid plan traditional in oriental garden design since Sassanian times. The field depicts compartments filled with trees and flowers, divided by water channels which form pools at the intersections (see 70d). Grid-plan garden rugs were particularly favoured by Safavid and Mughal rug weavers, and are found in later Joshagan and Bidjar rugs as well as certain tribal weaves such as those of the Bakhtiari.

Tree rugs

The tree is a time-honoured motif in oriental art; its fruit is a source of sustenance and its leaves give welcome shade. It also provides the weaver with a convenient way of filling the field with a directional design.

Tree and shrub designs are found in classical Indian and Persian rugs but their style is inspired more by contemporary miniature painting than by the archaic design found in Sassanian art, in which two animals are depicted nibbling at the lower branches of a tree (see 81c, 26a). It survives in a more traditional form in rugs made in Chinese Turkestan between the seventeenth and nineteenth centuries. It was also adopted as a tribal emblem and is found in nineteenth-century rugs by the Ersari, the Baluch, and the Qashqai. Rugs with the tree-of-life theme are still woven in Persia, at Heriz, Tabriz, Isfahan, Kashan, and Teheran.

Vase designs

An overflowing vase was the attribute of the Sumerian water goddess during the third millenium. Although it has long since lost its original religious significance, the vase continues as a recurring motif in oriental art right down to the present day.

One of the most attractive types of classical rug is the Persian 'Vase' group in which one or more vases serve as a pretext for the floral arrangement to extend over the field, either in the form of scrolling arabesques or in a lattice

a. Right *The field of this carpet contains a forked arabesque in which the shoots branch off in an axial stem arrangement. Cloud scrolls, palmettes, and delicate foliage can also be seen. Persia, seventeenth century.*
3.60m × 2.23m, 11′10″ × 7′4″.
Museum für Kunst und Gewerbe, Hamburg

arrangement (see 70c). Somewhat reminiscent of this composition is the design found in certain Transylvanian rugs, in which arabesques erupt from vases placed at each end of the field.

Rugs in which the tree-of-life and vase motifs are combined were woven in Chinese Turkestan and are made today in such centres as Kashan, Tabriz, and Meshed. Regional interpretations of vase designs were woven by Persian tribes, including the Qashqai and the Bakhtiari.

The above, like many other motifs, evolve over the course of time and the village weaver, in all likelihood unaware of their original significance, may interpret them in a manner which only distantly recalls the prototype. This has given rise to terminological misnomers of the 'wine-cup' and 'turtle' variety, given to motifs which superficially resemble the things they describe but which in fact derive from other sources. Permutations in design do not merely develop in a linear manner, however. It is clear that socio-economic events, and particularly trade, are also primary factors in the evolution of taste. Commerce and art are inextricably linked, and the design process will no doubt continue to reflect new ideas stimulated by trade as it has in the past.

Symbolism in Carpets

Among the few great carpets that have survived from the classical period of Persian rug weaving in the sixteenth and early seventeenth centuries are several richly ornamented with pictorial symbols. As one learns to read some of these highly complex symbol-groupings in their entirety, other carpet patterns from that period, and many of the more simply designed later rugs, begin to reveal their meanings also. In fact, the early Persian carpets can even provide clues towards understanding the patterns on rugs from other areas of Asia.

The large Persian carpets, called *khali*, were designed to be the principal decoration in a palace hall or the only floor covering in a Persian house. The pattern on these carpets was generally intended to present a small-scale plan of a part of the Universe: Heaven above, or Earth below.

The traditional Asian ideas about the Universe seem to have developed quite naturally from simple observation. In very early times, men who watched the sun rise in the east and then pass overhead from east to west, would soon have acquired a primary sense of spatial direction. Then, as they faced the rising sun at dawn with their arms outstretched in anticipation of a new day, the bilateral symmetry of their bodies would have made them aware of the other principal directions, north and south. This quite naturally led to the drawing of cross-shaped designs to represent the Four Directions and – by extension the World itself. Then, later, when they thought of the four intermediate directions, the X upon the cross gradually developed into the symbol of an eight-petalled flower, which has been used at the centre of rug medallions all over Asia to mark the centre of Creation.

The early people also thought of the sky as an enclosing dome, because a person standing on a barren plain sees the Earth as flat and the sky seems to fit down over it like a vast inverted bowl. They thought of the World Above as a realm beyond that dome, to be entered through a door in the sky, and this idea of a portal into Heaven was based on observation too. When the ancient sages tried to map the seeming movement of the stars in the sky – not realizing that this was caused by the Earth's rotation – their charts showed all the other heavenly bodies tracing circular paths around the North Star, which seemed to remain motionless. Since this particular star, gleaming so brightly, appeared on their charts as the centre of a concentration of star-circles, they thought it must represent an entrance to Heaven, from which streamed out celestial light.

This idea of a sky door leading into Heaven was not confined to Western Asia. The pierced dome of the Pantheon in Rome and the hole through the ceiling in Gothic cathedrals, like the symbolic 'hole' in mosque ceilings and the circular reserve guarded by a dragon in the ceiling of certain Chinese temples, all represent this universal concept; so it should not surprise us to find it featured on carpets that were intended to show an earthly reflection of the World Above.

The Muslims thought that this Celestial World consisted of several layers; one of these was the original Garden of

a. Opposite left *A detail of the Ardebil carpet, showing the eight-petalled flower that symbolizes the centre of the Universe.*
Victoria and Albert Museum, London

b. Opposite right *A detail of a sixteenth-century animal rug from Tabriz, Persia. The central medallion of this rug shows angels surrounding the Sky Gate.*
Musée Historique des Tissus, Lyons

c. Above *In the corners of this Sanguzsko carpet are heavenly figures, passing through the apertures in the sky to the Earth below. Detail, Persia, sixteenth century.*
Victoria and Albert Museum, London

d. Right *The Ardebil carpet. The lamps suspended from the central medallion symbolize the sun and moon and the inscription at the top records the date of the carpet. Persia, sixteenth century.*
10.51m × 5.53m, 36′6″ × 17′6″.
Victoria and Albert Museum, London

Eden, so often represented on Persian carpets by patterns of orchards, or gardens with exotic flowers and plants and unfamiliar animals.

At the very top of Heaven, beyond all paradises, they assumed there was still another portal: the Sun Gate, leading to the Throne of God. Its name did not refer to our actual sun, but to a symbolic Metaphysical Sun – another way of expressing the concept of Divine Light. Within that innermost circle, to be found at the core of the central medallion on many Persian carpets, one often finds a delicate trellis bearing tiny blossoms, surrounding the eight-petalled flower that symbolized the centre of the Universe. This motif is explained by the Arabic-Persian word for lattice, 'arsh, which makes a pun on another word that means the Throne of God. The Sun Gate is beautifully illustrated at the centre of the famous Ardebil carpet (see

a. Left The Figdor silk kilim. This design depicts a view of Paradise beyond the Sky, screened by hijāb *panels. Persia, possibly Kashan, late sixteenth century. 1.9m × 1.2m, 6'3" × 4'. Thyssen-Bornemisza Collection, Lugano*

b. Above A detail of a Persian carpet which also features hijāb *panels. The cartouches of the border contain elegant cloud bands. Tabriz, sixteenth century. The Metropolitan Museum, New York*

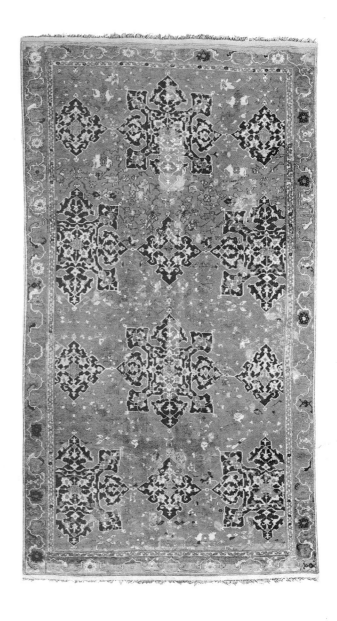

a. Above left *In this Turkish Lotto carpet the* hijāb *screen is composed of curving bars of gold and silver, studded with pearls and sapphires. It is an infinite design, overlaid by the border. Sixteenth century. 1.72m × 1.09m, 5'8" × 3'7". Victoria and Albert Museum, London*

b. Above right *A sixteenth-century Turkish rug in which the field design is conceived as an endlessly repeating pattern, extending under and beyond the cloud band border. Philadelphia Museum of Art, The Joseph Lees Williams Memorial Collection*

37a and d), which symbolizes the actual sun and the moon by two lamps. Some Persian rugs identify this portal still more explicitly by showing guardian angels around it (see 37b).

The people of Western Asia also imagined four more possible entrances through the fabric that covered the sky, providing other ways by which heavenly messengers could come down to Earth. They believed that these lesser apertures were located at the corners of the earth in the four intermediate directions, and imagined that our sun entered and left by means of them at the solstices. Again, these ideas seem to have been based on observation; on Mid-summer Day the sun appears to enter our world in the northeast and leave in the northwest, while on the shortest day in winter it enters in the southeast and leaves in the southwest. Therefore these corner apertures were considered to be lesser sun gates – this time, referring to our actual sun.

a. Left above *The field of this so-called Portuguese rug depicts the Earth as a mountain surrounded by water. In the four corners are foreign ships with alien people. Persia, sixteenth-century.* 4.41m × 1.93m, 14′6″ × 6′4″. *The Henry Francis du Pont Winterthur Museum*

b. Left below *The border of a carpet was seen to protect those sitting within its magic confines. This detail from a sixteenth-century Persian Herati carpet shows stylized Sunbirds, traditional symbolic guardians. Victoria and Albert Museum, London*

On many old Persian and Turkish carpets these corner gates were indicated by four corner medallions, usually conceived as being of the same shape and size as the central one. Although three quarters of each is generally overlaid by the border, they were imagined to be fully present, under and beyond the border. The Sanguszko carpet in the Victoria and Albert Museum shows heavenly messengers in the apertures at its corners (see 37c), while another in the Metropolitan Museum has figurative holes cut through the border to disclose similar angel figures within its hidden corner gates.

Persian artists apparently considered the covering of the sky-dome to be a screen composed of small, interconnected metal panels, or else an elaborate metal grillwork – such as they depicted on the ceilings of mosque domes in Isfahan, which were themselves symbolic sky-domes. This established a firm barrier between our world and the one beyond the sky. In addition, they imagined that behind the Sky Door there was another fence or screen to keep out the undeserving. This second barrier – called *hijāb* in Arabic and Persian – was supposed to exclude lapsed Muslims and unbelievers, though the refined souls of the Faithful could easily slip through.

On old Persian carpets depicting Heaven, the broad border – often figured with cloud scrolls and even angel figures – was apparently intended to portray the curtain of the sky, drawn back to disclose a view of the World Beyond; the latter may be partially obscured by an allover pattern of *hijāb* panels, between which are glimpses of Paradise behind it (see 38a and b). Some old Persian carpets have a border containing a continuous line of alternating light and dark motifs symbolizing successive days and nights, thus presenting a window-frame of Time through which to glimpse Eternity.

The field pattern on 'Lotto' rugs (from Turkey) also

seems to represent the *hijāb* barrier, as it shows a screen composed of curving bars of gold or silver, often studded with pearls and sapphires, within a border that may contain stylized clouds (see 39a). Other Turkish carpets from Ushak seem to indicate the same barrier by means of large, interlocking panels (see 39b). In both cases, these symbolic fences are interrupted by the border, showing that they were conceived as passing out beyond it. The Turks seem to have used red to symbolize the brighter world beyond the screen, whereas the Persians usually preferred dark blue, yellow, or gold.

In contrast with these portrayals of Heaven, a few Persian rugs presented a glimpse of the Earth, seen through the Sky Door as though by a God's-eye view. Among these were the so-called 'Portuguese rugs' from sixteenth-century Persia (see 40a). A broad border represents the curtain over the sky drawn back to disclose a conventionalized view of our World. Looking down through this figurative hole in the sky we see a quadrangular piece of land surrounded by four bodies of water, or four segments of an encircling sea, since the full extent of the water and the extremities of the land-mass are usually hidden beneath the overlaid border. In each of these are strange foreign ships – vaguely Portuguese, hence the very inappropriate name for this type of rug – along with dragons, giant fish, and a merman hailing the alien barbarians. All of these details emphasize the idea of distant seas at the rim of the known world, while the land-mass is represented as a mountain, built up in layers with four principal peaks and an eight-petalled flower at its centre to indicate the Cosmic Axis.

Many Persian carpets depict hunters killing wild beasts, or predatory animals tracking down their prey. Described as 'hunting carpets' or 'animal rugs', these have been considered to be earthly scenes (see 69b); but, especially when they have central medallions and angels in the border, they were obviously intended to show the World Above. People who enjoyed hunting as much as the Persian nobles did could not conceive that this sport would end with their physical death and even in Eden the larger beasts would retain their feral nature. Furthermore, these scenes were not to be taken literally.

Hafiz, who wrote the two lines of poetry quoted in the inscription on the Ardebil carpets, like other Persian poets constantly used puns and metaphors to present spiritual themes in seemingly worldly language. For example, he and the other poets often used the word *dām*, meaning 'snare', to refer to the transitory pleasures of this world, in contrast to the permanent delights of the World Above; but *dām* was also a general term for horned animals. Thus, the frequent depiction of a lion, tiger, or leopard, chasing and killing a deer, an antelope, or a wild ox, symbolized a Sufi mystic's obligation to destroy in himself the temptation of earthly pleasures that would hinder his journey towards the Sun Gate. Another Muslim requirement was holy war against paganism, and the wild ass (*gūr*), so often shown being annihilated as prey, made a pun on the word for 'infidel' (*gaur*) that was spelled the same in Persian script.

The concept of spiritual combat was also expressed by the numerous scenes of battle between a 'good' celestial Phoenix (the Sīmurgh) and an 'evil' underworld Dragon – the forms for which were taken from examples of Chinese art that had been brought to Persia. Other Chinese motifs occur on Persian carpets from the sixteenth-century classical period, but these likewise were reinterpreted to express Iranian concepts; for symbols seldom retain their meaning when they travel so far. Lastly, scenes of gardens – with or without animals – were also presenting views of Heaven, as the Persian word for 'garden', *ferdaus*, also meant Paradise. This was similarly true of Mughal carpets from India. Shortly after 1600 the Persian court required a return to stricter Muslim doctrines, and pictorial patterns were banned unless they showed merely flowers or trees. These, however, still symbolized Paradise to people of that arid land, and some of the later patterns even kept the middle medallion with its eight-petalled central rosette.

On still later Persian carpets, and on those from Turkey and the Caucasus, field patterns became more abstract and repetitive, though they often still symbolized Infinity beyond the Sky. The borders – still symbolic Sky Doors – usually contained the most significant motifs. Often the latter were ancient protective charms, to establish a kind of 'magic barrier' around the carpet, believed to turn away evil and guard anyone who sat within its protective confines. Persian carpets with the Herati pattern are good examples of this. Their field contains repeated designs that figuratively continue on under the border; while the latter has a continuous band of ancient 'Sunbird with Fish' symbols for magical protection (see 40b).

Moving over to the other side of Asia, the symbolism on old Chinese carpets is richer, more varied, and far more easily read by anyone who has some knowledge of the traditional culture. Although some of them may display familiar Buddhist or Taoist emblems – or the Yin-Yang symbol surrounded by trigrams, so dear to the Confucians – we find less emphasis on spirituality, and more on concrete, worldly thinking. Pictures of bronze tripods and vases show a reverence for Antiques; storks and pine trees symbolize Long Life; symbolic jewels suggest riches; many-seeded pomegranates express desire for many children; and, above all, an endless vine around the border suggests continuity of generations in the family line.

The Chinese language was more suited for punning than the Persian, so pictured puns and rebuses were common on rugs. For example, flying bats (*fu*) conveyed the idea of soaring happiness (*fu*), and various objects carried by these bats made puns on adjectives that specified the kinds of happiness desired. Punning wishes for promotion are also frequent. Background colours were very significant: yellow was reserved for the imperial family; red rugs were used at weddings, and white ones for periods of mourning. Certain types of dragons and phoenixes were private symbols for the emperor and empress until the last dynasty fell in 1912; but other symbolic animals and birds were common on carpets, along with auspicious flowers and plants.

In China, as in the Near East, the meanings of the old symbols have been forgotten. But, if we can learn to read the former symbols of Persia and China – both centres of cultural diffusion – this can add immeasurably to the interest of old rugs, and can help us to understand the thoughts and aspirations of the people who designed them, wove them, and used them in their daily lives.

A Caucasian dragon carpet.
The dragons for which the
carpet is named are the yellow,
spotted creatures in the
compartments at the top and
bottom of the rug. Seventeenth
century.
4.70m × 2.23m, 15′6″ × 7′4″.
Keir Collection, Richmond,
Surrey

History
of Carpets

Early Carpet Weaving

Everyone who is attracted by the richness of oriental carpets must at some time wonder by whom and where the earliest ones were woven. Unfortunately the perishable nature of textiles places a time limit on their survival, while their portable nature and their trade value means that they are often found far from the lands of their makers. Under such circumstances the examination of early rug fragments becomes a detective game, going beyond the art-historical analysis of designs and techniques. It also involves a search for geographical, social, and economic milieux favourable to the rise of a carpet-weaving tradition.

Literary sources through the ages make references to carpets in the Near East, where they were used as wall hangings and floor coverings. Early on, around BC250, the Greeks speak with great admiration of rugs from Babylonia and Persia. Later sources continue to refer to carpets, occasionally including descriptions of examples of such beauty or richness as to render them legendary. Arab writers of the seventh century AD tell of a rug like a garden, called the 'Spring of Khusrau', which was made of gold threads, embroidered with gems and pearls, and was kept in the Sassanian Persian palace at Ctesiphon. The problem with all these literary accounts is that they do not specify in what technique the carpets were woven. In the West it is the knotted pile rug which has attracted most interest, but the literary sources provide little information about early production of pile rugs.

We are left then to examine the earliest rugs themselves. For years the history of early carpets has focused on a group of Turkish rugs from the thirteenth or fourteenth century discovered in two mosques in central Anatolia, referred to as the 'Konya' carpets (see page 48). These were seen as examples of the earliest oriental rugs, woven perhaps in the initial stages of knotted pile carpet production in the Near East. The theory is that pile rugs originated among nomadic people in Central Asia, and were brought westwards by migrations of Turkic tribes in the eleventh to twelfth centuries. It is proposed that knotted pile was originally done in imitation of animal pelts to produce warm textiles for use in a harsh environment.

Careful analysis of various fragments of pile rugs from the Near East, pre-dating the Turkish migrations, has usually revealed that they were made in cut weft-loop pile rather than in a true knotted pile (see 44a). The process is different from weaving rugs by hand tying knots, and it is considerably less flexible in the design variations it allows the maker to introduce. In the Near East it is associated with textile production in an urban setting, rather than with the nomadic environment that is considered to be the birthplace of the knotted pile technique.

Genuine examples of knotted pile rugs were found by Sir Aurel Stein in archaeological expeditions to the Tarim Basin in Eastern Turkestan in the early years of this century (see 44b). There he unearthed small carpet fragments in various techniques dating from the third to sixth centuries AD. Some are tapestry-woven (flat weaves) and some cut weft-loop pile, but others have proved to be true knotted pile. Several variations of the 'Spanish' knot (see 18a) appear, as do examples of the traditional symmetrical or 'Turkish' knot (see 17b). The latter examples are particularly suggestive, for they share technical features with later Anatolian rugs, including knot type, unplied wefts in multiple shoots between the rows of knots and two-ply yarns for warp and pile. Their geometric designs are too fragmentary to decipher, but the structural resemblances here might lead one to conclude that these were the

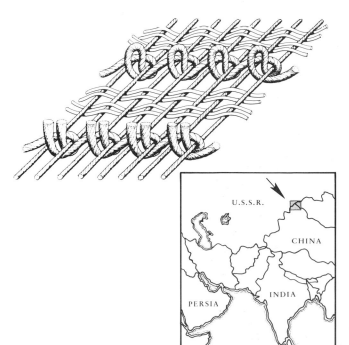

a. Left *Cut weft-loop pile weaving. In this technique looped wefts are inserted during the weaving and cut to form pile afterwards. The effect is similar to knotted pile but allows for less variation in the design.*

b. Left *A map of Central Asia showing Pazyryk, and the Tarim Basin in East Turkestan. Important early rugs have been found in these sites, including the celebrated Pazyryk carpet.*

a. Left *A drawing of a rug fragment from Fostat, Cairo, now in the Röhss Museum, Göteborg. The design on this piece identifies it as a fourteenth or fifteenth-century rug from Anatolia, similar to those seen in European paintings.*

b. Left *A drawing of a Fostat fragment now in Stockholm National Museum. This pattern is similar to the gul design on small-pattern Holbein rugs and could have been woven at any time between the thirteenth and sixteenth centuries.*

c. Left *The Pazyryk carpet. This is the earliest surviving carpet and was found in the 1940s in a Scythian tomb in southern Siberia. It dates from the fourth or fifth century* BC. *1.80m × 1.80m, 6′ × 6′. The Hermitage, Leningrad*

45

forebears of Anatolian Turkish rugs. However, the usual question must be raised as to whether the rugs were actually woven where they were found. Eastern Turkestan is situated on the east-west trade routes, and the variety of techniques in the fragments suggests the possibility of a variety of sources. As their designs and cultural context remain unknown they provide little information, other than proof that a knotting tradition did exist during the early centuries AD.

Another source of early carpet fragments, one somewhat more generous in revealing designs, is the rubbish heaps of Fostat or Old Cairo. Many pieces of old rugs, and other textiles reputed to have been found there, have surfaced on the art market over the years. Since they, were unearthed with no attention as to where and with what else they were found, dating can only be done by analysis of design, colour, and technique.

One group is composed of early Spanish rugs from the twelfth to fourteenth centuries, made in the single-warp knot. The rest appear to be Anatolian in technique and design, and represent various types. The drawing of some is reminiscent of the animal design carpets to be seen in European paintings of the fifteenth century (see 45a and 49b). Others are fragments of the Holbein-pattern rugs of the fifteenth and sixteenth centuries (see 50a and 51a). Still earlier examples bear close resemblance to certain Konya rugs. However, the most interesting scraps are those which appear to be Turkish rugs, but which are not quite like any known types (see 45b). Although they can often be seen as a variant of a familiar type, it is difficult to date them. Are they perhaps earlier than other known examples of a particular group, or are they lost design variants? Again there is the problem of a lack of context for any study. These fragments in isolation pose more questions than they give answers.

The focusing of attention on the Konya carpets and subsequent speculations that the Turks were the first weavers of knotted pile rugs were dealt a serious blow by an important archaeological find at Pazyryk in the Altai Mountains in southern Siberia in 1947 (see 44b). There, the Soviet archaeologist, Sergei I. Rudenko, began the excavation of a Scythian burial ground of some forty mounds dating from the fourth to fifth century BC. Early flooding and subsequent permanent freezing had kept the contents of the barrows in a surprising state of preservation. Among the mummified bodies of men and horses was a hoard of Scythian and imported art objects, including a well-preserved, finely knotted oriental rug (see 45c).

The rug measures about 2 metres (6 feet) square and is tied with the symmetrical knot at approximately 3720 knots per square decimetre (240 per square inch). The red field is covered with rows of squares containing radiating designs, surrounded by two major and three minor borders. The inner major border depicts a Eurasian deer (*Cervus dama* or fallow deer), while the outer one shows men riding and walking beside horses. Two of the three minor borders are composed of griffins in small squares, while the third repeats the motifs in the field. It is a technically accomplished piece, more finely woven than the Konya rugs of some seventeen centuries later, and it obviously stems from a tradition with some previous history.

The Scythians were a pastoral stock-raising people who ranged from the Black Sea eastwards. Those who inhabited the Altai Mountains were not true nomads, moving at most from pasture to pasture within a very limited range. They traded with the Greeks, Persians, and Chinese. Objects from these three cultures found at Pazyryk, provided the fourth or fifth century BC date for other items, including the rug. Nothing is known of the language of the Scythians; indeed, it is only through the Greeks that we have contemporary accounts of these people, in the writings of Herodotus.

The barrows revealed much about the material culture and art of these Scythian pastoral tribes. Many of the objects had never been seen before and among the most appealing are the textiles, including felt-appliqué work used as wall hangings and horse trappings (see 47b). As a pastoral, sheep-herding people, the Scythians were disposed to work in wool. Indeed the finds included not only the oldest surviving pile carpet and the oldest felts, but the oldest kilims as well (see 47a). The kilims are very similar to those woven up to modern times, including the use of the usual indigo and madder among the dyes. Derived from the materials at hand, these textiles are an artistic expression of a culture whose vitality remains undiminished even to modern eyes.

There is one crucial question: were rugs made locally or is the Pazyryk carpet imported? The barrows contained Chinese silks, so why not a Persian rug? The picture was made no clearer by the discovery in a nearby site of a small, even slightly older, knotted pile fragment whose design is no longer decipherable. It is almost twice as finely knotted as the complete rug and is woven in the asymmetrical knot. The difference in structure of the two pieces might indicate a difference in craft habits of two different weaving centres. As there is no design to study, it is not

possible to determine the origin of the fragment.

However, analysis of the design motifs on the complete rug does offer fascinating if inconclusive evidence. The crudely drawn men and horses in the border bear a striking resemblance to a depiction of men and horses on a frieze of similar date at the Persian capital at Persepolis. The man walking on the left side of the horse with his hand on its back, the knotting of the horse's tail, and the plumed forelock all closely resemble figures in the frieze. This similarity has led some scholars to attribute the work to the Achaemenian sphere of cultural influence, and therefore to see it as an imported object. Others doubt that a Persian artist would have been familiar with the appearance of fallow deer. The friezes at Persepolis depict all the peoples of the world, and the section with the men and horses is meant to represent the people of 'the North', possibly Scythians. Further, we have no evidence of rugs in Persia at this time, no depictions of them in use in contemporary Persian literature, metalwork, or stone carving.

Who wove the Pazyryk carpet is impossible to determine. Perhaps it is not so important to know despite some recent attempts, in the spirit of twentieth-century nationalistic pride, to identify it with this or that ethnic group. It stands in isolation, 1300 years and several cultural traditions removed from the history of the oriental rug as we know it. All it can tell us is that various people, at various times, have all explored the ability of knotted pile to communicate the beauty of their artistic expressions.

a. Opposite *Slit-tapestry weaves (kilims) were also found at Pazyryk and date from the fourth to the fifth century* BC. *It is not known whether they were locally made or imported, but they are very similar in design to flat weaves made in the Middle East to this day.*

b. Right *A Scythian felt appliqué, fourth to fifth century* BC. *A number of such felt carpets or wall hangings were found in the tombs at Pazyryk. They were probably of local manufacture.*

Early Turkish Carpets

The land of Anatolia, today the Asiatic part of the Republic of Turkey, has long been famous for its weaving traditions; documents from classical times onwards mention the practice of dyeing and weaving among the various peoples of Asia Minor. These medieval Hellenic traditions, and with them the political fortunes of the various groups within the Byzantine cultural orbit, declined after the battle of Malazgird in 1071. Meanwhile, the growing strength and westward movement of the Seljuk Turks eventually brought about a new balance of political and cultural power in Anatolia, today named Turkey after the invaders.

The Seljuks were Turkic peoples of Central Asian origin. Their conquests during the eleventh century had already brought Persia under their rule, and now they broke the power of the Byzantine Empire on the Anatolian plateau. They and their nomadic tribal allies, the Turkoman, brought with them a Turkic, Central Asian culture that over time both assimilated with, and in part supplanted, the age-old traditions that formed layer upon layer of the complex culture of Anatolia. Some of the invaders settled into village life, but many of them adhered to the nomadic pastoral patterns of their Central Asian past; even when the Turkoman nomads did settle into village or town life they often kept the traditional designs of their weaving art. As indigenous peoples converted to Islam, as the invaders adopted new ways of life, and as cultural and ethnic assimilation inevitably followed, the threads that formed the complex fabric of Anatolian culture intermingled to an extent that will never be fully explained or described.

In the realm of rug weaving, however, there remain identifiable links with the Central Asian, Turkic past that demonstrate a remarkable degree of continuity amid change. The Turkoman tribes that we associate with traditional rug weaving in Central Asia – Salor, Tekke, Saryk, Ersari, and Chodor – also formed part of the Turkic invaders and settlers in Anatolia in the aftermath of Malazgird. These people gave tribal names to hundreds of villages across Anatolia as they slowly abandoned their nomadic way of life over the succeeding centuries. Throughout the history of Anatolian Turkish weaving, we are constantly reminded of the links with old Central Asian traditions through rug design, genre, and the names of the weaving peoples, even though styles adapted and changed in the new cultural environment.

Anatolian rug weaving may be largely divided into two groups: traditional rugs intended for use in the village or nomadic milieu; and rugs and carpets woven for sale, either by traditional weavers as a sort of 'cash crop', or by weavers working within a totally commercial operation. The earliest Anatolian rugs to survive in substantial numbers, which probably date to the fourteenth century, belong to this second group. Discovered in the early part of this century in mosques in the towns of Konya and Beyshehir, these rugs and fragments are generally of a very large scale, woven on huge looms, and they show an entire repertoire of commercially-oriented designs. One indicates a high regard for the then-fashionable Chinese silk textiles in its use of lotus patterns from Yuan dynasty silks (see 48a); in

a. Above *A fragment of a pile carpet from the Alaeddin Mosque in Konya, with a design adapted from a Chinese silk of the Yuan period. Central Anatolia, fourteenth century.*
1.83m × 1.30m, 6' × 4'3".
Türk ve Islam Eserlei Muzesi, Istanbul

b. Above *A fragmentary pile carpet from the Alaeddin Mosque in Konya, with a design of gul forms on a white ground. Central Anatolia, fourteenth century. Detail.*
(6.08m × 2.66m, 20'6" × 8'8".)
Türk ve Islam Eserlei Muzesi, Istanbul

the red-on-maroon field, rows of blossoms with trailing stems have been adapted in somewhat geometric fashion from a much more curvilinear silk prototype. This field is contained within a traditional Islamic border of geometric strapwork forming eight-pointed stars. Another of the early Anatolian rugs recalls traditional Turkic tribal designs (see 48b) in its use of octagonal *guls* or tribal symbols in red on a simple white ground, the whole contained within a border adapted from calligraphic bands of architectural decoration common across the Islamic world. Other rugs found in both Konya and Beyshehir show geometric designs of strapwork stars and stylized plant forms associated with the Islamic repertoire of patterns known as arabesque (see 49a).

In all cases, these early Turkish carpets show one additional feature of great interest – their designs have not been conceived of as unified within the format of the carpet, but instead are infinite patterns, arbitrarily cut by the border of the carpet. The designs are also eclectic in nature and very roughly executed, the corner articulations being improvised and patterns often not centered. All this suggests that the weavers of the Konya and Beyshehir carpets may only recently have abandoned the weaving of small-format traditional rugs for large carpets more suitable for mosque floor covering. Two things seem clear with regard to these earliest surviving Turkish carpets: first, they are unlikely to have been original furnishings in the thirteenth-century buildings in which they were found; and second, we shall probably never know the exact nature of their relationship to the carpets Marco Polo saw in his passage through Konya and Karamania province in the thirteenth century, which he praised as "the most beautiful in the world".

Many early Turkish carpets can be dated by a collateral method: extensively exported to Europe, and even copied in various European countries, their prestige and cost led to their frequent depiction in dateable European paintings. Two small carpets dated to the fifteenth century, one in Stockholm and the other in Berlin, have close counterparts in fifteenth-century Italian paintings. Their geometric, almost totemic designs have remarkably different sources: the two birds flanking a tree in the Marby rug is an age-old design that has deep roots in Central Asian art and may have entered the vocabulary of Turkish art when Turkic peoples of Central Asia followed Buddhism (see 49b); the Berlin rug's design, abstracted either from Chinese porcelain or from Chinese woven or embroidered silk textiles, depicts the combat of the phoenix and the dragon, part of the vast repertoire of Chinese designs that entered the Islamic world in the aftermath of the Mongol invasions in the later thirteenth century (see 50b). In both cases the curvilinear prototypes have submitted to the iron discipline of the rectilinear weaving medium, with the result that forms have become heavily simplified and geometricized, a process known as stylization.

Because pictorial evidence has established an early date for the Stockholm and Berlin carpets, some recent writers have tended to date all such 'animal-octagon' rugs very early in the sequence of surviving carpets, that is, to the fourteenth and fifteenth centuries, and to associate them primarily with nomadic weaving traditions. It is true that such forms were popular in very early Turkish rugs from Anatolia, and their designs doubtless relate to the symbolism

a. Above *A fragment of a pile carpet from the Alaeddin Mosque in Konya with an arabesque strapwork star design. Central Anatolia, fourteenth century. Detail.* (3.20m × 2.40m, 10'6" × 7'9".) *Türk ve Islam Eserlei Muzesi, Istanbul*

b. Above *A small pile carpet discovered in Marby parish church, Sweden, with a design of birds flanking a tree. This is a very ancient Central Asian motif. Central or West Anatolia, fifteenth century.* 1.45m × 1.09m, 4'8" × 3'7". *Statens Historiska Museer, Stockholm*

a. Above left *This carpet, formerly in the Barbieri Collection, has a small-pattern Holbein design. The repeating* gul *appears to be a tribal emblem, possibly that of the Salor Turkoman. West Anatolia, late fifteenth century. 2.64m × 1.55m, 8′8″ × 5′. Wher Collection, Switzerland*

b. Above right *This famous rug was found in a central Italian church. The design depicts the combat of the dragon and phoenix, an ancient Chinese motif. Central or West Anatolia, fifteenth century. 1.72m × 0.90m, 5′7″ × 3′. Islamisches Museum, Staatliche Museen zu Berlin*

of nomadic peoples dependent upon their flocks and upon transport animals for their very existence. However, animal forms are also a logical element of pictorial design in rugs of all peoples living in traditional farming or pastoral environments at any period. Thus it is important to distinguish between forms that are linked to specific peoples and tribes, and those that are identified instead with the general social contexts of village or nomadic life. Both categories of design show amazing persistence throughout the history of carpet weaving.

Although it is clear that these designs continued over many centuries, recent scholarship has been able to assign many animal rugs to the period before 1500. Among these are carpets using the 'Holbein' and 'Memling' designs, named after the sixteenth-century European artists in whose paintings they were depicted (50a and 52a). Such carpets were made by weavers in Anatolia, the Caucasus, and Central Asia over many centuries. New discoveries of rugs and fragments in Anatolian mosques and Egyptian excavations suggest an age-old continuity of these patterns, stretching back historically to a period much earlier than the date of most of our surviving carpets. Dating of such very early carpets is generally based upon a mixture of archaeological evidence, technical analysis, the degree of stylization present in the design, and collateral comparison with other Islamic artistic media.

By the sixteenth century, several basic types of Turkish rug designs were well-known in Europe. The oldest (and probably those with the deepest Turkic roots) are the two Holbein patterns and the Memling pattern. The 'small-patterned Holbein' carpets show a repeating *gul* motif consisting of a knotted octagon, alternating with larger motifs composed of four split stylized leaves framing four lotus flowers (see 50a). The *gul* form, which was also seen in one of the Konya rugs, appears to be a tribal emblem, in this case quite possibly that of the Salghur or Salor Turkoman, who according to Turkoman tradition were the premier rug-weavers among these nomadic peoples. This particular knotted octagonal form is of remarkable longevity, appearing in Turkish rugs for over five hundred years, as well as in copies of Turkish rugs made in Europe. The cruciform 'four-lotus cross' motif from the small-patterned Holbein rugs appears in virtually all surviving artistic media, from architectural decoration to manuscript illumination, in fourteenth and fifteenth-century Islamic art from Anatolia, Persia, and Central Asia. Together these two forms – the repeating *gul* in its various guises, and the four-lotus cross – constitute one of the major forms of decoration in carpets associated with Turkic peoples, down to the present century. By varying the *gul*'s ground colour, the weaver of the Wher carpet illustrated here has created a most pleasing alternation of forms giving an overall effect of a lattice; one of the remarkable attributes of Turkish carpets, observable from very early examples onwards, is the manner in which the simplicity of repetitive emblematic forms is given complexity through variations in colour and in manipulation of small details of the design.

Another design found in early Turkic rugs, and extensively documented in Western pictorial arts, is known as the 'large-patterned Holbein' design (see 51a). Its principal element is a large octagon, often with exterior projections, again rooted in the tribal emblem or *gul*. It is frequently decorated in the centre with a typically Islamic strapwork geometric arabesque, and the relative degree to which this form has remained intact is often used by scholars in the sequential dating of such carpets. The larger octagonal forms often alternated with pairs of smaller ones, with a host of small interstitial forms used creatively in the field. The basic elements of the design appear throughout the history of rug weaving in Anatolia and the Caucasus, and their persistence is again linked to their tribal symbolism and perhaps also to their function as a sort of charm protecting the carpet and its owner from evil spirits. In the fifteenth-century Mediterranean world, these large octagons, like the designs of the small-patterned Holbeins, became so strongly identified with carpets that they were copied or paraphrased in the rug weaving of Islamic and post-Islamic Spain as well as that of Egypt.

Both of the Holbein carpet types use brightly-dyed wool in a variety of primary colours and show a similar technique. This features a medium-density weave with a sym-

a. Above *A large-pattern Holbein carpet. The design is named after the artist Hans Holbein, who depicts similar carpets in his paintings. West Anatolia, around 1500.*
4.29m × 1.90m, 14′ × 6′3″.
Museum für Islamische Kunst, Staatliche Museen Preussischer Kulturbesitz, Berlin (West)

a. Above left *The hooked* gul *motif of this carpet is known as the Memling design from its depiction in paintings by the artist of that name. West or Central Anatolia, late fifteenth century.*
1.70m × 0.93m, 5'6" × 3'1".
Iparmüvészeti Museum, Budapest

b. Above right *This design is known as para-Mamluk due to its resemblances to Egyptian Mamluk carpets. Anatolia, around 1500.*
1.78m × 1.25m, 5'9" × 4'2".
Philadelphia Museum of Art, Joseph Lees Williams Memorial Collection

metrical knot and warps on one level; the construction is entirely of wool with the characteristic counter-clockwise spin (and clockwise twist) of Anatolian carpets. Both also frequently employ a similar border design, whose use in Anatolian weaving was so ubiquitous that it was often taken over in European imitations. The 'kufesque' border, is so named because its forms are imitative of a geometric Arabic script named Kufic after the Mesopotamian town of Kufa. Its origins may lie in the Islamic practice of using bands of script as part of the basic repertoire of all decoration, whether in early textiles (the so-called *tiraz*) or in the decoration of architecture, ceramics, and metalwork. While no examples with legible words have survived in carpet weaving, they abound in other media, and the white, angular forms, often combined into complicated strapwork knots, are most characteristic of this group of Turkish carpets. Scholars tend to date those kufesque borders with floriated finials earlier than those with completely closed strapwork forms, as the former are considerably closer in their form to actual Arabic script.

Closely related in concept, technique, and colours to the Holbein family of early Turkish carpets are the smaller 'Memling' rugs, named after their appearance in paintings by the Flemish painter of that name. In Memling rugs the repeating *gul* consists of a stepped cross with small hooks in its corners, a design again found frequently in Anatolian, Caucasian, and north-west Persian rugs down to the

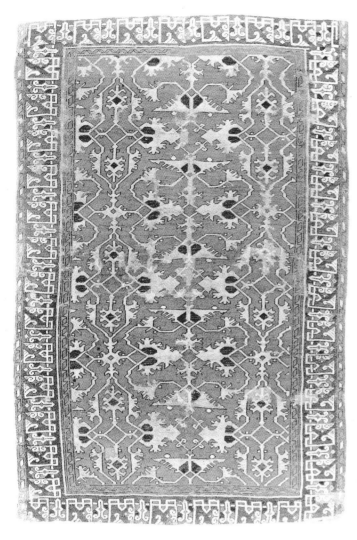

a. Above *A Lotto carpet in which the design is based on a repeating* gul *form used with a four-lotus cross. West or Central Anatolia, early sixteenth century.*
1.70m × 1.09m, 5′7″ × 3′7″.
Saint Louis Art Museum, Gift of James F. Ballard

present century. Of the few surviving early examples, one of the loveliest is a fragment in the Museum of Decorative Arts in Budapest (see 52a); unlike virtually all Memling rugs found in paintings, this example has *gul* forms in staggered rather than in parallel rows.

The Islamic preoccupation with geometrically-generated star strapwork, seen in the complex stone and wood decorations of Mamluk Egypt, the tile-mosaic of Morocco, and the wondrous carved stone portals of Anatolia, seems to lie at the root of another rug design. This is the much rarer fifteenth and sixteenth-century type known as the 'para-Mamluk' pattern, so named because some aspects of it recall the Mamluk carpets of Egypt (see 52b). The technique, the border designs, and the materials of rugs with the para-Mamluk patterns belong in the Anatolian artistic orbit, but their unusual colours, tending heavily towards a purply red and intense greens and blues, have been a subject of conjecture among scholars. The designs of the earliest surviving examples already show many differences from the supposed prototypes, as the number of angles at which a straight line can be 'drawn' in the carpet medium is much more limited than those employed in the seven, nine, eleven, and even thirteen-pointed stars sometimes found in wood and stone carving. In a process quite commonly encountered in the evolution of forms in Islamic art, and in Islamic carpets in particular, the generating 'straps' of the design have virtually disappeared in the surviving para-Mamluks, except for an eight-pointed central star strongly reminiscent of the small-patterned Holbein *gul*. What remain, small lancet or arrow-shaped forms scattered around the field, are the geometric interstices originally formed by the straps. Thus the ground has become the design, and the original design, the strapwork, has disappeared to become the red ground of these carpets. The unusually handsome example preserved in Philadelphia shows us not only the characteristic kufesque border and strapwork stars of the para-Mamluks, but an overall organization of form clearly related to the Turkoman tradition of the large-patterned Holbeins.

Either the popularity or the magical power of the strapwork star designs resulted in their appearing in other groups of carpets, including the so-called 'chessboard' rugs from south-eastern Anatolia or northern Syria, and a rare early Persian medallion carpet associated with the Turkoman rulers of Tabriz in the later fifteenth century. Other early Turkish carpets, the so-called 'Crivelli' rugs for example, also use variants on eight-pointed stars and are similarly related to large-patterned Holbein rugs.

Another carpet form stemming from the same general design tradition, which began to surface in Europe in very large numbers in the sixteenth century and which is documented in literally dozens of European paintings, is the so-called 'Lotto' pattern, named after the Italian painter Lorenzo Lotto (see 53a). Most Lotto carpets exhibit a design of a yellow lattice on a red ground, either contained within the popular kufesque border or using border designs of small cartouches adapted from other weaving traditions. The basis of the Lotto pattern is the repeating *gul* form used with the four-lotus cross. This forms a stylized pattern of great power and attractiveness which, in subsequent centuries, recurs with variations in carpets of Spain,

a. Left *The design of this Ushak carpet is derived from architectural motifs and book illumination. It is conceived as an infinite repeating pattern. West Anatolia (Ushak), sixteenth century.*
5.44m × 2.61m, 17′9″ × 8′6″.
Thyssen-Bornemisza Collection, Lugano

b. Opposite *A so-called double-ended prayer carpet with a cloud-band border. It is unusually large for a carpet of this type. Anatolia (Ushak), seventeenth century.*
2.34m × 1.39, 7′8″ × 4′6″.
Keir Collection, Richmond, Surrey

this point usually seem to be rooted in the carpet medium itself, an art form with strong ties to nomadic life and the necessities of nomadic economic and cultural existence. But the inherent design flexibility of the carpet medium – the potential for a field of coloured woollen knots of sufficient density to carry a virtually unlimited range of designs – led to a crucial division of labour in the production of commercial carpets, in which the function of designer was separated from that of weaver. As a consequence, the repertoire of designs began to expand beyond the traditional patterns derived from village and nomadic traditions. The designers, trained in the arts of book illumination and architectural decoration, began to impose new, curvilinear patterns on the rectilinear carpet medium. The central point of diffusion of this new development in Anatolia appears to have been Ushak, with its proximity both to ample sources of wool and dyestuffs on the central plateau, and to international markets. These were situated on the west coast of Asia Minor, which by the sixteenth century was firmly under efficient, trade-oriented Ottoman rule.

The designs found in Ushak carpets, especially the large examples showing centralized medallions (see 54a), have a number of roots. The general design layout is almost always architectural in inspiration, with the large medallions related to the architectural dome, and other forms to tiled wall decoration. The repertoire of smaller motifs clearly owes a great deal to the art of book illumination, especially as practised in Turkoman-dominated Tabriz and in Turkoman-influenced Istanbul in the last quarter of the fifteenth century and the first quarter of the sixteenth. The all-wool Ushak carpets adhere to the traditional Anatolian colours: two blues, one dark and one light, a brilliant yellow, bright red, dark brown for outlining, natural white, and occasionally a green. The prevailing motif of the great central medallions is the familiar four-lotus cross with its Central Asian Islamic associations. The ground ornament is usually a Turkoman-inspired chinoiserie foliage, or more rarely a traditional Turkic textile motif of Asian origin such as the three circles and wavy lines called *chintamani*. The Ushak carpet illustrated, from the collection of Baron Thyssen, is an especially lovely one; the infinite nature of the design is seen in the suggestion that the red-ground central medallion repeats, but is cut off by the border at each end of the carpet. Serrated light-blue medallions, with incorporated pendants, appear halved four times in the Thyssen example; in other shorter examples they might appear as quarters forming spandrels in the corner of the field. The yellow vegetal forms seen on the small portions of dark-blue ground between the medallions are rooted in fifteenth-century book illumination, while the four-lotus cross of the central medallion, as we have mentioned, appears to have taken its form from architectural decoration.

The same four-lotus cross is found in the central medallions of a group of much smaller carpets often attributed to Ushak, the curiously-named 'double-ended prayer rugs'. These small medallion carpets have corner spandrels bearing variants of the split-leaf *rumi* form found in their centres (see 54b). They are sometimes larger than the 1 by 1.5 metres (3 by 5 feet) *sejjade* or 'prostration rug' format suitable for one person's exercise of the Islamic prayer ritual. The lamp-like forms and stylized jewellery amulets

Anatolia, and the Caucasus. Large numbers of Lotto carpets were made from the late fifteenth to the eighteenth century in the small *sejjade* or prayer-rug format, while others, including many of the most splendid examples, were made in very large sizes.

The exact location of manufacture of these early Turkish carpets is rather a mystery. Ushak in west-central Anatolia and Bergama (ancient Pergamon) on the Aegean coast are both documented as prominent market centres; the former is also the source of some of the best-known commercial Turkish carpets of the sixteenth century and later. This has led to suggestions that the Holbein and Lotto carpets may have originated in one or the other area. Recent scholarship, however, tends to favour other areas, especially locations in the Konya and Kayseri provinces of central Anatolia, as the homeland of many of these rugs; but the matter will doubtless never be settled with certainty.

By the later fifteenth century, a phenomenon described by the late Professor Kurt Erdmann as the 'design revolution' began to occur in various carpet-weaving centres in the Middle East. The traditional design types examined to

a. Left *A Ushak carpet with a star design. These carpets were very popular in Europe. West Anatolia, sixteenth century.* 4.27m × 2.27m, 14′ × 7′5″. *The Metropolitan Museum, New York, Collection of Joseph V. McMullan*

b. Opposite left *This design is known as the 'bird' pattern and is influenced by the Iznik tile decoration on Ottoman buildings. West Anatolia, late sixteenth century.* 2.89m × 1.56m, 9′9″ × 5′1″. *Wher Collection, Switzerland*

c. Opposite right *The origins of this spot-and-stripe motif* (chintamani) *are complex and fascinating. Initially a Buddhist symbol, it later became the emblem of the Timurid state in Persia. West Anatolia, late sixteenth century.* 3.15.m × 2.02m, 10′4″ × 6′7″. *The Textile Museum, Washington, Arthur D. Jenkins Gift Fund*

 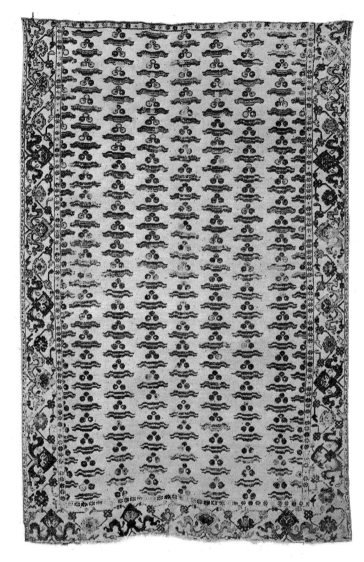

sometimes depicted hanging from one arch in such rugs are undoubtedly protective charms, and suggest that such rugs were woven to appeal primarily to a Middle-Eastern rather than to a European market. On occasion such small carpets incorporate an additional design motif roughly approximating an old-fashioned keyhole in form; interpretations of these so-called 'Bellini' designs vary, some seeing in them a mystical landscape of Chinese Buddhist origins, while others interpret them as depictions of an Islamic fountain or water course (see 30a).

Other patterns besides the ubiquitous medallion carpets (which enjoyed a vogue stretching into the nineteenth century) include the attractive 'Star Ushak' rugs with their cruciform medallions (see 56a). There are also other variations on medallion and cartouche forms, many of them strongly suggestive of fifteenth-century architectural tile decoration of Anatolia, Persia, and Central Asia. The best of these carpets exhibit a brilliant colouration along with a vibrant and lustrous wool pile, and their visual impact is powerful and effective; it is easy to see why their popularity in Europe began to wane as European furniture became more decorated and florid in Baroque times. In weaving associated with Ushak, the kufesque border seems to have become old-fashioned by the mid-sixteenth century and

was thought to be inappropriate to the curvilinear carpet forms then in vogue. While it continued to appear in village weavings up into the present century, its commercial appeal waned in favour of complex floral borders. These sometimes utilized forms made popular in the entirely separate group of carpets produced in Egypt and Istanbul under Ottoman court supervision in the later sixteenth and seventeenth centuries.

Another group of early Turkish carpets sometimes associated with Ushak, reflecting an entirely different set of design origins, includes a number of patterns almost always on a white ground. One pattern, of heavily stylized geometric leaves, was dubbed the 'bird' pattern by carpet scholars, no doubt due to the fanciful resemblance of some of its forms to two-headed humming-birds (see 56b). The bird pattern is clearly derived from another quite famous Ottoman Turkish artistic medium, the large fields of modular, polychrome, underglaze-painted ceramic tiles, mainly manufactured in Iznik, that decorate dozens of buildings of the period. The very same medium influenced the 'spots and stripes' carpets, whose design, sometimes called *chintamani*, incorporates a form with a long and interesting history in Islamic decorative arts (see 56c).

While they first appeared in west Anatolia in the mid-

a. Above top *The design of this*
sejjade *format rug is known as*
Transylvanian, since many carpets
of this type have been found in
Hungary. West Anatolia, early
seventeenth century.
Keir Collection, Richmond, Surrey

b. Above *A detail of a fragmentary*
kilim found in the Great Mosque of
Divrigi. East or Central Anatolia,
eighteenth century.
4.33m × 1.42m, 14'3" × 4'7".
Vakiflar Museum, Istanbul

sixteenth century, the bird carpets continued to be woven in smaller sizes, sometimes with rather clumsy borders and a rather coarse weave, in several other centres during the following centuries. The spot-and-stripe carpets with a white ground are rarer, although their design was on the whole much more popular in Turkic art over a much longer period. Appearing as early as the ninth century in the decorative pottery of Samarra in Iraq, the three circles became the emblem of the Timurid state in Central Asia in the later fourteenth century. They were later associated with leopard spots and tiger stripes, and were so named in early Ottoman documents describing these white-ground carpets. The original symbol however is of Buddhist origin, depicting three magical pearls borne on the waves of the sea, and its artistic peregrinations from the Far East into the white-ground *chintamani* rugs constitute one of the more fascinating voyages in the history of art.

By the seventeenth century one last important Ottoman Turkish carpet form begins to appear in European painting. The rugs are of small *sejjade* format, generally incorporating a centralized design with heavily stylized flowers and four corner spandrels (see 58a). Rug literature has named them 'Transylvanian', due to their appearance in very large numbers as votive gift furnishings in churches of what is today northern Rumania and southern Hungary. The Transylvanian rugs have a distinctive technique and repertoire of forms, all of which however can be easily related to Anatolian origins and prototypes. They were produced in usually large numbers and travelled widely in the carpet trade, even appearing in eighteenth-century America, documented in a portrait of the prosperous New England merchant Isaac Royall and his family by Robert Feke. The place of origin of the Transylvanian rugs has been widely debated among scholars, with some even maintaining that they were actually made in Eastern Europe. Most of the evidence now available suggests they originated in western Asia Minor.

Our knowledge of early rug weaving in Turkey was until recently confined almost exclusively to pile-woven examples. However, early tapestry-woven rugs, some of quite large size and bearing curvilinear designs related to the Ushak rugs and to Ottoman court carpets, have recently been discovered so it now seems that such traditional techniques as kilim weaving were not confined to the village ambience or to simple, geometric designs rooted in the nomadic tradition. An especially complex and beautiful example recently surfaced in a remote provincial Anatolian mosque, and included in its ground design are the tulips and hyacinths so beloved of Ottoman court artists of the sixteenth and seventeenth centuries (see 58b). Since that time almost a dozen other early examples have been discovered, and it appears that tapestry-woven rugs, so fragile and in later times so undervalued in comparison with their knotted-pile cousins, once occupied a prominent place not only in village and nomadic weaving in Anatolia, but in commercial weaving as well.

And what of Turkish village and nomadic weaving during these early times? There is ample evidence, both textual and stylistic, that rugs continued to be produced in abundance over the centuries in an immense variety of styles, genres, forms, and techniques. Many political and

a. Right *This carpet, found in the Great Mosque of Divrigi, may represent village production. East or Central Anatolia, possibly eighteenth century.*
Vakiflar Museum, Istanbul

economic developments affected this production: the constant warfare between Ottoman Turkey and Safavid Persia, the periodic Islamic religious revolts that sprang up across the complex ethnographic and cultural landscape of Anatolia, the continual migrations and resettlements of restless semi-nomadic peoples, and the gradually strengthening cottage industries, dominated by foreign or non-Islamic economic interests. Yet, while one local tradition or another might emerge or submerge, Anatolian village women continued to produce smaller rugs of great beauty and strength. Recent collecting of carpets from the village mosques of Turkey, under the auspices of the Vakiflar Museum in Istanbul, has revealed even more hitherto-unrecognized types of pile and flat-woven village and nomadic carpets (see 59a). Their actual age must remain a matter of conjecture for the present, but their designs and colours bespeak traditions of tremendous age and depth, linking them to shadowy forms of the distant past only hinted at in those carpets shown in European paintings.

The story of early Turkish carpets is one of the most interesting in the history of oriental carpets, both because of the unusual ties to Central Asian traditions exhibited in many of the surviving examples, and because Turkish carpets were the most familiar knotted carpets in Europe during the fifteenth and sixteenth centuries. Copied widely, and collected avidly in Europe, Turkish carpets by the sixteenth century were at least as familiar in the courts of Henry VIII of England and the Renaissance popes in Rome as they were in the lands of their origin. They were depicted in literally hundreds, if not thousands, of European paintings. So it should not surprise us that Turkish carpets were the first to be seriously studied in Europe, when the great connoisseur and director of the Berlin museum, Wilhelm von Bode, began to catalogue their basic types. Equally interesting is the historical legacy of early Turkish carpets in later weaving of Anatolia and the Caucasus. For the weavers of these later carpets, the designs of the sixteenth century remained a sort of classical repertory, and their impact was felt not only in commercial carpets, but in village and even nomadic weaving as well. And finally, early Turkish carpets have maintained over the centuries a high place in the symbolic consciousness of the West, where their bold colours and delightful patterns, often first encountered in paintings in close proximity to the Virgin Mary, to saints, kings, and persons of great importance, have brought them into close association with wealth, power, and holiness, in a context far removed from their nomadic and Islamic roots.

Mamluk and Ottoman Carpets

In the mid-thirteenth century, a Turkish slave in the service of the Ayyubid sultans of Egypt, who had risen through military ranks to become a general in the Ayyubid armies, took control of the Egyptian state. He founded an unusual system of government that was to persist in Egypt until the early sixteenth century. In this regime only foreign slaves of Turkic origin could rise to power, and this military caste, known as Mamluks, built a powerful and prosperous state in Arabic-speaking Egypt, while adhering to their own culture and language.

No group of oriental rugs has been the cause of more speculation and misunderstanding than Mamluk pile carpets. Their purported place of weaving, Cairo, fulfils none of the usual geographical and social requirements for a carpet-weaving environment; their designs and colour schemes, while vaguely suggestive of contemporary weavings from elsewhere in the Islamic world, are strange and indeed unique; and their unusual technique, employing clockwise or S-spun yarns, is found nowhere else in the Islamic world. Even their place of weaving, despite fairly conclusive evidence of their Egyptian provenance, continues to be a subject of debate, along with the origins of their designs and the pattern of their artistic evolution.

Mamluk rugs as a group are easy to identify. Technically, in addition to the S-spun yarns, these rugs utilize a very strong, four-ply woollen warp. The pile, with only one exception, is woven entirely of wool, and uses an asymmetrical knot open to the left. The colours include a lac-dyed purply red, and highly saturated blue and green hues, while one group also has golden yellow, other blues, and a small amount of off-white. Very rarely, however, do we see white wool and never do Mamluk rugs incorporate either black or near-black in their colour scheme. Their field designs almost always include a focal medallion or medallions and a host of complex filler forms, while their borders, with few exceptions, have a pattern of alternating one-centred and elongated cartouches. In size they vary from very small carpets of roughly 1.5 by 2 metres (4½ by 6½ feet) to gigantic carpets up to 11 metres (36 feet) in length.

The unusual designs, environment, and technique of Mamluk rugs have brought forth a host of theories over the past fifty years, but a consensus is now gradually emerging. Mamluk rugs appear in Egypt for three reasons. By the later fifteenth century, carpets were a recognized accoutrement of royal courts and the ruling classes throughout the Islamic and Mediterranean world. According to documents, they were manufactured in Spain, North Africa, Syria, Anatolia, and Persia, as well as in Egypt. The Mamluk rulers of Egypt, of Turkish origins and culture, would naturally favour the use of carpets. Also, the Mamluk state was competing in the Mediterranean market for luxury goods, where political and economic rivalries fed upon each other; this must have added an economic incentive for the establishment of a carpet manufactory in Egypt, almost certainly with state support if not control.

When, sometime in the fifteenth century, the Mamluk carpet manufactory was established in a setting without indigenous carpet-weaving traditions, the result was a peculiar amalgamation of technique, design, and commercial adaptation. Clockwise spinning was traditional in Egypt, and was quickly adapted to imported wool, for neither the fertile Nile valley nor the Egyptian desert was suitable for the raising of sheep. The Mamluks shared trade, culture, and long borders with Turkic Anatolia and the Turkoman principalities of western Persia and Iraq, so it is easy to see how the strong four-ply warp and the asymmetrical knot common in north-west Persian carpets might have been adopted by a new weaving establishment. The Mamluk rugs are dyed with imported dyestuffs, no doubt explaining in part their unusual colouration. The prevailing standard of rug design in the fifteenth century, from Azerbaijan to Andalusia, was the Turkish model, and it is therefore natural that in their basic layout Mamluk rugs echoed both the early Turkoman medallion carpets of Azerbaijan and the *gul* forms dominant in Anatolian weaving. Truly synthetic innovation is rare in Islamic art but it does occur in Mamluk carpets, and the visual evidence in the carpets themselves strongly supports this hypothesis of their origins.

In colour scheme, Mamluk rugs fall into two categories: an earlier group with a more limited palette, and a later group with additional hues of white and yellow added to the basic red, green, and blue. In the matter of size and format, Mamluk rugs are unique in Islamic weaving in the variety they demonstrate within a uniform style. The great Medici carpet in the Pitti Palace is almost 11 metres (36 feet) long, and repeats the medallion form three times over its length. Numerous smaller Mamluk carpets show both the proportions and single-medallion designs reminiscent of their Anatolian cousins, the 'para-Mamluk' and large-pattern Holbein rugs. Two small Mamluk *sejjade* or prayer-rug sized carpets exist; one uses a border of Chinese cloud bands plainly derived from north-west Persia, a field design of the Bellini type from Anatolia, and the crowning-arch form of an Islamic prayer rug. The other, recently discovered in a synagogue in Italy where it had been used as a Torah curtain, bears a Hebrew inscription and a design derived in roughly equal parts from the prevailing Egyptian rug style, Ottoman textiles, and Hebrew book art; new research suggests it may even have been woven by a Cairene weaver of Jewish extraction in Italy.

A small and well-preserved Mamluk carpet of almost square format in the Boston Museum of Fine Arts (see 61a) provides a typical example of Mamluk design and colouration. The central medallion is octagonal, filled with small vegetal forms derived, in the opinion of some scholars, from the age-old papyrus forms in Egyptian art. The eight-pointed star that surrounds the medallion has a scalloped edge strongly reminiscent of the 'cloud collar', ultimately of Chinese origin, that surrounds the medallions in early north-west Persian carpets. Both the field and the beautifully articulated border, with its alternating cartouches are typical of Mamluk rugs.

Among the most splendid of all Mamluk carpets is the Simonetti Mamluk now in the Metropolitan Museum, with its five consecutive focal areas (see 61b). In this carpet it is

a. Above *This rug shows typical Mamluk design and colouration, with its octagonal central motif and cartouche border. Egypt (Cairo), first half of the seventeenth century.*
2.69m × 2.79m, 8′9″ × 9′2″.
Museum of Fine Arts, Boston, The Harriet Otis Cruft Fund

b. Right *The design of this early sixteenth-century carpet, with its mosaic-like assembly of motifs, recalls Egyptian inlaid marble flooring of the same period. Egypt (Cairo).*
9m × 2.41m, 29′5″ × 7′10″.
The Metropolitan Museum, New York, Fletcher Fund

a. Above *This is the only
Mamluk carpet with a silk
pile. Its huge size and strong
palette create a splendid effect.
Egypt (Cairo), sixteenth century.
Österreichisches Museum für
angewandte Kunst, Vienna*

b. Right *A Mamluk carpet, in
flawless condition, found
recently in the Pitti Palace.
Documents record that it was
acquired during the reign of
Grand Duke Cosimo I
between 1557 and 1571. Egypt
(Cairo).
10.88m × 4m, 35'6" × 13'3".
Palazzo Pitti, Florence*

a. Left *This carpet demonstrates the Ottoman court style, known as the* saz *style, that was adopted by Cairene weavers after the Ottoman conquest. Egypt (Cairo), seventeenth century. 10m × 3.30m, 32'7" × 10'9". Palazzo Pitti, Florence*

b. Above *A prayer carpet of* sejjade *format. This is one of the finest carpets in the* saz *style and is related to Ottoman ceramic tile designs. Turkey (Istanbul or Bursa), late sixteenth century. Österreichisches Museum für angewandte Kunst, Vienna*

easier to see the mosaic-like assembly of small interstitial forms, including small elongated lancet-like motifs similar to those seen on the para-Mamluk rugs; this great complexity is heightened by the use of seven colours. The 'assembled' aspect of Mamluk rug design, in which stock elements are put together in a collage-like manner, has caused some to compare their designs with Egyptian inlaid-marble flooring of the Mamluk and Ottoman periods, which the Mamluk rugs resemble in concept if not in actual detail.

The unique silk Mamluk carpet in Vienna, probably made in Egypt several decades after the Ottoman conquest in 1517, is at once the most splendid and the most problematic of Mamluk rugs (see 62a). Its design of three great medallions is set in a mosaic-like field of crowded polygons abutting against each other in an almost arbitrary fashion. Here and there appear Turkmen *gul* motifs, small paraphrases of the 'two-one-two' large-patterned Holbein rugs of Anatolia, and also the strapwork stars of the para-Mamluk rugs. All are assembled in an almost overwhelming variety of geometric compartments of every shape imaginable. In addition to the remarkably eclectic and assembled nature of its field design, the main border, a somewhat weak arabesque, does not articulate in the corners. The Vienna rug is as splendid a sight as exists in the world of oriental carpets, and its combination of the intense Mamluk palette with a silk pile is breathtaking in its effect; but the designers were clearly less than comfortable with its great size and scale, especially its width which is, unprecedented for Mamluk carpets.

Ottoman carpets

The young Italian dealer and scholar, Alberto Boralevi, recently discovered two remarkable rugs from Egypt, forgotten in storage in the Pitti Palace in Florence. The first was the largest Mamluk carpet yet to come to light, a huge wool carpet with three medallions in virtually flawless condition (see 62b). Documents discovered in the inventories of the Medici wardrobe mention its acquisition during the reign of Grand Duke Cosimo I, sometime between 1557 and 1571, describing it as a "Cairene carpet 19 *braccia* long by 7 wide". Its immaculate condition further supports the hypothesis that carpets using the Mamluk design repertoire continued to be produced in Cairo long after Egypt had become an Ottoman province.

The second carpet discovered by Boralevi was executed in a technique very similar to that of the first, but its design is completely different (see 63a) It is in fact an Ottoman court carpet, and its design derives from the work of court artists in Istanbul who made designs for all artistic media, from architectural ceramic revetments to textiles and metalwork. The link between Cairene weaving and Ottoman court designs is both clear and logical. Documents from the fifteenth century onwards suggest the existence of court rug weaving under state control in the Ottoman empire, but apparently none of these early examples has survived, probably due to the periodic fires which swept the Topkapi Palace in Istanbul. When the Ottomans conquered Egypt they found in the Mamluk workshops a state-controlled commercial establishment whose products were more finely woven than the West Anatolian rugs of the time, and whose palette was very much in tune with the then-prevailing Ottoman court taste. By the middle of the sixteenth century, when the Ottoman court style of feathery curved leaves, rosettes, lotus palmettes, and stylized flowers known as the *saz* style emerged, it was quickly taken up by the Cairene weavers. A document from the Medici inventories states that the Grand Duke received this "large good Cairene rug 17 bracchia long by 5 and ⅔ braccia wide" from the explorer and admiral Verrazzano in 1623, and travellers' accounts speak of the Cairene rug industry flourishing well into the seventeenth century.

In the year 1585 the Ottoman sultan Murad III ordered eleven weavers from Cairo to move to the court of Istanbul, bringing with them almost 1900 kilos (2 tons) of dyed wool. The movement of artists around the Ottoman empire seems to have been a fairly common phenomenon, and this migration of a small number of Cairene artisans to Istanbul or its vicinity, as we have seen, did not mean the end of weaving in Cairo. Which carpets of Ottoman design were in fact woven in Turkey, and which in Cairo, is still an open question, although those examples with a silk warp are generally assigned to a weaving site, possibly Bursa, in the general vicinity of Istanbul. Among several lovely small *sejjade* carpets in the Ottoman court style, the superb example in the Museum of Applied Arts in Vienna, with its silk warp and weft, and its use of white and light blue cotton in the pile, is generally counted among the very best (see 63b). The design of a complex arch form, with ornate upper spandrels and quarter-medallion spandrels in the

is closely related to Ottoman ceramic tile designs from the late sixteenth century, and originates in the same workshop.

Carpets with Ottoman court designs were woven over a considerable period, and among them are examples quite definitely of commercial quality, as well as others that may well have been woven for use among the Ottoman ruling classes. As exemplars of the 'official' state style of the Ottoman empire, these carpets exercised a profound effect on commercial and even on village rugs, their sinuous curvilinear designs capturing the imagination of weavers from all parts of Ottoman society. The court design most popular with village weavers was an unusual form of *sejjade* rug with an architectural design incorporating coupled columns, of which the finest surviving example is to be seen in the Metropolitan Museum of Art in New York (see 65a). Over the centuries the architectural design of this rug was subject to innumerable mutations, as it joined the stock repertoire of village rug weaving across the Turkish realms.

Para-Mamluk carpets

Two other groups of carpets are often included in the Mamluk orbit, primarily on the basis of technique. These are the para-Mamluk rugs, which were evidently woven in Anatolia, but which use an asymmetrical knot open to the left (see 17c and 52b); and a group of rugs evidently woven in Syria, among which the most familiar examples use the so-called 'chessboard' design of repeating compartments ornamented with eight-pointed strapwork stars (see 65b). The use of repeating *gul*-like motifs in these carpets suggests a strong link with Turkoman weaving traditions. This is quite feasible, for Turkoman tribes populated northern Syria as well as the south-central Anatolian hinterland in the sixteenth century, about the time that rugs of this pattern began to appear in European paintings. Recently a number of designs, in addition to the chessboard pattern, have been identified with the same technical production. This, by a combination of historical inference, stylistic, and technical evidence, and a process of elimination can be placed somewhere in the neighbourhood of Mamluk and later Ottoman Damascus. Characteristics of these carpets suggesting their commercial origin include first, their technical resemblance to Cairene carpets both in colouration and the use of the asymmetrical knot open to the left; and second, their invariably well-planned corner articulation in the borders, no matter how arbitrarily the field motifs are cut. This again points towards an entrepreneurial production aimed at Mediterranean markets, and consequently either emulation of, or direct competition with, the Cairene rug manufactory.

The Cairene Mamluk rugs and their Syrian and Ottoman cousins constitute an especially interesting chapter in the history of rug weaving, and demonstrate clearly the fluid state of much rug scholarship at the moment. New documentary discoveries, and the dramatic emergence of unknown examples of unusual size, condition, or design in various European collections, have fundamentally changed our ideas about these carpets in the very recent past, and there is no reason to suppose that these new discoveries have yet exhausted fate's storehouse of surprises for scholars and lovers of these beautiful works of art.

a Opposite *Ottoman court designs were copied by village weavers and this* sejjade *design with coupled columns was particularly popular. Turkey (Istanbul or Bursa), late sixteenth century.*
1.67m × 1.27m, 5'6" × 4'2".
The Metropolitan Museum, New York, Gift of James F. Ballard

b. Above *The weaving technique of this carpet relates it to Mamluk work but the design, with its* gul-*like motifs suggests Turkoman influence. Possibly Syria, sixteenth century*
3.77m × 2.43m, 12'4" × 8'.
The Textile Museum, Washington, Gift of George Hewitt Myers

Early Persian Carpets

Carpet weaving is an old and well-established tradition in Persia, although the earliest surviving carpets date only from the end of the fifteenth century. Arab records from the tenth century list Fars, Majanderan, and Gilan as carpet-weaving towns, and considerable documentary evidence from the period of the Il Khanid dynasty (1220–1380) indicates that carpet production was by then well-established. The emperor, Genghis Khan, is known to have donated Persian carpets to a mausoleum in Damascus; Marco Polo noted the abundance of carpets as he passed through Persia in the thirteenth century; and the fourteenth-century traveller Ibn Battuta recorded that carpets were spread before him as a token of honour in Persia.

By the fourteenth century carpets were being clearly depicted in Persian miniature paintings (see 67a). These show carpets with small-scale, repeating, geometric patterns, the field usually divided into squares containing different types of stars and rosettes. The colours – orange, red, and green – are extremely bright, but it is not known if these were the true colours of the carpets, or the colours which harmonized most with the decorative effect favoured by the painter. It seems clear that there are similarities between the geometric patterns on these carpets and those on the carpets and fragments found at Konya and Beyshehir in Turkey, and at Fostat in Egypt. Often the borders of the Persian carpets display kufesque characters which are reminiscent of the Anatolian pieces; although it should be noted that the hexagonal and octagonal motifs of the Anatolian carpets are less common in Persia. Scholars assume that some form of relationship must have existed between these two carpet-weaving areas, but as no Persian carpets from this period have survived, it is not possible to establish the exact nature of the interaction.

Chinese influence had been evident in many aspects of Persian art before the fourteenth century, and it became increasingly important after 1380 when Timur (Tamberlain) began to attack Persia from his base at Samarkand, finally becoming ruler and establishing the Timurid dynasty in 1405. The Timurids, of mixed Mongol and Turkic descent, had cultural and trading links through Central Asia to the Far East, and China become increasingly important in Persia. By the middle of the fifteenth century the Timurids had developed a new decorative style, based largely on Eastern curvilinear designs, that was to have a profound and lasting effect on the arts of the Islamic world. First appearing on book-bindings and in manuscript illuminations, it is characterized by the combination of blossoms and scrolling leaves. However, for several decades the older geometric patterns continued to be depicted on carpets in Persian miniatures.

It was in the second half of the fifteenth century that illustrations show the old, small-scale patterns of crosses, stars, and rosettes being replaced by medallions, which emphasized the centre of the field and were surrounded by blossoms and arabesques. The motifs included the lotus, peonies, leafy palmettes, fantastic and composite blossoms, as well as a split-leaf motif, or *rumi*. Such carpet designs did not suddenly and totally supersede the geometric style, and both types are sometimes depicted in the same painting (see 25a); however, by the end of the fifteenth century the floral style prevailed. No carpet in the geometric style is known to have survived, but it is possible that some of the early floral carpets, which may date from the end of the fifteenth century, illustrate a combination of the two styles. One carpet with a medallion and corner-piece composition and a field of blossoms and swirling stems, is clearly designed on a geometric grid (see 68a); and other late-fifteenth and sixteenth-century carpets have fields divided into regularly placed cartouches (see 68b), which suggests that the geometric tradition did survive for some time.

Contemporary miniatures and documents show that carpets were used to adorn the floors of palaces, mosques, and even garden pavilions, often forming the only item of furnishing. Different carpets would be displayed on special occasions. A Venetian traveller to Persia in 1474 commented that the monarch "caused certain silk carpets to be brought forth which were marvellous fair"; and an Italian visitor to the summer pavilion of Shah Abbas (1587–1629) at Ashraf described a charming, open-air evening reception with chandeliers, soft music, and rich carpets spread out for the guests. Such carpets are likely to have been made in highly sophisticated court workshops, but other weavers, both nomadic and settled, were also producing carpets for similar domestic use. These no longer exist, destroyed by centuries of hard, everyday wear, so our knowledge of fifteenth and sixteenth-century Persian weaving can only be derived from the surviving 'court' carpets.

Safavid carpets

In 1499 the Safavids began their conquest of Persia. Shah Ismael I defeated the enfeebled Timurids in 1501, was crowned in 1502, and was succeeded by Shah Tahmasp in 1524. Under Tahmasp, several royal factories (*karkhanes*) were established for weaving textiles, including carpets. The major ones were at Kashan, Kerman, Isfahan, and Tabriz. The artists were under pressure to produce new designs for carpets, which were used to furnish the royal palaces and government buildings and were sent abroad as diplomatic gifts.

Towards the end of the fifteenth century a revolution occurred in carpet design when miniaturists and book illuminators became involved. They introduced medallions, arabesques, flowers, trees, animals, figures, and even calligraphy. No longer were the weavers active participants in the design; now they were merely technicians. These stylistic changes were partly made possible by the use of the fine, asymmetrical knot and of silk for the warp and weft, later for the pile itself; this enabled the weavers to achieve greater density of pile and to imitate accurately miniature painting (see 69a). Because the surviving carpets were woven in different factories but under the same royal patronage, it is not always possible to distinguish the products of one workshop from another, and Safavid carpets are usually divided into categories based on design – such as Medallion carpets, Garden carpets, Hunting carpets – and sometimes on technique.

a. Above *This fourteenth-century Persian miniature shows carpets with the brightly coloured geometrical motifs of the period. It depicts gold coins being poured over Humay as he leaves Humayan's room after their wedding. British Museum, London*

Only three sixteenth-century carpets are dated: one, in the Poldi Pezzoli Museum, Milan, is inscribed with the name Ghiyath al-Din Jami (possibly the weaver). The date is either 929 (1522/3) or 949 (1542/3); until recently most scholars favoured the latter, but now the actual authenticity of the carpet has been questioned. The other signed and dated examples are the two renowned Ardebil carpets, one in the Victoria and Albert Museum, London (see 37d) and one in the J. Paul Getty Collection in the Los Angeles County Museum. Both are said to be from the Shrine of Shaikh Safi at Ardebil and both bear the date 946 AH (1539/40) along with two lines from an ode by the fourteenth-century poet Hafiz: "Except for thy haven, there is no place for me in this world, / Other than here, there is no place for my head." They are signed "The work of a servant of the Court, Maqsud of Kashan". It is not certain whether Maqsud was the master weaver or the man who commissioned these carpets. Their place of manufacture is also unknown, and although Kashan seems logical, scholars at the beginning of the twentieth century favoured Tabriz, despite the fact that Tabriz was under Ottoman rule from 1533 to 1555.

A series of smaller rugs were probably woven at Kashan, also in the first half of the sixteenth century; they measure approximately 4.4 by 3.7 metres (14½ by 12 feet) and were woven entirely in silk. There are two basic groups: four surviving carpets have all-over patterns of animals grazing and in combat (see 69b), and ten others have floral arrangements around a central medallion (see 70a). These few carpets, although not identical, share many features and must have had a common design source – either a pattern book or a limited number of cartoons – which was adapted by the weavers in the same workshop.

An important but small group of Safavid carpets, the so-called 'Sanguszko' group, is represented by about fifteen whole carpets and fragments. It is named after a medallion carpet now in the collection of Prince Roman Sanguszko in Paris and said to have been taken at the battle of Chocim in 1621. Although no definite classification has been formulated, it is generally considered that the main characteristic is a medallion combined with animals (see 70b). They differ slightly from the classical medallion-and-animal carpets in their use of soft colours and the composition of the border. The lobed medallions in the border, containing bird, animal, and human forms, are very similar to some mosaic panels in a *medresseh* or religious college in Kerman, which was commissioned by the governor, Garj Ali Khan, at the beginning of the seventeenth century. On the basis of this, and similar evidence, it has been suggested that this group of carpets was woven in Kerman. However, as artists and master weavers seem to have moved, or been moved, from place to place, it is never possible to identify with any certainty the provenance of one carpet or one type of carpet.

A similar problem, of classification and origin, surrounds a group called 'Vase' carpets. These can be defined in two different ways: either by design, or by a particular weaving technique (see 17a) which unifies carpets of widely differing designs. Generally speaking, when classified by design alone, these carpets do not have a centralized pattern and can be viewed from only one direction. They seem to

a. Above *The basic grid of this rug is strictly geometrical, but it also shows the transition to a more floral style. Persia, late fifteenth or early sixteenth century.*
5.30m × 2.22m, 17'4" × 7'3".
Museu Calouste Gulbenkian, Lisbon

b. Above *The cartouches of this floral-style carpet contain dragons, phoenixes, lions, and birds against flowering stems. Persia, sixteenth century.*
8m × 4m, 26'3" × 13'1".
Musée des Tissus, Lyons

a. Above left *The delicate drawing and graceful design of this Garden carpet indicate the involvement of court artists. Persia, early sixteenth century. 7m × 3.65m, 23' × 12'. Los Angeles County Museum of Art*

b. Above right *A detail of a silk rug which depicts animals in combat in a landscape. Persia (Kashan) seventeenth century. The Metropolitan Museum, New York, Bequest of Benjamin Altman, 1913*

be a riot of flowering blossoms, of lotus, peony, and pomegranate, with feathery palmettes and curved lanceolate leaves. Sometimes vases are dispersed among them, hence the name. On close inspection, however, it can be seen that each element is part of an elaborate lattice pattern formed by two or three systems of stems upon which the blossoms are placed at regular intervals. Although only a fragment, the carpet in Berlin (see 70c) is a particularly vivacious example of the three-plane-lattice composition. It is probably one of the earliest to have survived, and dates from the second half of the sixteenth century, although the dating of this group of carpets is a matter of debate, with many people assigning them all to the seventeenth century and later. Kerman again is often credited as the centre of production. Some of the carpet motifs, and the way they are arranged, are found in late-sixteenth-century mosaic and tile decoration in that city.

If the Vase group is defined on technical grounds it encompasses numerous design types, including Sanguszko carpets and certain 'Garden' carpets. All these carpets feature a depressed warp (see 17a) and three shoots of weft after every row of knots. The first and third shoots are wool and the second one is either silk or cotton; the warp is also cotton. This particular structure is very similar to the one used in Kerman carpets of the nineteenth and twentieth centuries.

The Wagner Garden carpet (see 70d) is, in its technique, part of the Vase group. The field represents a garden divided into four compartments by a canal system with a central pool. These *chahar bag* (four garden) carpets faithfully depict, from a bird's-eye view, classical Persian

a. Above *A small silk carpet with a medallion and corner pieces on a field of blossoms and cloud scrolls. Persia (probably Kashan), mid-sixteenth century.*
2.45m × 1.85m, 8′ × 6′.
Mobilier National, Paris

b. Right *A Sanguzsko carpet with a central medallion and animals in combat. Persia, late sixteenth century.*
5.09m × 2.75m, 16′8″ × 9′.
Thyssen-Bornemisza Collection, Lugano

c. Opposite left *A Vase carpet based on a three-plane-lattice composition. Persia (probably Kerman) late sixteenth century.*
2.45m × 1.44m, 8′ × 4′8″.
Museum für Islamische Kunst, Staatliche Museen Preussischer Kulturbesitz, Berlin (West)

d. Opposite right *This carpet depicts a classical Persian garden with pools and flowers. Persia (probably Kerman) seventeenth century.*
5.30m × 4.31m, 17′5″ × 14′2″.
Burrell Collection, Glasgow

gardens in which high walls enclose pools and tiled water channels, bordered by trees, rose bushes, and many types of flowers and shrubs. Fish swim in the channels and pools, and sometimes animals browse, while birds survey them from the branches of trees. When compared to similar motifs in earlier Persian carpets it is clear that these animals have lost their vivacity, the trees are stiffer, the leaves and flowers less charmingly observed. Later garden carpets, dating from the eighteenth century, are often ascribed to Kurdistan.

Trees, flowers, animals, and birds were a highly important feature of Persian art. The country is an arid plateau ringed by mountains, and the people's love of water and shade, of paradisical settings in which animals and birds roam, is reflected in their carpets. From the sixteenth to the eighteenth centuries, beautiful floral carpets were woven in Herat, the former Timurid capital now inside Afghanistan. They have a deep red field and a dark greenish-blue border, and are characterized by the use of serrated leaves, usually in pairs around a composite blossom (see 33a).

The influence of these carpets was widespread, both in west and east. A great number were imported via Isfahan into Europe in the seventeenth century and are represented in paintings by such Dutch artists as Rubens, Vermeer, de Hooch, and Van Dyck. Weavers from Herat were prob-

ably recruited by the Mughal emperor Akbar (1556–1605) to work in his carpet workshops, and as they would have continued to weave carpets to their traditional designs, it is possible that many of the carpets once catalogued as Persian were really woven in India (see 72a). This lack of certainty has led many people to call carpets with the Herati colouring and dense floral pattern 'Indo-Persian'. Their influence should not be underestimated: it can be seen in many nineteenth-century Persian carpets, and in the products of twentieth-century looms in Iran, Afghanistan, and Pakistan. Even the English manufacturers of machine-woven carpets in the second half of the nineteenth century relied heavily on Herati designs.

One of the largest surviving and best documented groups of Safavid carpets are sometimes known as 'Polonaise'; at the Paris International Exhibition of 1878 they were wrongly assumed to be Polish, and the misnomer has persisted. Despite the fact that many are coarsely woven, often on a cotton warp and weft, they are commonly accepted as the epitome of the lavish courtly taste which prevailed in Shah Abbas' glittering cities, Kashan and Isfahan. The silk pile is woven in vivid colours – bright greens, blues, pinks, and yellows – and is enriched with brocaded gold and silver thread (see 72b). Such carpets were highly esteemed in both Persia and Europe, and many

a. Above *These Indo-Persian carpets with Herati designs were made in both India and Persia. This one may be Indian. Seventeenth century. 2.77m × 1.47m, 9'1" × 4'10". Thyssen-Bornemisza Collection, Lugano*

b. Above *A Polonaise carpet with silk pile and silver and gold brocading. 4.83m × 2.15m, 15'10" × 7'. The Metropolitan Museum, New York, Gift of John D. Rockefeller Jr., 1945*

a. Above *A silk kilim with the arms of the king of Poland. It appears from contemporary documents that this was executed in Kashan in 1602. 2.38m × 1.32m, 7'9″ × 4'4″. Bayerische Verwaltung der staatlichen Schlösser, Gärten und Seen, Residenzmuseum, Munich*

of the surviving ones were originally diplomatic gifts to European monarchs and ambassadors. The first known appearance of these carpets in Europe was in Poland in 1602, and in the following seventy years there are many references in royal inventories to 'gold and silk carpets'.

Closely related to such carpets are a number of flat-weaves or kilims. One bears the arms of Sigismund Vasa III, King of Poland (see 73a). A document dated 12 September 1602, preserved in Warsaw, is an account rendered by an Armenian, Sefer Muratowicz, who had been sent to Kashan by Sigismund to purchase silk carpets. It notes the prices he paid for six pairs of carpets, recording the price of five crowns extra for the inclusion of the King's arms in one carpet, and it seems probable that the account related to this kilim. The field of silk kilims usually follows the same basic design – a central medallion or diamond with bar-and-palmette appendages at the top and bottom, and quartered medallions in the corners. Because the designs often include animals and birds and are woven in bright colours, the group is usually assigned to Kashan and is considered to be the probable successor of the sixteenth-century silk pile carpets from that city. The rarest type of silk kilim, sometimes called the multiple-medallion kilim, is represented by only three examples. One is privately owned, but on loan to the Victoria and Albert Museum, and another has been in Japan since the sixteenth century; it was used as a campaigning cloak by the samurai warrior, Toyotomai Hideyoshi, who died in 1598. The third example is in the Thyssen-Bornemisza Collection (see 38a). The colours have faded – the soft orange must once have been a bright flame and the black outlines of the motifs have decayed. When first woven, the silver and gold thread must have glittered in a way not usually associated with the rich, mellow colours of most surviving Persian carpets.

Although the death of Shah Abbas in 1629 is usually taken to mark the end of Persia's golden era, the principles of the classical style were not abandoned. Carpet production did suffer from a decrease in court patronage and a certain degree of stiffness and stylization became common, but it has been seen that magnificent carpets continued to be woven in the seventeenth century. Safavid rulers struggled on for a further century, sustained more by the glories of the dynasty's past than by their own merits. They were overthrown in 1722 following an Afghan invasion which left Persia in a state of political and economic turmoil. There seem to have been no marked artistic developments in carpet design during the eighteenth century, but the traditions survived in town and village production. It was for the Qajar dynasty (1787–1925), that emerged paramount at the end of the century, to restore order and provide the impetus for a revived interest in the arts and a new look in carpets. A revised vocabulary of ornament, based on classical designs, was introduced, and when Persian carpet production was revived on a commercial basis about 1875, the influence of sixteenth and seventeenth-century motifs was discernible.

Early Caucasian Carpets

The area known as the Caucasus is the wide isthmus that separates the Black and Caspian seas. The Greater and Lesser Caucasus Mountains extend in two ranges from northwest to southeast and form a jagged barrier across this landbridge between Europe and Asia, creating its rugged surface of valleys, ravines, foothills, and plains before finally giving way to coastal lowlands.

Inhabiting the complex terrain of the Caucasus is a human population of even greater complexity. From pre-classical antiquity onwards, so many successive waves of foreign invaders and immigrants settled here that a four-teenth-century Arab geographer dubbed the region *jabal al-alsun* – the Mountain of Languages. By modern count, the area is occupied by over fifty separate peoples, of whom indigenous mountain tribes, Georgians, Armenians, Slavs, Ossets, Kurds, and Azeri Turks are the most numerous ethnic groups, and Christianity and Islam the predominant religions. The last of the outside conquerors of the Caucasus was Russia, in a drive that began under Peter the Great and was completed in the late nineteenth century. The region now comprises the Soviet Socialist Republics of Georgia, Armenia, and Azerbaijan, and the very southernmost parts of the Russian Republic, which includes Daghestan.

Caucasian village rugs of the nineteenth century were produced mainly to the south of the Lesser Caucasus Mountains in an area traditionally known as the Transcau-casus, and in the eastern coastal region bordering the Caspian. It is quite probable that tribal and nomadic peoples in these areas wove small-scale rugs – and then completely used them up – long before nineteenth-century trade introduced the descendants of these rugs to the West.

The oldest existing Caucasian rugs are now thought to date from the early seventeenth century onwards, a period when the southern and eastern Caucasus were subject to Persian control. These old survivors are considerably larger than most tribal or nomadic weavings and exhibit intricate, formalized patterns that suggest their reliance either on cartoons or on other rugs with designs originating in court workshops. At the same time, the Caucasian rugs are much more coarsely knotted than carpets made in workshops serving the Persian court. They are therefore thought to be products of a cottage industry set up in villages or urban centres of the Caucasus, products destined for export. A large group of them have indeed been collected from mosques along the trade routes throughout Turkey and are now in the museums of Istanbul.

The length of early Caucasian rugs often exceeds 5 metres (16 feet). Their width is comparatively narrow – usually not more than half the length. Primary colours – especially red and dark blue – dominate their palette. They are most frequently surrounded by a single, rather narrow, main border, often flanked only by unornamented guard stripes. All of them have wool pile and are symmetrically knotted, with a knot count that exceeds 1550 knots per square decimetre (100 per square inch) only in later examples. Their foundation material, too, is usually sheep's wool; the wool warps exhibit a variety of natural colours,

and the thinner wefts are nearly always some shade of red. Only in one rather rare category of these rugs, and in occasional later examples of several types, is cotton used in the foundation.

In much of the older rug literature, early Caucasian rugs in various designs have been called 'Kuba' carpets. But Kuba, a small town in the eastern province of Daghestan that is known as a source of nineteenth-century rugs, was probably established only in the mid eighteenth century, well after the earliest 'Kuba' carpets were woven. Further-more, in contrast to the small, fine, nineteenth-century products associated with Kuba, early Caucasian rugs are big and relatively coarse. Both their weaving characteristics and their designs suggest their genesis further south and west, in the areas of Shirvan and Karabagh.

The oldest and most numerous family of early Caucasian rugs are called 'dragon' carpets. The field of a typical early dragon rug – usually red, but sometimes blue or brown – is divided into irregular compartments by a two-colour lattice (see 42a). This latticework is formed of jagged-edged leaves, paired in giant upright and inverted Vs. The points of these Vs are overlapped by large palmettes or rosettes. The compartments that flank these palmettes are filled with angular S-forms – the dragons for which the carpet group is named. Highly stylized, these creatures nevertheless have identifiable crests, rear legs, curving tails, and flames that sprout from their shoulders and haunches. They often boast colourfully spotted coats.

In older carpets, including the example in the Keir Collection illustrated here, the dragons are accompanied by other creatures: lions battling *chi'lins* (composite beasts with dragon heads and stag bodies) in large compartments unoccupied by dragons, and ducks and pheasants squeezed into the lattice itself. The very earliest dragon carpets also include, in some of the smaller compartments, pairs of deer flanking single trees; in later carpets these motifs are replaced by palmettes. Even in the oldest existing rugs, the whole bestiary is geometrized almost to the limit of recognition. The distant ancestry of the dragons and their animal associates (the Near-Eastern tree-flanking deer excluded) is Chinese, but they probably come to the Caucasus more directly from Persian court art, which represents them all with greater naturalism in its own carpets of the later sixteenth century.

Persian carpets, notably the floral 'Vase' carpets of seventeenth-century Kerman (see 70c), also anticipate the overall trellis pattern and uncentralized, single-direction design of the dragon rugs. Even one of the stranger structural features of the Kerman carpets – a heavy, single weft added at periodic intervals, perhaps to facilitate tight packing of the knots – recurs on many dragon rugs and on early Caucasian carpets in other designs.

Early in this century it was proposed, and it has sometimes been reasserted, that the design of dragon carpets originated in Armenia. One of the arguments supporting this contention was based on the identification of a purple dye used in dragon carpets with a particular, insect-produced purplish colour found in thirteenth-

a. Right *An eighteenth-century Caucasian dragon carpet. Here the dragons have usurped all the large compartments, and the central pair are reversed, altering the one-directional scheme of earlier dragon rugs.* 4.45m × 1.91m, 14′6″ × 6′4″. *The Textile Museum, Washington*

b. Far right *This is probably a nineteenth-century Kurdish adaption of the original seventeenth-century Caucasian dragon carpet. An inscription at the top records the name of the weaver — Husayn Bek.* 4.45m × 1.83m, 14′8″ × 6′. *The Textile Museum, Washington*

century Armenian manuscripts. This comparison presupposed that dragon rugs were far older than is now admitted, in the light of their derivative relationship with Kerman rugs of the seventeenth century. But there do exist carpets, inscribed in Armenian, with designs apparently derived from dragon rugs. These testify, as do copious inscriptions on nineteenth and twentieth-century Caucasian rugs, to the importance of Armenian artisans and clients in the rug production of the Caucasus, production that occupied numerous peoples in that diversely populated region.

Throughout the seventeenth and eighteenth centuries, the design of dragon rugs underwent inevitable modification. In some examples, all other animal and bird forms have disappeared, leaving only dragons to dominate the larger compartments. Even the dragons themselves are occasionally replaced with spiky, flowering plants. Another tendency of the weavers of later dragon carpets

was to transform the original single-direction pattern into ones that might be read from either end of the rug. This was sometimes accomplished rather tentatively, by reversing a few palmettes in the central compartments. A rug in the Textile Museum in Washington (see 75a) shows the process taken a step further; although its dragons have become tortuously abstract, the pair of them in the middle can nevertheless be seen to stand on their malformed heads while their brethren above and below them are upright.

In the most extreme cases, one-way design was jettisoned totally in favour of a centralized format, with end-to-end symmetry and a single medallion imposed upon the carpet centre. Another Textile Museum rug with the dragon design is thus organized; its dragons and most of its other fauna and flora appear in mirror image around a star-shaped central medallion (see 75b). Inscribed in Arabic with the name Husayn Bek and a date that can be read as

a. Above *The Niğde carpet.
The lattice divides this
beautifully preserved carpet
into diamond-shaped
compartments filled with floral
motifs and cloud bands. The
Caucasus, seventeenth century.
Detail.
(7.52m × 3.05m, 24'10" × 10'.)
The Metropolitan Museum,
New York, Gift of Joseph V.
McNullan*

b. Right *An eighteenth-
century Caucasian sunburst
carpet. The sunburst, with its
white, pronged rays, survives
to dominate the famous
nineteenth-century carpets
known as 'eagle Kazaks'.
5.31m × 2.31m, 17'6" × 7'8".
The Textile Museum,
Washington*

c. Opposite *In this carpet the
repeat pattern, which includes
in-and-out palmettes, may
have been derived from
brocaded textiles. The
Caucasus, eighteenth century.
2.29m × 4.48m, 7'6" × 15'.
The Textile Museum,
Washington*

either 1592 or 1689, this carpet was once cited as evidence of the role of Muslim Turks in the creation of early dragon carpets. The whole repertory of animals found on the oldest dragon rugs is indeed present on this one, not just undiminished, but augmented by new creatures. The extra animals, however, are adventitious little striped quadrupeds and birds-in-boxes, looking suspiciously like the ones that appear in nineteenth-century Caucasian rugs. The palmettes and leaf-lattice of the Husayn Bek rug are atypically inelegant, and its colours and structure unusual. In short, the rug is now thought to be a copy – or rather an inventive adaptation – of Husayn Bek's early dragon rug, by a nineteenth-century Kurdish weaver. It demonstrates the persistent attraction and durability of dragon carpet design, and the competing tendency over the years to render that design centralized and symmetrical.

The bold latticework that so tenaciously organizes dragon rugs – even later rugs on which the dragons have become abstract mutants or have altogether vanished – also dominates the designs of other early Caucasian rugs that were never host to animal decoration. A seventeenth-century carpet now in the Metropolitan Museum of Art, obtained in the early 1900s from a mosque in the central Anatolian town of Niğde, provides a splendid example of lattice-patterned floral design (see 76a). The red, stem-like lattice of the Niğde carpet creates diamond-shaped compartments with two sorts of ornamentation. Leaf-surrounded cruciform medallions containing four palmettes fill some of the diamonds; in alternate compartments, crossed palmettes and blossoms are embraced by pairs of cloud bands. These cloud bands, by the angular standards of Caucasian weaving, are remarkably sinuous. Like the animals that occupy dragon rugs, they are Chinese motifs, introduced to the Caucasus by way of Persia.

The Niğde carpet, although uniquely well preserved, is one of at least five museum-held rugs in closely related, lattice-patterned floral designs. In the Museum of Turkish and Islamic Art in Istanbul, for instance, there are two very worn fragments from a nearly identical carpet. These fragments and the Niğde rug, unlike other groups of early Caucasian carpets, have cotton warps and wefts. Their designs – and perhaps their use of cotton – appear directly indebted to a species of Kerman Vase carpet that also includes blossoms inside variously coloured, diamond-shaped compartments. The two fragments were found in a dervish *tekke*, or meeting house, in Bursa, far to the west and north of Niğde. While these lattice-patterned floral rugs doubtless did not share the enduring popularity of the dragon carpets, they too must represent a design type commercially distributed outside the Caucasus.

New rug designs appear from the Caucasus during the eighteenth century. In some of them, compartment organization breaks up, leaving only vestiges of leafy latticework to protrude from or embrace large, discrete, and increasingly medallion-like floral forms. An arresting version of this design appears on rugs that are sometimes called 'sunburst' carpets, after one of their dominant motifs. Like dragon carpets, these usually have red grounds. The sunburst itself is an angular, diamond-centred blossom with projecting buds, strikingly surrounded by white, pronged rays. It is accompanied by giant pairs of curved leaves that

hold tilted palmettes or sawtoothed medallions in octagonal embrace, and by a different species of palmette – ovoid, open-ended, and upright. Often the arrangement of these elements is symmetrical and centralized, with the sunburst in the middle, leaf octagons above and below it, and palmettes distributed around the periphery. An example in the Textile Museum, however, maintains end-to-end symmetry only in the halved elements at its sides, and boldly stacks all the motifs up the middle (see 76b).

a. Left *The small-scale floral repeat of this eighteenth-century Caucasian fragment is known as the Afshan pattern. It became fashionable at this period and continued throughout the nineteenth century.*
2.49m × 3.71m, 8'3" × 12'4".
The Textile Museum, Washington

also include prominent 'in-and-out' palmettes (see 33a). But the design scheme of the Caucasian rugs, as exemplified by a carpet in the Textile Museum (see 76c), can also be read as an arrangement of repeated diamonds without the lattice. These diamonds are formed of larger, horizontal palmette-pairs and smaller, vertical palmette-pairs combined in floral quartets, as are the palmettes within the diamond medallions of the Niğde carpet.

The most common of all repeat floral designs has become known by the name 'Afshan', from the Persian word meaning 'scattering'. This design did not originate in the Caucasus but – like the in-and-out palmette design – appears in an earlier and more curvilinear form on carpets from Persia and Mughal India.

Caucasian rugs of Afshan design have dark blue or – less often – red grounds, overgrown by vertical rows of contiguously stacked, S-shaped vines that connect fringed diagonal leaves with horizontal palmettes and end in lily-like, forked blossoms. Between the vines appear small lobed or starlike medallions. A fragmentary Afshan carpet in the Textile Museum (see 78a) has four series of vertical S-vines; a few carpets have as many as six.

The elegant monotony of the Afshan design seems to have gained such great favour in the late eighteenth century that it continued to be reproduced, essentially unchanged, in nineteenth-century rugs from several districts of the Caucasus.

If this selective survey of early Caucasian carpets demonstrates the wide variety of their designs, it also shows an abiding tendency to treat these designs in a characteristic way. However refined and elegant the concept on which the pattern of an early Caucasian rug is based, that pattern will always be rendered, not in graceful curves, but rather in a series of straight and angled lines. However early the carpet, its animal and plant forms will be stylized and abstract. Such angularity and abstraction are naturally due in part to the purely technical limitations of coarse knotting. But to endure and flourish as they did, early Caucasian rugs must also have satisfied a distinct aesthetic preference. The innate tension of their designs – sophisticated yet rustic – makes these rugs fitting representatives of the complex area in which they originated, and, to modern eyes, they remain fascinating art.

Sunburst carpets, like dragon carpets, were commercial hits, and many specimens remain in Turkish, European, and American museums. A spectacular matched pair, 6.6 metres (21½ feet) in length, was recently uncovered in the Great Mosque of Divriği, in eastern central Turkey, and has now been transferred to the Vakiflar Museum in Istanbul. The sunburst motif itself has had a prominent solo career; it occasionally shows up as the central medallion in later dragon carpets, and eventually appears, singly or in multiples, in the many nineteenth-century 'eagle Kazaks' now thought to have been produced, like their sunburst carpet ancestors, in Karabagh.

Some Caucasian rugs of the eighteenth century are host to designs that seem the very antithesis of the bold, large-scale motifs of sunburst carpets. Their floral patterns tend to be relatively small, ceaselessly repetitive, and without central focus – characteristics that may point to an origin in finer, brocaded textiles.

One popular floral design, which usually occupies carpets with blue fields, features stepped and fringed horizontal palmettes that point inwards and outwards along the carpet length. Such a layout is immediately reminiscent of a large group of sixteenth and seventeenth-century 'Indo-Persian' carpets, of which the far more curvilinear designs

Carpets of Mughal India

It is impossible to say how far back the history of the pile carpet in India extends. Carpets were certainly in use by the fourteenth century, when the Moroccan traveller Ibn Battuta describes them, but there is no real evidence for their manufacture before the Mughal period. The absence of a local tradition of carpet weaving is reflected in words such as *gilim*, *qalicha*, and *farsh*: all terms used in India for a pile carpet, but all of foreign origin. The Mughals were of course 'foreign' to India themselves: Babur, who created the Mughal empire by defeating the Afghan Lodi dynasty and taking Delhi in 1526, was a Turk from Ferghana in present-day Uzbekistan. It was during the reign of his grandson Akbar between 1556 and 1605 that the empire consolidated its power, and in 1598, Akbar's prime minister and confidant Abu'l-Fazl completed a great survey of the empire, the *A'in-i Akbari* or 'Institutes of Akbar'. In it he relates how the emperor caused carpet workshops to be set up, manned by experienced weavers and established in every town, especially the imperial cities of Agra, Fatehpur Sikri, and Lahore. The carpets made in these workshops were apparently so splendid that those of Persia and Turkestan were "no longer thought of", though he admits that carpets were still being imported from Persia. It is probable that Akbar's "experienced weavers" came from Persia. We are told, again by Abu'l-Fazl, that Lahore "is the resort of people of all countries, whose manufactures present an astonishing display", and it is not unreasonable to suppose that carpet-weavers were among the foreign craftsmen there. Akbar's enthusiastic patronage of the arts, and the splendour of his court, must have lured many Persian craftsmen as well as miniature painters to his capitals. Certainly there is a fusion of Persian and Indian elements to be seen in carpets as well as paintings.

No carpet exists today that can be indisputably dated to Akbar's reign. Identifying carpet types from miniature paintings is notoriously problematic, but it is worth noting that the vast majority of carpets depicted in illustrated manuscripts of this period show floral designs with lotus palmettes on scrolling stems. These motifs are reminiscent of the controversial 'Indo-Persian' group of carpets, also known as 'Indo-Isfahan' or 'Herat' carpets (see 72a), which at one time were attributed solely to Persia. It is now widely accepted that at least some of these carpets were made in India, possibly by Akbar's expert craftsmen in his new workshops. Strikingly similar designs using lotus palmettes and cloud bands occur in architectural decoration of the Akbar period at Fatehpur Sikri and Akbar's tomb at Sikandra, near Agra. The Persian examples appear to have been made in Herat, the city from which Akbar would probably have recruited his weavers. Many of this immense group of rugs are undoubtedly Persian, but some have Indian characteristics including a particular red colour in the field and a relatively empty background. The colour scheme of red field and blue-green border is one that continued to be popular throughout the Mughal period.

Another carpet which may be datable to around 1600 has an extraordinary design of fantastic animals (see 79a). About a dozen fragments survive, but no overall design is discernible; though rows of heads on some pieces suggest an analogy with Persian 'Vase' carpets. In a stylistically related, but more finely-woven piece with a blue ground, in the Musée des Arts Décoratifs, the animal heads are incorporated into a scrolling arabesque, a motif popular among Persian manuscript illuminators since the fourteenth century. A striking parallel to the blue-ground piece is found in the animal-headed scrolls of Timurid illumination of the fifteenth and early sixteenth century; this taken in conjunction with the fineness of the weave, despite its early date, may indicate that the blue rug is Persian (probably from Herat) rather than Indian, even though it has the coloured silk warps associated with Mughal rugs of the seventeenth and eighteenth centuries.

Pictorial elements came to dominate carpet design during the first quarter of the seventeenth century. Three particular rugs from this period illustrate the interrelation between

a. Above *The stylized treatment of the animals and flowers in this rug seems to antedate the naturalism of the Jahangiri period. India, early seventeenth century.*
1.29m × 1m, 4'3" × 3'3".
Burrell Collection, Glasgow

miniature painter and carpet designer. The first (see 81a) is a rug in the Museum of Fine Arts, Boston, which has a lively asymmetrical design, far removed from the formal repeating pattern of comparable Persian animal rugs, although the border of palmettes separated by long-tailed birds does recall those of the Kashan silk animal rugs of the sixteenth century. The foliage and human figures suggest Indian miniatures of the Akbar period, while the woman and child in one corner recall Rajput painting.

The second is the famous 'Peacock' rug in Vienna, which is even more 'painterly' than the Boston carpet – surely neither of these was ever meant to be put on the floor, but at approximately 1.5 by 2.5 metres (5 by 8 feet), both are of a manageable size to hang on a wall. Like the Boston carpet, the Peacock rug has a bright red ground with an asymmetrical design, but here the inhabitants of the rug are trees, flowers, and birds. It is sometimes suggested that Mansur, the renowned animal and flower painter at the court of Jahangir (who ruled between 1605 and 1627) was the designer, but once again the trees and foliage are more in an Akbari style, recalling particularly the decorative stone carving at Fatehpur Sikri. It is difficult to determine how long it took for motifs used in architecture to appear in the decorative arts; Fatehpur Sikri was abandoned as an imperial city in 1584, yet it seems unrealistic to suppose

that these rugs could date from much before 1600.

The third pictorial rug, the animal carpet in the National Gallery of Art, Washington, is related to the first two in style, but is larger and more formalized, and has a design more recognizably appropriate to a carpet. Although it shows a large number of animals dashing in several directions, it is in fact a symmetrical design. It is likely that this rug was made in the 1620s, at a transitional stage between the experimental freedom of the early pictorial rugs and the more formal pieces of the Shah Jahan period. All three of these rugs have curious borders of grimacing faces in palmettes. They also share the characteristically Mughal feature of pinkish-red elements, usually leaves and flowers, superimposed on the darker red of the background with no dividing line between the two shades. This adventurous and attractive concept, also executed in blues and greens, is often used for the pointed wisteria-like clusters of flowers which embellish many animal and floral rugs.

In the 1620s, a great passion for flowers overtook the Mughal court, apparently brought on by a springtime visit by Jahangir to Kashmir. The artist Mansur accompanied him and painted over a hundred flower studies to satisfy the emperor's love of nature. The new taste for floral decoration coincided with the introduction into the Mughal court of European herbals, and their botanical renderings of

a. Far left *These scenes are influenced by miniature painting and their asymmetrical arrangement is typical of the period. India, early seventeenth century. 2.43m × 1.54m, 7′11″ × 5′. Museum of Fine Arts, Boston*

b. Near left *This flamboyant rug has over 1000 knots per square inch. The single plant and cusped arch were favourite decorative motifs in Shah Jahan's reign. India, 1625–50. 1.25m × 0.90m, 4′1″ × 2′10″. Thyssen-Bornemisza Collection, Lugano*

c. Right *Tree rugs are not uncommon in Persian weaving, but are very rare in India. This rug combines Mughal naturalism with Persian elements in the border. India, circa 1635–45. 2.27m × 1.92m, 7′5″ × 6′3″. The Frick Collection, New York*

flowers added a new dimension to the Mughal style. In royal Mughal albums, miniature paintings were mounted in borders decorated with flowering plants, painted singly and realistically as in the herbals. Their use spread, and during Shah Jahan's reign (1628–58) the flowering plant was the dominant motif in architectural decoration, manuscript illumination, and the decorative arts.

A small group of carpets from the second quarter of the seventeenth century shows how the simple, almost austere, flowering-plant design could be used to splendid effect. They all show a single plant with several blooms, standing in a cusped arch and flanked by smaller flowers. It is probable that they are prayer rugs, as indicated by their mihrab-like arches and small size, but it should be remembered that textiles with similar architectural elements are frequently shown hanging on the interior walls of palaces in Mughal miniatures.

The most striking of this group is the flamboyant rug in the Thyssen-Bornemisza Collection (see 81b). The intensity of the deep-red ground is accentuated by the lustre of the soft goat hair (*pashm*) used for the pile. The drawing of the main plant recalls Persian painting rather than the stolid woodcuts of the herbals, while the small wispy clouds, as well as the rocks and stream at the bottom, are Chinese in origin but introduced through Persia. The plant is flanked by cypress trees, which recur in the same role in the 'millefleur' prayer rugs of the eighteenth century. The unusually narrow borders, and the fact that the field has been repaired with pieces from an almost identical rug, indicate that this rug may have been one niche of a *saf*, or multiple prayer rug.

A more sober but equally beautiful prayer rug is in the Pincket collection in Belgium. It shows a formal chrysanthemum-like plant against a delicate light-brown back-

a. Above *Finely woven trellis carpets became popular in Shah Jahan's reign. This one recalls Persian Vase carpets with its palmettes in the trellis. India, mid-seventeenth century.*
2.94m × 1.37m, 9'8" × 4'6".
The Metropolitan Museum, New York

ground, devoid of ornamentation such as the previous rug's clouds and cypress trees. This rug has over 31,000 knots per square decimetre (2000 per square inch), achieved by the use of silk warps and wefts and finest goat hair for the pile. This almost incredible fineness of knotting is surpassed only by a fragmentary rug of the same group, part of which is in the Metropolitan Museum, New York, which has 39,500 knots per square decimetre (2,550 per square inch). No other carpets have ever been as densely knotted as Mughal carpets of this period.

Another version of this rug illustrates the practice, relatively widespread in the Mughal workshops, of making a less fine version of certain top-quality rugs. The coarser counterpart of the Pincket rug, also in the Metropolitan Museum, has a modest 3480 knots per square decimetre (225 per square inch). With its bolder palette and coarser drawing, it lacks the simple elegance of the Pincket rug; but, though it suffers by comparison, it is nonetheless a striking rug and a rare complete example of the flowering-plant design.

The same two-tier production system was used for a unique carpet now in the Frick Collection, New York (see 81c). Datable, like the prayer rugs, to the early part of Shah Jahan's reign, it has a design of trees, alternately leafy and flowering, on a deep-red ground. The trees and flowers are drawn with exquisite naturalism using a subtle range of colours. This is another of the silk foundation, goat hair pile rugs, and a large piece of its equivalent, in cotton and sheep's wool, is now in the Textile Museum, Washington, though the flowering trees have become disproportionately large bunches of flowers.

It was probably during Shah Jahan's reign that the greatest number of top-quality Mughal rugs were made. Sadly, most are now fragmentary, but several impressive pieces remain to bear witness to the perfection of the workmanship and design of this period. The motifs on these rugs are predominantly floral, frequently combining the typically Mughal single flowering plant with elements borrowed from contemporary Persian carpets – such as the sickle-shaped leaves enclosing a palmette. In several cases, one idiom appears in the field and the other, contrasting with it, in the border, a partnership that may be seen in the Frick tree rug, which has Persian elements in the border and Mughal naturalistic trees in the field.

Another magnificent rug of this period is the Altman trellis carpet (see 82a), which has an unusual and beautiful tree border. With its ogival-trellis pattern imposing a certain rigidity on the design, this carpet is one of the compartmental rugs popular in Shah Jahan's reign. While retaining the fine naturalistic drawing of the flowers, many of this group draw on European models for the curling trellis. But another ogival-lattice carpet (to be seen in fragments in the Victoria and Albert Museum, and in Dusseldorf) lacks any baroque twists and turns; instead, both the form of the lattice and its serrated edges recall the Turkish velvets and brocades that were being imported into Mughal India at this time.

The rugs which for many people embody the Mughal carpet style are the red-ground pieces with rows of single flowering plants (see 83a). These are seen as the archetypal Mughal rug because, with their empty background, red field, dark blue border, and unmistakably Mughal plants,

a. Above *A shaped floral carpet made for the palace at Amber near Jaipur. A label on the back bears the date 1689. India, Lahore.*
1.21m × 4.33m, 4′ × 14′3″.
Maharaja Sawai Man Singh 11 Museum Trust, Jaipur

b. Left *The splendid rug of which this is a detail has an unusual arrangement of two adjacent medallions in the centre. The label on the back of the carpet states that it was acquired in 1667. India, Lahore.*
(11.58m × 4.41m, 38′ × 14′6″.)
Maharaja Sawai Man Singh 11 Museum Trust, Jaipur

a. Above *A beautiful, though fragmentary, floral rug knotted on a silk foundation. India, mid-seventeenth century. Detail.*
(5.64m × 1.25m, 18'6" × 4'.)
Museu Calouste Gulbenkian, Lisbon

b. Above *This rug dates from Aurangzeb's reign when dense patterns of small flower heads came into vogue. India, early eighteenth century.*
2.10m × 1.47m, 6'9" × 4'9".
Ashmolean Museum, Oxford

they are far removed from Persian carpet styles. Also there are enough of them, or fragments of them, still in carpet collections and on the art market for them to have become relatively familiar. A large number of these rugs are still to be found in the palace at Jaipur (now a museum); these were originally made for Raja Jai Singh for his palace at Amber, which was completed in 1630. Many of the rugs in this important collection still bear their original labels, the floral rugs labelled as coming from Lahore. Most of the rugs of this type now scattered throughout the world can be traced back to the palace at Amber.

Although the hallmark of carpets from the Shah Jahan period was the naturalistic flowering plant, there were nonetheless some more fanciful, but equally meticulously drawn, variations. Foremost among these is a stunning piece in the Gulbenkian Museum, Lisbon (see 84a), which is finely knotted on silk warps and wefts. The design features a swirling arabesque with pin-wheel rosettes, long variegated frondy leaves, and feathery palmettes, all enclosed by a double-scroll border enlivened by Chinese clouds.

Far better known, valued both for its documented history and its qualities as a work of art, is the Girdlers' Carpet. It was commissioned in 1631 for the Worshipful Company of Girdlers in London, to whom it still belongs, as a gift from the Master, Robert Bell, who was also a director of the East India Company. Made in Lahore, it incorporates into the Persian-style floral design the coats of arms of Robert Bell and the Girdlers' Company, with St. Lawrence and the gridiron which is the company's symbol. It was designed to lie on a table, the usual position for a carpet in seventeenth-century England, and it still bears ink stains as a memorial to board meetings long past.

Robert Bell was not the only Englishman to commission a personalized carpet: we are told that Sir Thomas Roe, James I's ambassador to Jahangir's court from 1616 to 1620, also ordered one, but it does not survive, unlike the Fremlin carpet in the Victoria and Albert Museum. This is an animal rug, commissioned by William Fremlin in about 1640, and it incorporates into both field and border the arms of the Fremlin family. We can infer from its shape and the disposition of the coats of arms in the border that it was also intended as a table rug.

The European presence in India is also suggested by the notoriously controversial group of carpets known as 'Portuguese', in allusion to the figures in European dress in the boats which fill the corners (see 40a). Originally attributed to Goa because of its strong Portuguese connections, these rugs have also been associated with Gujarat and both

northern and southern Persia. The overgrown central medallion has no parallel in any of these centres, and the erratic structure of the rugs, including the use of symmetrical, asymmetrical and jufti knots, adds to the confusion. The maritime scenes draw on miniature painting in a rather Mughal way, and the colour scheme, including the juxtaposition of pink and red, might be said to be more Indian than Persian; but no hard evidence for an Indian origin has yet come to light, and the borders are of a type associated with Safavid rather than Mughal carpets.

Shah Jahan's younger son Aurangzeb defeated his brother, the cultivated, art-loving Dara Shikoh, to seize the throne in 1658. Aurangzeb is habitually written off as an austere, bigoted monarch who actively discouraged music and the arts. However true this may be, the Mughal empire actually expanded under Aurangzeb, attaining its greatest ever area with the annexation of the Deccani kingdoms of Bijapur and Golconda in 1686 and 1687. Such a huge empire required many officials of high status, so demand for high-quality goods such as carpets was still strong. Fine-weave trellis carpets continued to be produced, as well as new types such as the floral rug in the Ashmolean Museum, Oxford (see 84b). Here an all-over Persian design is combined with Mughal characteristics such as the superimposition of red on pink, the meticulous drawing of the flowers (facilitated by the use of goat hair for the pile), and the use of silk warps arranged in bands of green, yellow, red, and white. This rug is related in its use of dense floral decoration to the 'millefleurs' group, which includes prayer rugs with cypress trees flanking a flowering plant in a mihrab-shaped niche. In these rugs, however, instead of the stately single plant that was used in the Shah Jahan period, the space is crammed with flower-heads, with no attempt at realism. The borders, too, are filled with multiple flower-heads, where earlier in the seventeenth century, we would have seen a rather sparser scrolling-leaf-and-flower pattern.

With Aurangzeb's death, the decline of the empire accelerated, and its fate was presaged in 1739 when Nadir Shah of Persia invaded Delhi and carried off a large part of the Mughal treasury. The empire struggled to maintain its territories but the British gradually took over, in spite of a succession of Mughal emperors still nominally in power. This was no milieu for the production of prestigious carpets; the days of imperial patronage of brilliant and innovative craftsmen were over. When the Indian carpet industry did start up again, it was to provide copies of favourite Persian rugs for the Western market.

*An early nineteenth-century
prayer kilim from Eastern
Anatolia.*

Gazetteer

A guide to the carpet-producing
countries of the world

TURKEY

a. Left *Women returning from work across the fields in Western Turkey*

For centuries the carpets of Turkey, or Anatolia, have been so well known in Europe that they have almost been taken for granted. Early European painters showed rugs draped from balconies and covering tables and floors from early in the fourteenth century, and when proper research began into the origins of Turkish carpets, these early patterns were given the names of painters, such as 'Lotto', 'Holbein', and 'Memling'. Similar designs were still being made, virtually unchanged, down to the second half of the nineteenth century. It is only in relatively recent years that scholarly research has begun to attribute pile carpets and flat weaves to their genuine origins, thus creating a complex and fascinating picture of Turkish carpet weaving.

In discussing the carpets of Turkey, it is important to be aware that from the seventeenth century BC when the Hittites first formed a recognizable state, until the establishment of the Osmanli or Ottoman empire in the fifteenth century AD, Turkey was simply part of the vast land mass which stretched from Peking across the roof of India into East Turkestan, Afghanistan, Persia, Syria, the Balkans and beyond. Through conquest and migration, displacement and defeat, the high Anatolian plains were buffeted by waves of cultures and civilizations, including the Scythian, Lydian, Thracian, Armenian, Persian, Greek, and Roman. The majority were of Indo-European stock, but in the

paths of conquerors such as Alexander the Great, Ghenghis Khan, and the Seljuk Turks, other peoples – Mongolian, Chinese, and later, Arab and Slav – were absorbed into the heterogenous mixture which today constitutes the population of Anatolia. Nor should it be forgotten that, at its height, the Ottoman Empire stretched from Anatolia to Armenia, the southern territories of the Caucasus, and Turkestan; across the entire coast of North Africa, and north into Europe as far as the gates of Vienna. As late as the turn of this century Palestine, Arabia, Mesopotamia, Syria, and the Lebanon were under Ottoman rule.

The primary source of traditional carpet weaving in Turkey, with the greatest influence on both pattern and construction, is Konya, capital of the Seljuk dynasty from the thirteenth century until its overthrow by the Osmanli Turks at the end of the fifteenth century. The Seljuk Turks were of Central Asian Turkic stock and fragments of early Turkish pile-woven carpets have a pattern which is closely linked to Turkoman *guls* (see 163b). Old Konya carpets sometimes feature an additional upper and lower band with a repeating gable pattern which is still used by some Turkoman tribes in their weaving today. The other noticeable feature of the older tradition was the use of a red-dyed weft, which apparently was almost universal until the beginning of the sixteenth century and the overthrow of the Seljuk dynasty. In addition, some tantalizing flat-woven pieces suggest that an even older, pre-Turkoman tradition still survives in isolated areas of Anatolia.

It is important to keep this historical background clearly in mind since there are traces of many different cultures in the symbols, motifs, patterns, and techniques still used in Turkish weaving today. And it is becoming more and more evident that the names and attributions of many highly individual types of carpet and prayer rug may be no more than the merchants' identification for work done over a much greater area, possibly made specifically for trade. The carpets from the Bergama region, which sometimes resemble the Lotto and Holbein patterns of the fifteenth and sixteenth century, may have continued to be made principally for the European market, while the people themselves made flat weaves and pile carpets in an older, quite separate tradition. Meanwhile, some motifs and patterns made for merchants' orders may have been incorporated into tribal work because they were found adaptable and pleasing. Bearing these factors in mind, it is extremely difficult to make broad generalizations beyond the fact that the patterns tend to be geometric and abstract, with virtually no representations of humans or animals. The symmetrical knot is used almost universally in Anatolian pile weaves, and even the finest work is coarser than that of Persian or Turkoman tribal work.

The people being mainly Muslim, there is great emphasis on a wide variety of prayer rugs, though some of these feature a cross-like motif in the border which suggests that the weavers may have been Armenian. Prayer rugs made in

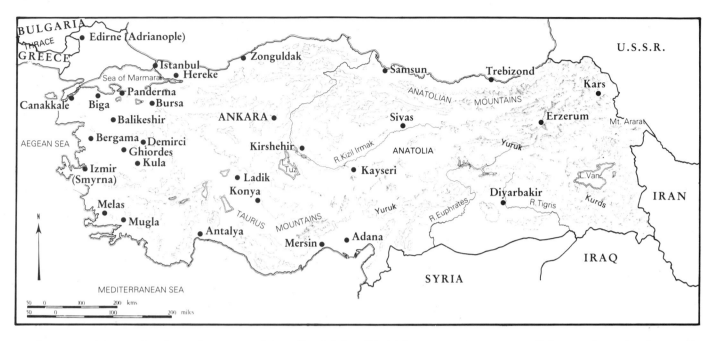

rural communities tend to have the centre of the mihrab left plain, except for an edging of flower heads around the inner outline. There may also be an almost abstract shape, representing a hanging holy lamp, suspended from the central arch of the mihrab. In larger towns and in more sophisticated carpet-weaving centres, there may be a single row of flowers in a panel at the bottom of the mihrab representing the garden of Paradise, or two columns down either side symbolizing the pillars of wisdom. The arch of the mihrab is almost always angular and may be stepped; though in the Persian-influenced patterns made originally by the court manufactories it is often curved, as in most Persian prayer rugs. This less common mihrab-shape derives ultimately from the 'Cairene' tradition. Spandrels above the prayer arch are almost always filled with a representation of flowers or leaves. A tree of life occasionally fills the mihrabs, in particular those from Demirci where, like Ghiordes, a carnation motif is common in the borders. Elsewhere, in traditional Anatolian patterns such as Ladik, the tulip, indigenous to Turkey, is common.

One other prayer mat made in Turkey is notable – the so-called 'graveyard' or 'cemetery' rug (*mazarlik*) with a small gabled house flanked by two cypress trees, or a mausoleum or mosque shape with two gables and a central dome overshadowed by tall abstract tree shapes. These designs are produced mainly in Kula, Ladik, Ghiordes, and Kirshehir.

Cotton has been used in the foundation of Turkish carpets since the end of the eighteenth century, making them rather more supple than those from other carpet-weaving countries. White cotton was also used, as in Turkoman weaving, for small highlights in the pile. Where traditional red-dyed wefts are not used, the groundweave is usually undyed natural beige or grey wool. In rural and nomadic carpets it is often natural dark brown, and goat hair may be found in the groundweave. In colouring

Turkish carpets give an overall impression of red, usually derived in the past from madder though towards Eastern Anatolia cochineal was more common.

After more than a hundred and fifty years of commercial exploitation at the expense of tradition and creativity there has recently been a renaissance of the old designs and dyes. With the virtual demise of carpet manufacture in Iran, Turkey is fast becoming the world's principal producer of pile-woven carpets. Many carpets are being made with traditional geometric designs again, related to those made in the sixteenth century and once the most coveted in all Europe. Many more, though, are still being made in ugly colours and derivative, meaningless versions of Anatolian and Caucasian designs. Some high-quality copies of traditional Caucasian designs appear on the market, beautifully knotted and made of fine wool, but many of the carpets are cheaply made and eclectic in design.

The flat weaves of Anatolia were so underrated that until relatively recently they were used to wrap bales of carpets for shipment. However, with the renaissance of the carpet-weaving industry and the growing importance of Turkish weaving, the Turks have rediscovered their ancient heritage in the remote regions and villages, and now not only value but over-value the kilims and prayer kilims which they once disregarded. Commercial pressures have forced many genuinely traditional pieces to appear on the market, a situation which occurs when a culture or a way of life deteriorates in the face of political upheavals and economic factors, and the people are forced to sell their treasured possessions. It is a sad reflection of local conditions that more and more authentic prayer mats, prayer kilims, carpets, and rugs are reaching the West from the more remote and increasingly unsettled districts of Anatolia. But it is the newly-discovered existence of these very pieces which has called into question many assumptions concerning the rugs and carpets woven in Anatolia.

Hereke including Panderma and Kum Kapou

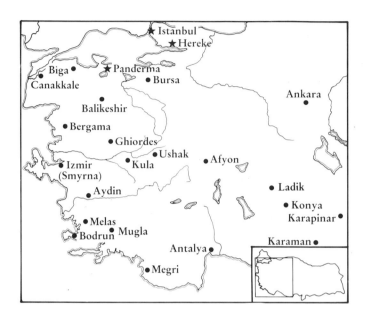

The fine silky-piled wool carpets and silk rugs made in Hereke are greatly admired by Europeans for their elegant quasi-Persian patterns, but connoisseurs of traditional weaving tend to be dismissive about them. It was from Hereke in the nineteenth century that many of the 'Turkey' carpets came, in the standard blues and reds of mahogany-furnished houses of the day. Exported from the port of Smyrna they were known in England as 'Smyrna' carpets.

Established in 1844, the Hereke manufactory was intended specifically to produce fine carpets for the Ottoman court. Although the quality of both materials and craftsmanship remain of the very highest, the Hereke manufactory follows no Turkish carpet-weaving tradition, nor has any individual style. Rather than returning to the strict geometric patterns of early Ottoman carpets, it concentrated on producing large rugs for the sultan's palaces, with Persian designs which were considered to be far superior to those of Turkey. Here too were woven many of the presentation carpets given by the sultan to the crowned heads of Europe.

In recent years, as traditional Turkish weaving has risen in esteem, the Hereke manufactory has been using patterns and motifs copied from early Ushak and Ottoman designs, as well as continuing to produce French and Persian styles.

The districts around Istanbul and the Sea of Marmara were ideal for the production of silk carpets, for Bursa is the centre of Turkish silk production. No carpet-weaving industry exists in Bursa today, but there are thriving manufactories in *Panderma* by the Sea of Marmara, and in Kum Kapou in the Armenian quarter of Istanbul. Of the two, Kum Kapou is most worthy of note, since Panderma produces mostly copies of traditional prayer rugs and rugs of Persian design. Early Panderma prayer rugs, woven up to the beginning of this century, were curiously delicate and small-patterned, with narrow multiple borders of small floral motifs and a single arabesque panel above and below the prayer arch.

Until relatively recently some of the work from *Kum Kapou* was attributed to Persian Safavid ateliers, so fine was the weaving and so rich the glitter of gold and silver threads. Other rugs, carpets, and prayer rugs were woven in Ottoman 'Cairene' patterns, with curved mihrabs undulating arabesques, palmettes, and arabic script, all subtly interwoven with flower heads and leaves. This remarkable work was in fact woven by Turkish Armenians, who had moved from Kayseri to the Armenian quarter of the capital at the end of the last century. The mistaken attribution can partly be explained by the use, almost unique in Turkey, of the Persian or asymmetrical knot which was possibly introduced to Kayseri in the mid-nineteenth century by an influx of weavers from Tabriz and Heriz.

TYPICAL SPECIFICATIONS

Warp
Natural greyish-white wool, or natural white silk.

Weft
Natural greyish-white wool, or natural white silk with metal thread. Two shoots.

Pile
Silk or silky wool. Medium low.

Knot
Symmetrical or asymmetrical. 2000–12,000/dm^2 (133–800/sq. in.).

Ends
Plain weave.

Sides
Two to three pairs of warps, bound with yellow supplementary weft.

Handle
Soft, velvety, and pliable.

a. Opposite *A fine silk carpet woven in the Kum Kapou workshops in Istanbul. This carpet has a floral Persianate design and is woven with the asymmetrical or Persian knot. Late nineteenth century.* 1.86m × 1.32m, 6'1" × 4'4".

b. Right *The Hereke workshops were established under royal patronage in 1844 and produced very fine silk rugs. The design of this prayer rug is based on Ottoman court designs. Nineteenth century.*

Bergama including Balikeshir, Yacebedir, and Yuncu Yuruk

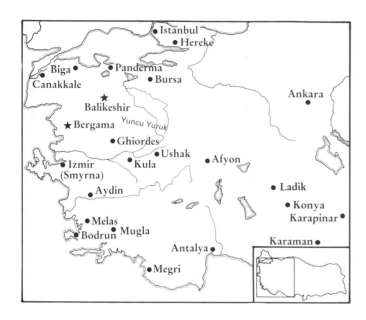

Although there has been no carpet weaving in Bergama for some time, the name is still given to carpets made in the surrounding district. The patterns ascribed to Bergama, however, are the descendants of the geometric patterns of the fifteenth and sixteenth centuries, and demonstrate the common ancestry of the Seljuk, Turkoman, and Caucasian designs. No trace of Persian influence is discernible, and instead, some Bergama patterns may be confused with those made in the Kazak-Gendje district of the Caucasus. Fine wool comes from sheep raised around Balikeshir, and Bergama carpets are of high quality, though some of the dyes are rather dull and tend to diminish the lustre of the pile. Larger versions of the Bergama designs are woven in Cannakale, and some particularly fine versions in Enzine. Bergama rugs and prayer rugs are generally very restricted in colour, using only red, blue, and white. The field colour of prayer rugs is generally a natural white or red.

Pile-woven rugs and prayer rugs from *Yacebedir* have fine dyes, in particular a deep inky blue black and a dark red, but the wool is harsher and more granular. The area inside the mihrab is often reinforced with extra weft threads, and a typical prayer arch is stepped and often ends in a small V-hook. In secular rugs the hooked motif is common. Saw-edged leaves, angular stars, and rosettes are reminiscent of Caucasian patterns, but as in most Anatolian prayer rugs the borders are wider, the rugs more square.

From *Balikeshir* come multi-niched prayer kilims in exaggeratedly elongated shapes in which there are no vertical lines. They are woven on a fine white wool warp in the limited palette of Bergama rugs. Early examples used madder for the red dye, later ones cochineal. Typical also of the Bergama-Balikeshir district are interlocking latch-hook patterns in an extremely formalized 'tree' shape, with no formal borders and ends woven with narrow stripes. Unusually, the red dye used by some weavers in this district may corrode the wool, giving the pile-woven pieces a relief effect.

The pile and flat weaves made by the local population for their own use are more adventurous in their use of colour. Ten or more colours may be used, in a typical olive-tinged spectrum of yellows, greens, blues, and browns as well as the limited Bergama palette. Today, the rugs made by nomad tribes around Bergama and Balikeshir are generally attributed to the *Yuncu Yuruk* rather than the towns and villages where they are bartered or sold to merchants.

TYPICAL SPECIFICATIONS

Warp
Wool, natural white and/or grey, sometimes dyed red. Occasionally goat hair; cotton in recent work.

Weft
Wool, dyed red or red-brown. Two to six shoots.

Pile
Wool; sometimes natural white cotton for highlights. Medium height.

Knot
Symmetrical. 600–1200/dm^2 (40–80/sq. in.).

Ends
Plain weave, red with stripes of various colours.

Sides
Two to four pairs of cords, bound with warp, usually red.

Handle
Flabby and heavy.

a. Opposite *The designs of Bergama carpets are often descended from sixteenth and seventeenth-century Turkish weavings, and may also be related to Caucasian rugs. In this example the eight-pointed star of the border is adapted from large-pattern Holbein carpets, and the hooked Memling gul can be seen in the field. Bergama, second half of the nineteenth century.* 1.95m × 1.67m, 6′5″ × 5′6″.

b. Right *This carpet has the geometric motifs and orange and olive colouration associated with Yuruk weaving. The design, of octagons within squares surrounded by Memling guls, is similar to that of large-pattern Holbein rugs. Around 1880.* 2.28m × 1.16m, 7′6″ × 3′10″.

Kula including Ghiordes and Ushak

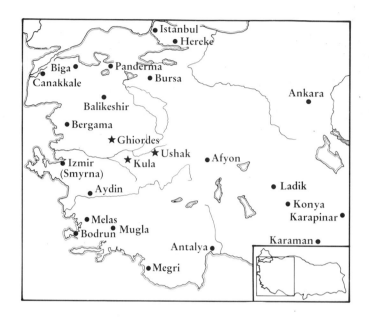

The town of Kula lies between the ancient carpet-weaving centre of Ushak and the port of Smyrna (Izmir). Though little remains today of the famous 'Star' and 'Medallion' Ushak patterns of the seventeenth and eighteenth centuries, some elements can still be seen in the large diamonds and star-shaped medallions of recent weaving from this area. An angular wave-pattern is often used in the border, in conjunction with an arrow-headed diamond which is probably from an older tradition and resurfaces in many areas of Anatolia. Prayer rugs made in Kula have a distinctively flattened prayer arch and a series of narrow borders, often flanked by two wider bands of scroll-pattern. Two broad bands of flowerheads often almost fill the mihrab, on a blue, red or apricot field. Cemetery rugs (*mazarlik*) are also made in Kula.

Prayer rugs known as *Ghiordes* but almost certainly made in many villages in the surrounding district, including Kula, also have a red and yellow palette. The pile is short, the wool more granular and less lustrous than Kula rugs. The mihrab is squat, short, and steeply pointed, almost crowded out by arabesque panels, spandrels, and broad flower-filled borders – huge stylized carnations being typical. The flat weaves of Kula, Ghiordes, and the surrounding areas are remarkable for their continuity of designs inherited from a remote past. *Kis-kilims*, made for a bride's dowry, show the traditional angular wave-patterns, as well as a curiously shaped medallion of roughly hexagonal form with two short diagonals pointing to the four corners. This shape is a formalized representation of a flayed animal pelt, and can be found in many primitive and nomadic pieces of extreme antiquity.

Ushak today produces little of merit, though remnants of past traditions linger in the red-dyed weft and in the weakened versions of the 'Star' and the 'Medallion', formed from a large leaf pattern or a hexagonal medallion on an empty field. The knotting is loose, the wool coarse and loosely spun, and the pile is thick enough to disguise the poor knotting and give an erroneous impression of density and richness.

In the villages north of Kula and Ghiordes, recently discovered flat-weave patterns may reinforce the theory that designs for pile carpets arose from simple geometric patterns woven centuries before by settlers more ancient than the Turkoman, Seljuk, or Ottoman invaders. Simple hexagonal and repeated diamond medallions, perhaps the forerunners of the 'Star' and 'Medallion' Ushak, are still being woven in small villages near Afyon and around Kutaya, as well as a pattern resembling either a comb or rows of birds in flight. The dyes may be garish, the weaving coarse, but the patterns and designs have caused considerable reassessment of standard theories concerning Turkish carpets.

TYPICAL SPECIFICATIONS

Warp
Kula – natural ivory wool, sometimes white cotton in later work. Ghiordes – wool, natural white, sometimes blue.

Weft
Kula – wool, natural white or brown, sometimes dyed yellow; sometimes cotton, goat hair, or jute and wool; two to four shoots. Ghiordes – wool, natural white or dyed red; sometimes white cotton; two shoots.

Pile
Kula – silky wool, sometimes silk; medium height; pile lies in opposite direction to design. Ghiordes – wool, sometimes white cotton; low.

Knot
Symmetrical. Kula – 850–2000/dm² (57–133/sq. in.). Ghiordes – 1200–2400/dm² (80–160/sq. in.).

Ends
Plain weave, white, red, or colour of warps. Fringes plaited.

Sides
Kula – two to four cords, bound with weft. Ghiordes – two to four cords, bound with white, green, or blue supplementary weft (sometimes cotton).

Handle
Thin and floppy.

a. Opposite *A Ghiordes prayer rug with the typical flattened niche and flower-filled spandrels. The border features an angular and stylized flowering plant. These rugs were woven in villages around Kula and are derived from eighteenth-century Ottoman court designs. Early nineteenth century.*
1.54m × 1.24m, 5′1″ × 4′1″.

b. Right *A Kula carpet with fine, clear colours. The borders contain a number of stylized flower patterns, as well as geometric motifs and an attractive wave pattern which is derived from the borders of earlier Ushak carpets. This forms an effective contrast to the open, delicately ornamented field. First half of the nineteenth century.*
2.08m × 1.44m, 6′10″ × 4′9″.

Melas including Megri and Aydin

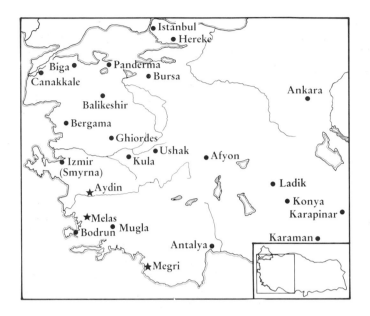

Melas is known mainly for its prayer rugs, which are quite different from any other Anatolian examples, in that the prayer arch is seldom stepped and almost always waisted, like an angular truncated form of the 'head and shoulders' shape. An unusual amount of yellow is used together with reds, oranges, tans, and small amounts of dark tones, usually aubergine. In many Melas rugs the spandrels have grown and squashed the mihrab, while the rest of the central panel is filled with rows of leaves or serrated flower heads, probably carnations. The borders, separated by guardstripes filled with rosettes, often feature a version of the palmette, or angular stems joining formalized flower shapes with small squares in the centre. The *Ada-Melas* rugs, made between Karaova and Bodrum, have geometrical designs and a comb-like border surrounding the mihrab, which is long and narrow. In secular rugs a tree-of-life motif often appears, as well as tulip heads and boteh.

From *Megri*, at the southernmost tip of Western Anatolia come prayer rugs of a very individual design, sometimes known as 'Rhodes'. These may have a central mihrab with the unusual feature of a candelabra standing at the base. The most typical are clearly divided into two halves with different designs in each panel, one of them almost always containing a toothed lozenge repeating down a central spine.

From *Aydin*, north of Melas, come a variety of kilims, in strong bright colours, many of them in extremely large sizes and made in two halves, or in a curious construction which appears to be unique to this area. The wide borders are woven as two strips, and the central field as a third, with the join on the border line. These may have been made as door coverings for mosques; the wide top panel would have been attached to the lintel and the central panel would act as a door flap, while the two borders would cover the door frame. Aydin kilims are often woven in an almost *trompe-l'oeil* pattern, with either dark blue hexagons on a white field, or white trefoils on a dark blue ground.

TYPICAL SPECIFICATIONS

Warp
Natural, undyed greyish white wool. Sometimes goat hair.

Weft
Wool, dyed red, sometimes blue, or brown. Two to four shoots. Sometimes goat hair.

Pile
Soft, lustrous wool. Short to medium.

Knot
Symmetrical. 900–2500/dm^2 (60–166/sq. in.).

Ends
Plain weave, red. Fringes plaited.

Sides
Two to four pairs of warps, bound with weft or red or blue wool.

Handle
Light, soft, and velvety.

a. *Opposite above Prayer rugs from Megri are often known as 'Rhodes' carpets. This typical design is divided into two halves, the right-hand panel containing the characteristic hooked lozenges repeating down a central spine. The colours of these rugs tend to warm and strong, and the central panels usually have a red or dark blue ground.*
1.52m × 1.01m, 5′ × 3′4″.

b. *Opposite below A Melas prayer rug with stylized carnations above the niche and a flowering plant within it. The waisted prayer rug is typical of the region. The main border contains stylized palmettes. Mid-nineteenth century.*
1.54m × 1.09m, 5′1″ × 3′7″.

c. *Right An unusual and very fine Melas prayer rug. The flowers of the zigzag border are ultimately derived from Ottoman weavings. Early nineteenth century.*
1.70m × 1.10m, 5′7″ × 3′7″.

Konya including Ladik, Karapinar, and Karaman

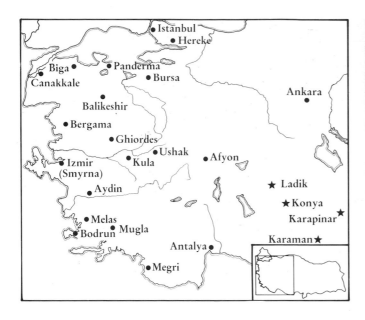

Konya has the oldest tradition of carpet weaving in Anatolia, rich with Turkoman, Seljuk, and Ottoman symbols and motifs. Traditional weaving, made for the local population, flourishes in the whole district and the kilims are of particular interest.

Among the most formal and well-known designs is the Ladik prayer rug, made not only in *Ladik* itself but also, with variations, in Konya. These sophisticated rugs have a triple arch supported by two graceful columns, with straight-stemmed tulips in a panel above the mihrab. The more simple versions, made in the surrounding villages, are less well-defined, often with two columns of flowers or tree shapes below a flattened arch with two smaller arches on either side. The panel of tulips springs downwards from below the mihrab, or alternatively, there are large formalized carnations in the panels and borders. Even simpler versions have a stepped arch terminating in an arrowhead which may have older origins. An arrowed diamond is frequently used in graduated interlocking patterns for *kiskilims*, made as dowry pieces and often interwoven with silver thread.

In the kilims from the districts surrounding Konya are to be found symbols and motifs not found in the pile-woven rugs, many of them probably of extremely ancient origin. Some secular kilims have a white ground, strong deep colours, and a corrosive black dye but no red. The patterns include hexagons down the field, and often a horizontal long-bodied insect or animal with two legs is repeated down the sides, which have no formal border. Another design can be attributed to *Karaman*, an area so famous for its kilims that not long ago Karaman was the generic term for flat weaves in Anatolia. This features intricate interlocking lozenges and the use of different colours produces an effect of diagonal lines across the field, which is bordered by a black and red toothed edge. Prayer kilims from this district have wide mihrabs, often with double hooked gable ends and borders of S-shapes in small rectangles or hexagons. Another form has repeated prayer arches, three or four down the field with a border of serrated leaves or a wave-and-comb pattern. As further evidence of the deep layers of compacted cultures, a cross-like motif is often to be found in the borders of prayer kilims, possibly pointing to a long-forgotten heritage of Armenian weavers. From *Karapinar* come multiple-niche prayer kilims of extremely ancient origins, possibly intended as shrouds for the dead, with the arches representing 'gates' to Paradise.

Yastik (cushion covers) and *heybeh* (saddlebags) of great imagination, as well as tent bands, floor coverings, and tent hangings, are made in the villages and by pastoral nomads who range over a wide area south and west of Lake Tuzo.

TYPICAL SPECIFICATIONS

Warp
Konya – wool, natural ivory white or grey brown. Ladik – wool, natural white or yellow-dyed. Cotton in later pieces.

Weft
Konya – wool, natural ivory white or grey brown, or dyed red or yellow; sometimes goat hair. Ladik – wool, natural brown or red-dyed. Two to six shoots.

Pile
Konya – soft lustrous wool, medium to high. Ladik – wool, medium height.

Knot
Symmetrical. 900–1500/dm^2 (60–100/sq. in.). Ladik – up to 2500/dm^2 (166/sq. in.).

Ends
Plain weave, either in colour of weft or in multicoloured stripes. Fringes plaited.

Sides
Two to four pairs of warps wrapped with weft. In Konya the warps may be wrapped with additional weft.

Handle
Konya – heavy, floppy, and soft. Ladik – firm, compact, and fine.

a. Opposite *The triple arches of this elegant Ladik prayer rug are derived from Ottoman court designs, but the flower-filled compartments of the border are related to Transylvanian rugs. Early nineteenth century.* 2m × 1.39m, 6'7" × 4'7".

b. Right *This unusual Konya rug combines a mihrab and a medallion design. Protective amulets hang below the niche and the border features a carnation pattern which is so highly stylized as to be almost unrecognizable. Early nineteenth century.* 2.10m × 1.50m, 6'9" × 4'10".

Kirshehir including Mudjur

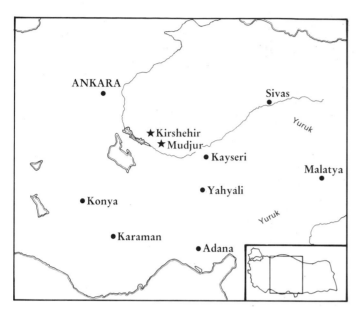

In Kirshehir were woven the famous 'Medjid' carpets named after Sultan Abd el Medjid in the mid-nineteenth century – rich floral carpets much influenced by European designs, with rococo swirls on a white ground. Many Kirshehir carpets still maintain a highly stylized floral pattern; but the central field may have an *odshalyk* (a double mihrab with a stepped gable at each end) with a curious mixture between a traditional arabesque and a floral pattern in top and bottom panels. The field colour is often a bright, distinctive cherry red, or a clear leaf green. Kirshehir prayer rugs can be distinguished by a rather sketchy mihrab, often no more than an outline on a green, white, or occasionally yellow field which is left empty. Here too are made 'graveyard' or 'cemetery' rugs (*mazarlik*) with a brighter, more extensive colour range than those of Kula, Ladik, or Ghiordes, and wider border stripes filled with repeating formalized leaves, flower heads, stylized carnations, and S-scrolls. Kirshehir and the region around produces a fine range of kilims, often related to pile-woven patterns, with floral borders. These are loosely woven in shiny lustrous wool with very pronounced slits, and some are very large, often as wide as 3 metres (10 feet). The designs of some of the smaller kilims suggest a Turkoman *hatchli*-type influence – squares of diamonds and lozenges are set in a definite frame like a wooden door.

Prayer rugs from *Mudjur* have the richest palette of all Anatolian prayer rugs, and an exuberance which is almost Caucasian. Patterns and motifs are strictly geometrical, with stylized rosettes, diamonds, and small zigzag wave-pattern borders. The prayer arch is stepped, sometimes outlined in different colours, and the crest of the arch is a single or double-headed arrow – a motif often repeated in the upper panel. The borders are wide, with each repeating motif squared up and of a different colour so that the effect is of tiles. A distinctive ewer shape, unique to Mudjur, is often woven into the spandrels. Kilims from this area have strong colouring, using bright tomato red, wine red, green, yellow, and a rich dark blue.

TYPICAL SPECIFICATIONS

Warp
Natural wool, white or ivory, sometimes dyed red or green in Kirshehir. Cotton in later Mudjur work.

Weft
Wool, usually dyed red or brown. Kirshehir – two or three shoots. Mudjur – one or two shoots.

Pile
Wool, soft in Kirshehir, hard in Mudjur. Medium.

Knot
Symmetrical. 600–2000/dm^2 (40–133/sq. in.).

Ends
Plain weave, the same colour as the weft. Fringes plaited.

Sides
Kirshehir – one to two pairs of warps bound with weft. Mudjur – two to four pairs similarly bound.

Handle
Soft and pliable.

a. Opposite *A Kirshehir carpet woven in the Medjid style much influenced by the European rococo. The design has a three-dimensional effect that is rare in oriental carpets, but the central field features a traditional Turkish odshalyk or double-ended prayer niche. Second half of the nineteenth century.*
2.70m × 1.10m, 8′10″ × 3′4″.

b. Right *A typical Mudjur prayer rug with a red niche and borders formed of neat geometric designs, broken up to give a speckled effect. Mid-nineteenth century.*
1.83m × 1.34m, 6′ × 4′5″.

Kayseri including Yahyali

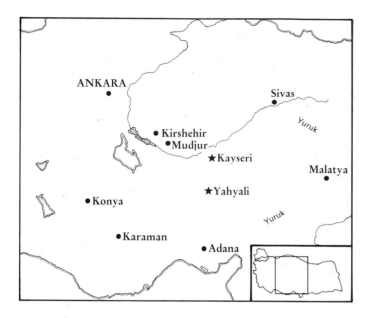

In strange contrast to the neighbouring towns, *Kayseri* has long been the centre for the production of large quantities of silk or silk and cotton carpets for export, using old Anatolian or Persian patterns. Confusingly many of the fine 'silk Pandermas', as they were called by the merchants, were made here. These are characterized by the use of a pale celadon green, similar to the colouring of Persian Ferahans. Kilims from the surrounding area show the innate skill of local weavers who make flat weaves in designs featuring graduated diagonal lines, extremely difficult to achieve, in a series of interlocking diamonds or arrow-headed diamonds repeated down the field. Unlike the wide kilims of Kirshehir, which are woven in a single piece, Kayseri kilims are usually woven in two long strips. Older kilims have a soft colour spectrum of greens, browns, yellows, and reds, but more recent work shows a hardness of tone in deep blues, cochineal reds, a strong bluish green, and considerable areas of white, often cotton.

South of Kayseri lies the small town of *Yahyali* where some of the most authentic village rugs are made today, using a fine quality wool and natural dyes. Many prayer rugs are woven in Yahyali as well as small carpets, in traditional, delightfully naive patterns. Before the growing interest in Anatolian rugs and carpets attributed this work correctly, they were known as 'Konya Yuruk' since they were similar in construction and design to nomad work and were generally sold through the central carpet-trading centre of Konya.

a. Opposite *A fine Kayseri rug woven with silk and metal thread. The delicate scrolling design is of Persian rather than Turkish origin. Early twentieth century.*
1.88m × 1.35m, 6′2″ × 4′5″.

b. Right *A yastik or small door mat, woven in long lustrous wool and fine natural dyes. Carpets of this type were formerly known as Konya Yuruk. Nineteenth century.*
1.17m × 0.66m, 3′8″ × 2′2″.

Sivas including Village Sivas and Malatya

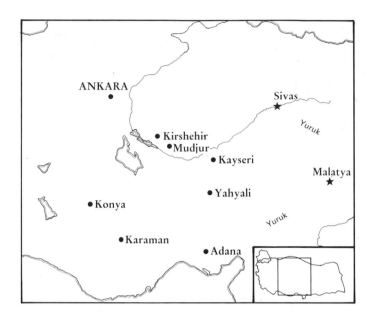

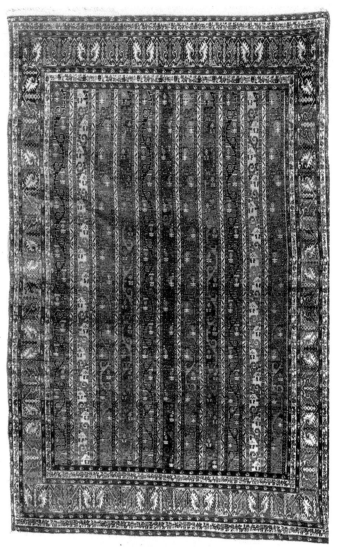

This is the most easterly carpet-producing town in Anatolia, responsible for great quantities of finely woven pile rugs based on traditional Persian patterns. Although their designs and craftsmanship are remarkable, they do not have the luminous clarity of most fine genuine Persian carpets. This is partly due to the fact that they are knotted with a symmetrical knot which tends to present a rather flat pile, but more to poor dyeing which results in a shadowed, blue effect. Sivas town carpets also suffer from taking design motifs indiscriminately from many sources, crowding them together in an incoherent fashion. Sometimes an *odshalyk*, or double-ended mihrab, is discernible in a truncated form, set inside an overgrown stepped double mihrab with an outline obscured by over-decorated spandrels. Here, it would seem, commercialism has triumphed over aesthetics.

Village Sivas rugs, on the other hand, are refreshingly primitive and simple. Coming from a region where a considerable number of settlers from East Turkestan now live, many of the designs have more traditional roots. The usual red-dyed weft is absent, and alone among all Anatolian weaving the construction is often similar to the Caucasian Kazak group. Only one end is fringed, and the top kilim end is turned over and stitched to the back of the rug. Some rugs sold through Sivas show signs of Turkoman colouring in the use of rich wine reds, while the proximity to Armenia may account for a cross-like motif which appears in the borders of some village Sivas prayer rugs.

The area around Sivas, stretching down to the south and *Malatya*, has a long tradition of kilim weaving, particularly of 'compartment' kilims with a distinctive design of panels filled with a variety of archaic motifs repeated down the field. The panels in the field are enclosed with border patterns and often outlined with a white crenellated line. The colours are limited and harmonious, in soft tones of blue, green, red, mauve, and white. From this district also come *saf* kilims with each compartment in a 'head and shoulders' mihrab shape, and a cross-like motif or a 'running dog' pattern in the borders. Curiously, this area does not seem to produce any single prayer kilims. From Malatya come some striking and easily recognizable 'band' kilims, many of them inordinately long and measuring up to 5 metres (16½ feet). Their colouring may indicate a Kurdish origin, since sombre dark blue, madder and cochineal reds, and dark brown are the most typical. The designs depend to a certain extent on their construction, which is in two long strips. Unlike other kilims made in this way, Malatya kilims have each piece matching in design and independent, not as two halves of one single pattern. These designs are a series of parallel bands of diamonds, latch-hook motifs, S-shapes and lozenges, sometimes quite wide. All but rare exceptions have a brilliant-white four-barred grid repeated at regular intervals down the length. This feature may also appear as part of the band design in red or blue.

a. Opposite *The design of this Sivas rug is not a traditional Turkish one but is derived instead from Persian woven silks. Nineteenth century.* 1.83m × 1.09m, 6′ × 3′7″.

b. Right *A Malatya compartment kilim. The design, composed of hooked lozenges in harmonious colours, has a classical and archaic feeling. First half of the nineteenth century.* 5m × 1.65m, 16′5″ × 5′5″.

Kurd and Yuruk and Aleppo

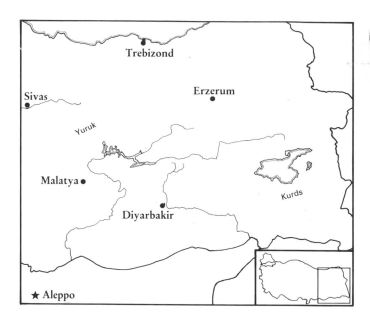

Kurdish tribes are scattered throughout Central Anatolia and used to wander freely over the borders between Turkey, Iraq, and Iran. Most now live in the area around Lake Van, with another group centred around Bayazid, one of the main trading centres for Kurdish work. This varies in quality, and much of it is very poor. The wool is harsh, the knotting loose, and the unevenly stretched warp and weft cause distortion. The work is generally sombre in colouring and the pile is short. Kurdish kilims are hard to identify except on the basis of colouring, since it is only in recent years that flat weaves have been attributed to particular regions of Anatolia, in many of which Kurdish tribes also live. This is notable in the eastern regions, where even the terms 'Kurd' and 'Yuruk' are easily confused.

The *Yuruk* are nomadic and semi-nomadic people who roam across the less-inhabited regions of Anatolia. Apart from the Yuncu Yuruk whose work is now being recognized, much of the Yuruk weaving comes from Eastern Anatolia, and can be identified mainly by the long shaggy pile, thick wefts (which are often dyed in bright colours), and the excellent quality of the wool. Yuruk patterns contain many variations on the hexagon, diamond, and hooked, stepped lozenge, as well as a zigzag pattern in both the border and the field. Until recently it was thought that the Yuruk had adapted Caucasian designs, but it is now known that all these designs belong to the ancient weaving tradition of Anatolia. Yuruk kilims are hard to identify, and probably many of them belong with the more recently attributed flat weaves of Malatya and other Eastern Anatolian groups.

The finest kilims from this part of Anatolia are those woven in and around *Aleppo*, just over the Syrian border. Here kilims were as important as pile-woven carpets and many of them were made specifically as door hangings and curtains. The remarkable range of designs is not limited to the bold primitive work of other regions. They are subtle in colouring, employing cochineal in particular to achieve many different tones of red. The borders are almost always white, either wool or cotton, and other colours include soft apricot, a clear blue, yellow, and a leaf green. In some examples a border of a meander and vine leaf are specific to the region, while others show a wide variety of curving hook-shapes, palmettes, and diamonds.

TYPICAL SPECIFICATIONS

Warp
Natural undyed wool, brown, ivory or grey, sometimes with goat hair.

Weft
Wool, natural brown, or dyed blue, red, or orange. Sometimes goat hair. Two to four shoots.

Pile
Wool, with occasional highlights in white cotton. Short to medium.

Knot
Asymmetrical. $500-1500/dm^2$ ($33-100/sq.$ in.).

Ends
Plain weave, the same colour as the weft, occasionally brocaded. Fringes plaited or grouped in long tassels.

Sides
Groups of two to three warps, bound with weft and reinforced with variously coloured wool.

Handle
Pliable and heavy.

a. Opposite *The nomadic and semi-nomadic Yuruk are to be found throughout Anatolia. Their weaving is characterized by bright colours, fine wool, and repeating geometric forms. The hexagonal motifs in the borders of this prayer rug are often used in the field. Nineteenth century.*
1.60m × 1.24m, 5'3" × 4'.

b. Right *An Aleppo kilim with the wide range of cochineal reds, the clear blues and yellows, and the white borders typical of the region. This kilim is woven in two matching halves and may have been made as a door hanging. First half of the nineteenth century.*
3.04m × 1.21m, 10' × 4'.

Modern Carpet Production in Turkey

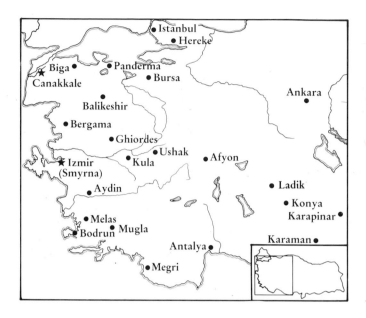

Much of the appeal of oriental carpets in the West derives from the fact that they are handmade. Yet anyone with a knowledge of antique carpets who visits one of the huge warehouses in which new and semi-antique pieces are offered for sale is likely to be disappointed. Everything is handmade, thousands of people have been provided with livelihoods, but something vital is missing. The carpets have no soul, and the spirit of individual creativity that pervades antique carpets has disappeared. Commercialism has taken over. The colours are poor chemical dyes, the designs are debased, and the wool is machine-spun and of the worst quality.

This uninspiring picture reflects the declining standards of modern rug production throughout the orient today, in which any possible measure is taken to keep down the costs of production. Turkey is no exception, and many villages have stopped making carpets altogether while others have been persuaded to weave the more 'commercial' Persian and Caucasian patterns. A few continue to weave their ancient traditional designs, but all the villagers have forgotten the old vegetable-dye recipes; the loss is such that six years ago there was only one place in the whole of western Turkey where madder was used and could be bought, although it grew as a weed in the cotton fields. The villagers have adopted instead imported, factory-produced dyestuffs, and these cheap dyes give harsh and ugly results.

Now under the influence of Dr Harrald Böhmer of Marmara University in Istanbul, a weaving renaissance has begun in Turkey. The project is known as the Dobag Project, a name deriving from the Turkish words for research and development into natural dyes, and it began in 1981 on the Aegean coast where local weaving styles go back many centuries. Two centres of production have developed so far, one around Cannakali and the other in the Yuntdag mountains near Izmir.

The villagers have been persuaded that a return to the use of natural dyes and the formation of a marketing cooperative would enable them to earn more money. These people were already wool producers, experienced in sorting and spinning, but they had to be taught the old dyeing recipes. After many difficulties resulting from threatened commercial interests and internal political squabbles, carpets began to be produced which continue the traditions of the past.

Strict conditions are imposed on the weavers; only natural dyes and pure indigo can be used and all the patterns have to be local and traditional. The carpets are woven with high quality, handspun wool, and are divided into three grades. The first two are bought by the cooperative, and the third must be sold on the free market for less money. The carpets are not bleached, treated with agents to increase the wool lustre, washed with optical brighteners, 'antiqued' with chemicals to tone down the colour, or artificially aged by cutting down the black wool. Each carpet is sold with a guarantee concerning the dyes used, and the dealers must agree not to try to enhance the carpets' appearance with a chemical treatment before sale.

In comparison with commercially 'finished' carpets, these may at first seem a little rough, but in the same way as a good wine matures with age so these carpets steadily improve. During normal household use a natural lustrous patina develops and the colours acquire the mellowness of old vegetable-dyed pieces. Furthermore, these untreated carpets will outlast any 'lustre-washed' carpet.

The project may also be seen as a social experiment in the economics of village life. It is not merely engaged in finding work for poor villagers but is also reviving lost crafts in a living community. It is gratifying that in those villages which are involved in the cooperative the people are earning enough to buy more land and build new houses, instead of leaving for the cities. Moreover, the knowledge of dyeing has become diffused outside the cooperatives and for the first time in this century there is a flourishing free market in new carpets with natural dyes.

Every year the work improves as the weavers learn new skills, demonstrating that the great art of carpet weaving has not entirely died under the impact of the commercial pressures that arose at the end of the nineteenth century. The success of this project should serve to encourage other weavers in the Middle East to return to the high standards established during the centuries of fine weaving.

a. Opposite *A detail of a carpet woven in western Anatolia under the direction of Tolga Tollu, who is using natural dyes and interpreting traditional designs with great sensitivity. 1984.*

b. Right *The recently established Dobag Project encourages the use of natural dyes and traditional patterns. This design is derived from Bergama carpets. West Anatolia, 1984.*
1.96m × 1.30m, 6'5" × 4'9".

THE CAUCASUS

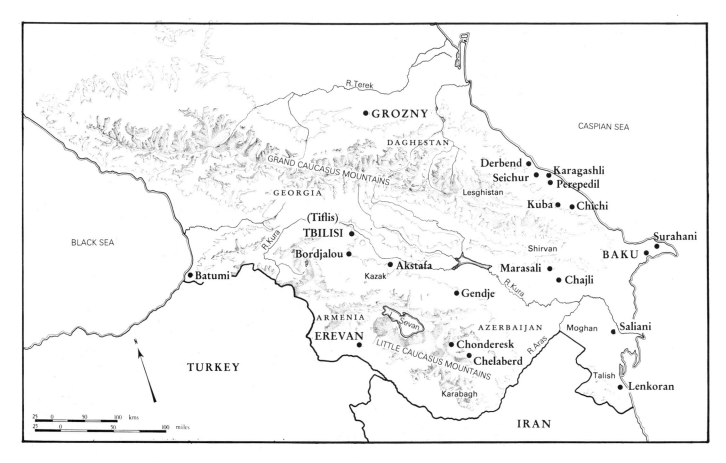

By permission of Dr Ulrich Schürmann much of the following material has been derived from his book, Caucasian Rugs. *However, some of it has had to be adjusted to fit the format of the present book.*

There was remarkably little scholarly interest in carpets from the Caucasus until about ten years ago, and virtually no documentation to set beside the innumerable works on carpets of almost every other oriental country. Little was known about the pastoral nomads and settled tribes of this remote land before it became part of the USSR and since then there have been many changes. It seems that these tribes wove little in the way of decorative trappings or tent hangings, unlike the Turkoman tribes to the east of the Caspian Sea. Apart from some tent bags, saddlebags, and coverings for ox-drawn carts, little survives to suggest that anything other than rugs, carpets, and prayer rugs were ever made in the Caucasus.

In terms of construction, Caucasian weaving appears to fall into two distinct groups with quite different characteristics. The 'Kazak' group which lies south of the Caucasian mountains includes Kazak itself, the largest rug-producing district, together with Bordjalou, Karachov, Chelaberd, Lambalo, Lori-Pombak, Karaklis, Gendje, Karabagh, Shusha, Talish, Lenkoran, and Moghan. North and east of the mountains the 'Kuba' group has a different construction. These are the rugs from Kuba, Chichi, Seichur, Perepedil, Karagashli, Baku, Surahani, Saliani, Daghestan,

Lesghistan, Shirvan, Marasali, Chila, and Derbend. The majority of prayer rugs woven in the Caucasus belong to the second group, whose people are almost without exception Muslim. Rugs with Christian symbols are more likely to be found among the 'Kazak' group where there are large settled communities of Armenian Christians.

'Kazak' rugs are recognizable by the fact that they have a fringe at one end only, or no fringe at all. In setting up the loom, the warp thread is passed over the top beam, down the back of the loom, and around the bottom beam. When the rug is finished the pegs holding the top beam to the horizontal frame are removed and the beam is pulled out, leaving a row of flattened loops. These are sometimes taken back into the carpet, or woven into a narrow band of kilim which is then folded over and stitched to the back of the rug. Rugs and carpets woven on looms with fixed beams must have their warp threads cut when they are finished and thus have a fringe at either end. It is this characteristic which distinguishes rugs of the 'Kazak' group from the rugs of the 'Kuba' group.

Colours and dyes can sometimes provide additional evidence for the origin of some carpets. The most significant is the use of cochineal reds and violets which are mainly confined to Karabagh, Shirvan, and some carpet-weaving centres along the Caspian Sea. Elsewhere in the Caucasus, the root of the madder plant produces a red dye which is less brilliant, ranging from a clear brick red through to a dark purple, quite different from the violet

a. Right *A carpet shop in the Maidan, Tiflis around 1900. Both kilims and pile weavings are displayed.*

obtained by using cochineal dye. One of the greatest delights of Caucasian rugs is their subtle changes of tone within each colour. This change, known as an 'abrash', is due to the different strengths of each batch of dye, and it enhances rather than diminishes the charm of the piece.

Length of pile can also provide some clues towards defining the district of origin. More warmth is needed in the mountains and the pile is consequently thick and high, whereas in more temperate areas the pile is lower. Cotton is only available in a very few parts of the Caucasus and its presence in a carpet will further narrow the field. Many Caucasian rugs today are worn down and no longer have their full length of pile. Nevertheless it is possible to see from the design that the pile was originally high. Detail is lost in a thick shaggy pile so designs are far more bold and simple than in rugs woven with a medium or low pile. The most intricate patterns of all are woven in a low pile.

There is a great profusion of symbols and patterns in Caucasian rugs but they have become so stylized down the centuries that their meaning can no longer be defined. Some motifs would seem to have come from Persia, like the angular Caucasian version of the boteh and rugs depicting animal fights, though the latter are normally woven across the width of Caucasian carpets and not down the length as they are in Persia. The dragon and cloud band, both found in carpets from the eastern districts of the Caucasus, are believed to have come from the Far East and from China. A stiff, formalized dragon appears in the earliest surviving Caucasian pieces, but it is only conjecture to state that this dragon was reduced to the simple 'S' motif found in the same districts hundreds of years later.

Caucasian carpets today are among the most treasured of all oriental and tribal work, for their Golden Age has passed. Where other countries may still weave traditional designs, unchanged except for more modern methods of weaving and dyeing, in the Caucasus most of the tribes have been settled and the identity of their traditional designs, symbols, and patterns has been lost for ever.

Kazak including Bordjalou, Karachov, Lambalo, Lori-Pombak, Karaklis, and Shulaver

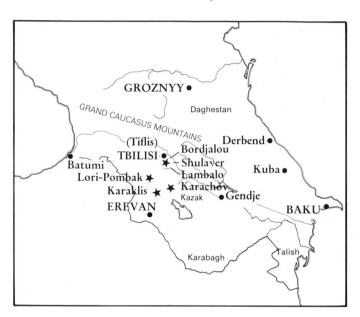

The first and largest district in the 'Kazak' group is *Kazak* itself, stretching from Erivan in the Armenian Caucasus to Tiflis on the borders of Georgia, and with Karabagh to the south-east. The khanate of Kazak produced both high-piled rugs from mountainous areas and low-piled rugs from the valleys, villages, and settlements, many of which have their own easily recognizable characteristics. All have uncut looped top ends and a fringe at the bottom only. The stepped hooked polygon recurs frequently and is seen at its boldest in the shaggy deep-piled rugs of *Lori-Pombak*, which also feature massive geometrical medallions on a plain field. A refinement of these bold patterns is seen in the silky, tightly woven rugs from *Karachov*, often typified by a unusual, luminous green ground, and a corner design of geometric rosettes on a light ground. Rugs from *Lambalo* often have geometrical flowers in the main border, and the field is left plain to show off the beautiful dyes and fine, silky wool. From *Shulaver* come very similar rugs, but the detail is greater and the ground is often covered with an all-over pattern.

The low-piled rugs of *Bordjalou* are much larger and more intricately patterned, with repeating geometrical designs in the field, often in white on a natural black-brown ground. The town of *Karaklis*, on the railway line from Tiflis to Erivan, produces the largest rugs woven in this district, on the same traditional black-brown ground but rich in flower and bird designs. These show the influence of the French-style carpets made in the southern Caucasus for noble Russian households at the end of the eighteenth century.

TYPICAL SPECIFICATIONS

Warp
Double, usually three-ply natural wool.

Weft
Red wool. Up to four shoots.

Pile
Wool. Lori-Pombak and Karachov – long and shaggy. Karachov – short, silky, and tightly woven. Lambalo and Shulaver – medium. Bordjalou and Karaklis – short.

Knot
Symmetrical.
560–1100/dm^2 (37–73/sq. in.).

Ends
Uncut top fringe, often woven into a plain weave band, turned over and stitched down.

Sides
Two or three cords, overcast with red, blue, or brown wool.

Handle
Varied, but usually thick and heavy.

a. Opposite above *Although the pile has been worn low this is still a fine rug for the design has great clarity, rare in Caucasian rugs. The border has a 'leaf and wine glass' motif. Lori-Pombak, mid-nineteenth century.*
2.36m × 1.29m, 7'9" × 4'3".

b. Opposite below *The borders of this carpet illustrate the difficulties that weavers encounter if they are not using a cartoon. The green of the field has kept its colour and is enhanced by the abrash. Bordjalou, nineteenth century.*
2.74m × 1.37m, 9' × 4'6".

c. Right *The depth of colour, lustrous wool, and inventive design of this carpet combine the best features of Kazak weaving. The fine yellows and greens are particularly notable. Dated 1866.*
2.20m × 1.60m, 7'2" × 5'3".

Gendje including South Shirvan

Many rugs ascribed to *Gendje* were woven in outlying areas and brought into this railhead town, where the caravans converged halfway between Tiflis and Baku. This district also produced French-style carpets in the eighteenth and nineteenth centuries to be freighted to Russia, and their influence still shows in a palette which is paler and more pastel than most South Caucasian rugs. The population is mainly Armenian so patterns and designs stem from their traditional and religious sources. In particular, a saw-edged leaf pattern is frequently used in the main border. The diagonal rows of stars, hexagons, and rhomboid shapes is perhaps reminiscent of Talish patterns.

Gendje rugs vary immensely in quality, both in the wool and the standard of knotting and weaving. The best have a medium pile and are made from fine silky wool. Some Gendje rugs, perhaps those made in quantity for export, have three or more weft threads between each row of knots. These rugs tend to have a higher pile, using thick mountain wool, and are easily recognizable because the pattern is scarcely visible from the back, which looks a dirty beige. Much use is made of the typical stepped hooked polygon, either as large medallions or in a smaller all-over pattern.

Rugs from *South Shirvan*, to the north-east of Gendje, have the same construction as all the 'Kazak' group of rugs, with uncut fringes at the top ends. Their design and use of patterns and symbols, however, belong more to the second group of 'Kuba' rugs. The warp threads are always natural brown or brown mixed with white, while true rugs of the Kazak group always have a natural white wool warp.

TYPICAL SPECIFICATIONS

Warp
Natural white wool. South Shirvan – natural brown, or brown and white wool.

Weft
Wool, red or natural white. Often three or more shoots.

Pile
Wool, fine, silky. Medium height, or thicker and longer.

Knot
Symmetrical.
500–1200/dm² (33–80/sq. in.).

Ends
Uncut top fringe. Narrow flat-woven ends, often red.

Sides
Two or three cords, overcast with red, blue and red, or brown wool.

Handle
Varied, soft and silky in the best.

a. Opposite *The medallions are placed on a fine, deep blue field adorned with boteh. The border design is typical of Gendje carpets. Nineteenth century.*
2.65m × 1.10m, 8′10″ × 3′7″.

b. Right *This Gendje prayer rug is dated 1873. The diagonal stripes and the latch hook are typical of the region. Nineteenth century.*
1.32m × 0.86m, 4′4″ × 2′10″.

Karabagh including Chelaberd, Shusha, Chondoresk, and Goradis

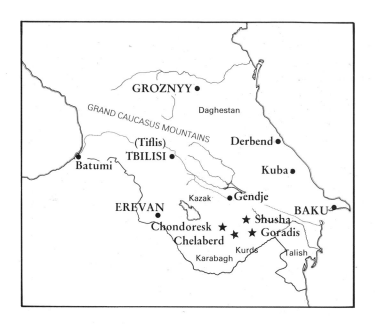

The rugs most usually associated with *Karabagh* are those with an all-over flower design in brilliant blues, cochineal reds, and violets. Many have purely Persian patterns, in particular the continuous Herati motif. Others, notably the famous 'eagle' Kazaks or 'adler' Kazaks have bold geometric splashes of brilliant colour. These rugs were actually made in the *Chelaberd* district.

From *Chondoresk* come the distinctive 'cloud band' Kazaks, with a design which may have originated as far east as China, where the motif is very familiar. Far to the south, on the borders of Moghan is *Goradis*, producing rugs with a unique design of stylized scorpions or crustacea in a fluid all-over pattern, and Herati borders. In *Shusha* patterns is found a Caucasian version of the Persian boteh in an astonishing variety of colours, on a ground of ivory or cochineal red. In Shusha too are made the flower-and-vase carpets so reminiscent of Persian rugs, though the brilliant use of cochineal red as the ground colour is completely individual.

There is a large proportion of Muslims to the east, on the shores of the Caspian Sea, so gables and stepped gables, derived from prayer-rug mihrabs, frequently appear in Karabagh designs. The mihrab motif can also be seen in rugs made by the Kurdish tribes of this district, interwoven with rigidly stylized dragon shapes, hooked polygons, flowers, and plants.

The French-style carpets of the late eighteenth century were largely produced in Karabagh, and their intricate patterns of roses and flowers are to be seen in later carpets from the region.

TYPICAL SPECIFICATIONS

Warp
Natural white wool, occasionally brown.

Weft
Wool, undyed brown or white, sometimes red or blue. Cotton sometimes used in Goradis. Karabagh – double weft between every two rows of knots.

Pile
Wool. Medium height, longer in Kurdish rugs.

Knot
Symmetrical.
800–1200/dm² (53–80/sq. in.).

Ends
Uncut top fringe, some have plain weave finish in white, or brown and white.

Sides
One to three cords, overcast with red wool.

Handle
Fine, soft, and silky. Mountain rugs – thick and harsh.

a. Opposite above *The design of this Karabagh carpet, with its florid scrolls and foliage, is European in inspiration. Nineteenth century.*
4.11m × 1.42m, 12′6″ × 4′8″.

b. Opposite below *The famous 'eagle' or 'sunburst' Kazaks come from the Karabagh district. The motif was first developed in the eighteenth century. Chelaberd, nineteenth century.*
2m × 1.42m, 6′7″ × 4′8″.

c. Right *The cloud-band motif, from which this carpet derives its name, originated in China. The field is scattered with a variety of motifs, including horses and a human figure. Chondoresk, nineteenth century.*
2.06m × 1.58m, 6′9″ × 5′2″.

Talish including Lenkoran and Moghan

Talish rugs are easily recognizable by their long, narrow shape and distinctive design. They are woven by Tartars – pastoral nomads with the greatest skill in rug-making of all Caucasian people. The wool is lustrous, the length of pile medium, and the knotting denser than either Kazaks or Karabaghs. The main borders are always on a natural ground, and the inner field is sometimes left plain, usually blue, less commonly red. More often the field is filled with rosettes, small squares, or stars set in squares. The rich, velvety thickness of Talish rugs is increased by stepped warp threads and extra, short weft threads, generally blue, running 2 to 3 centimetres ($\frac{3}{4}$ to $1\frac{1}{4}$ inches) from the sidecords towards the centre. The top fringe is left uncut and the bottom fringe is usually plain.

Moghan rugs are distinguished by a more symmetrical use of colour and a field which is packed with small blossom-heads arranged in squares or pyramids. Inner borders may have typical Talish rosettes, but the main border is not always on a natural ground. *Lenkoran* rugs are very similar but darker in colour and cochineal reds are used which are seldom found in Talish work. The central field is often filled with small medallions made of repeating S-shapes as distinct from the angular hooks of other Kazaks. From Lenkoran, too, comes a group of fine soumaks and a flat weave, 'djidjim', which is heavy, tightly-woven and clearly intended as a floor-covering.

Kilim, soumak, and djidjim have large abstract geometrical shapes and the hooked motif is common, sometimes appearing as a 'tarantula' within a cartouche. This southern group of flat weaves are woven without borders, but the edges are often filled with a zigzag pattern.

TYPICAL SPECIFICATIONS

Warp
Natural brown or white wool, stepped.

Weft
Wool, undyed, red, or blue. Two shoots.

Pile
Wool, lustrous. Medium height.

Knot
Symmetrical
$900–2000/dm^2$ (60–133/sq. in.).

Ends
Uncut top fringe. Narrow white strip of plain weave. Flat weaves have knotted or braided ends.

Sides
Two to four cords, overcast with blue wool.

Handle
Soft, heavy, and velvety.

a. Opposite above *This formal modular design has been enlivened by the variety of detail within each unit. The deep skirt with a floral motif is unusual. Moghan, mid-nineteenth century.*
2.28m × 1.57m, 7′6″ × 5′2″.

b. Opposite below *A djidjim with a repeating 'tarantula' motif. The colouration, varying in each unit, is particularly harmonious. Nineteenth century.*
1.98m × 1.52m, 6′6″ × 5′.

c. Right *Talish rugs are always long and narrow. The field may be filled with stars as in this carpet, or be left plain. Nineteenth century.*
2.20m × 1.10m, 7′3″ × 3′7″.

Kuba including Chichi, Seichur, Perepedil, and Karagashli

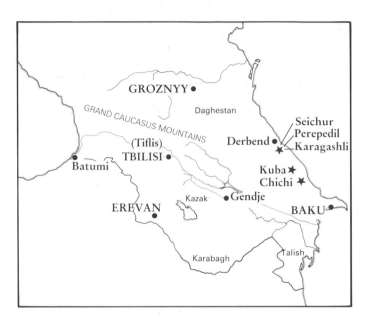

The largest rug-weaving centre in the second, 'Kuba', group is Kuba itself, where some of the finest Caucasian rugs were made, some intended as bedcovers and wall hangings, others as floor coverings. There is a considerable Muslim population, and prayer rugs were woven in Kuba with characteristic Caucasian all-over patterns and an imposed mihrab. Kuba rugs frequently have stepped warp-threads, both ends of the fringe are cut and sometimes knotted, and often the band of kilim at either end is strengthened with blue wool or cotton in soumak stitch. Rugs in the Kuba group have a low pile with medium-density knotting and are generally rich, heavy, and dense. Patterns are more sinuous, and many rugs have kufesque borders or trailing tendril motifs.

From *Perepedil* comes a distinctive ram's horn device, and an all-over pattern of flowers and leaves on a deep indigo or black field with a Herati border, showing considerable Persian influence. *Karagashli* rugs are typified by a design of wild lilies splaying out from medallions. The field is often plain, usually red, or filled with flowers, blossoms, bouquets, and rosettes.

Chichi rugs are woven by an isolated tribe of Chechens and generally have small stepped polygons in the central field, which is usually deep blue or indigo, and a main border of diagonal bars alternating with rosettes. Rugs from *Seichur* have a broad 'X' repeated down the field which is often ivory, yellow, or more rarely green. Also typical is their use of the 'running dog' border and a particularly clear red in the inner border. From Seichur also comes the 'carpet of roses', a Caucasian version of Aubusson designs with the field packed with cabbage roses in vivid, almost strident reds.

TYPICAL SPECIFICATIONS

Warp
Undyed wool; cotton in more recent pieces. Seichur – alternate warps depressed.

Weft
Natural wool. One or two shoots.

Pile
Wool. Short to medium.

Knot
Symmetrical.
900–4000/dm^2 (60–266/sq. in.).

Ends
Finely knotted fringes at both ends. Flat weave reinforced with blue soumak stitch.

Sides
One or two cords, overcast with deep blue or white wool, or cotton.

Handle
Densely knotted, silky.

a. Opposite above *The delicate colours of this Chichi rug are unusual. Originally, before the black outlines were corroded, the effect would have been crisper. Some of the black has been crudely restored.*
1.52m × 1.09m, 5′ × 3′7″.
Nineteenth century.

b. Opposite below *A unusually small Kuba rug with a kufesque border. The flowers of the field, endlessly repeating, are carefully drawn and coloured in a random but controlled fashion. Nineteenth century.*
1.36m × 1.21m, 4′6″ × 4′.

c. Right *The design of this prayer rug, with scorpions in the field and a kufesque border, appears to be earlier than many of the more commercial Perepedil carpets. Nineteenth century.*
1.47m × 1.17m, 4′10″ × 3′10″.

A large group of important flat weaves comes from the Kuba district and the weaving technique known as soumak even takes its name from Shemaka, south of Kuba. The kilims are woven in designs of considerable antiquity, usually on the same pattern as pile carpets, with a main field enclosed within borders. These are usually of two main types: the continuous meander-and-bar pattern, or a single repeated motif, which is sometimes remarkably similar to the hooked stepped border patterns in Memling carpets of the fifteenth century. Unlike almost any other group of kilims, the Kuba group have clearly delineated design motifs, many of an angular medallion type, commonly known as 'tarantula' on a plain field which is often scattered with small ornaments, including birds, animals, flowers, and an angular boteh similar to those found in Marasali prayer rugs.

a. Opposite left *This kilim has a bar-and-meander border and a central field with the geometric medallions and vertical lines that are typical of Kuba kilims. Nineteenth century.*
2.99m × 1.57m, 9′10″ × 5′2″.

b. Opposite right *The field of this kilim is composed of large 'kochak' medallions. The hooked motifs of the main border are similar to those of Memling carpets of the fifteenth century. Kuba, nineteenth century.*
2.31m × 1.39m, 7′6″ × 4′7″.

c. Right *A pile carpet from Seichour with the X-shaped motif characteristic of this region. Nineteenth century.*
1.96m × 1.30m, 6′5″ × 4′3″.

Shirvan including Marasali, Chajli, and Akstafa

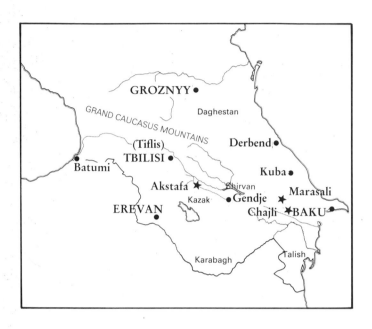

Rugs from the prolific carpet-weaving district of *Shirvan* have characteristics of both 'Kazak' and 'Kuba' groups. The top ends are not cut to form a fringe, and the bottom fringe is either knotted or braided. Warp threads lie on one level, unlike the stepped warps of most Kuba rugs. To the east, tribal rugs from the foothills of the Caucasus, such as those from *Chajli*, use typical Kazak motifs and geometric designs in clear bold colours. There are many settled Armenian Christians in Shirvan so rugs often have cruciform motifs as well as stylized animals and Persian-influenced border patterns. Eastwards, along the shores of the Caspian Sea, the population is mainly Muslim and there is a large production of prayer rugs, often featuring diagonal lines of white across a dark-coloured ground. The highly-prized *Marasali* prayer rugs have a velvety appearance and are very flexible and soft. A typical pattern has the Caucasian version of the boteh covering the field in diagonal lines on a ground that is often dark blue. The borders may also have an extremely simplified boteh facing alternately left and right.

To the west, in the district of *Akstafa*, the principal symbol is a curious, angular bird, thought by many to be an interpretation of the peacock from Persia. The 'akstafa' is found in many other rugs woven up the coast of the Caspian Sea, and is often to be discerned among the crowded figures and flowers characteristic of other more central Shirvan rugs.

Shirvan also produces some fine kilims, in particular those with broad bands of hooked medallions and others consisting of a series of narrow bands of varying widths, often woven in a chevron or arrowhead pattern. Large Shirvan 'band' kilims were used as coverings for ox-drawn carts. Small flat-woven prayer rugs were also made, with designs similar to those of pile rugs.

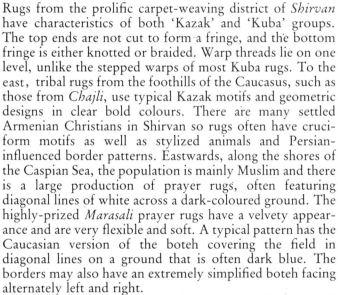

TYPICAL SPECIFICATIONS

Warp
Wool, natural brown, or brown and white. Shirvan – cotton in later pieces.

Weft
Mainly white cotton. Some very old pieces use wool. Two shoots.

Pile
Wool. Short to medium.

Knot
Symmetrical.
1000–3000/dm² (66–200/sq. in.).

Ends
Uncut fringe at top. Bottom fringe braided or knotted. Also flat weave with embroidered decoration.

Sides
Natural wool, one cord, overcast with white wool. Marasali – double cord, overcast white wool. Akstafa – double cord, overcast blue wool.

Handle
Full-bodied and soft. Marasali – velvety and flexible.

a. Opposite above *A typical, slightly elongated Chajli runner. It is finely woven and adorned with octagons and latch hooks. Nineteenth century.*
4m × 1m, 13′ × 3′3″.

b. Opposite below *This runner displays the highly stylized 'akstafa' bird which resembles a peacock. The low pile gives a clearly defined design. Akstafa, nineteenth century.*
3.17m × 1.16m, 10′4″ × 3′10″.

c. Right *A kilim from the Shirvan area, with the characteristic hooked medallions in bands of different colours. The design has no border. Nineteenth century.*
2.67m × 1.63m, 8′9″ × 5′4″.

Baku including Chila, Surahani, and Saliani

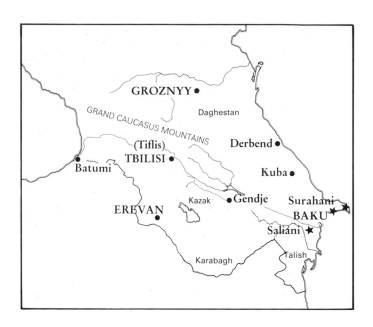

Carpets made in *Baku*, like those of Shirvan, also have features in common with both the 'Kuba' and 'Kazak' groups. Warp threads lie on one plane and top fringes are left as loops, though sometimes both ends have cut fringes. Low-piled Baku rugs tend to be soft and flabby compared with the velvety texture of Shirvans, and the quality and density of knotting is looser and often of a lower standard. It is their colours above all which distinguish Baku rugs from those of any other district. More blue is used, from the palest tones through aquamarine to darkest turquoise, with a ground colour of dark blue or black. Baku patterns are disciplined and repetitive, often featuring interlocking lozenges or medallions as well as small stylized animals.

Chila produces rugs with a strong Persian influence, with patterns frequently composed of boteh, each row usually facing in alternate directions, whether in a stepped pattern or in straight vertical lines. These rugs are known as 'Boteh' Chila as distinct from 'Avshan' Chila which have a more muted palette and a central field design derived from the Herati pattern. The 'barber's pole' is a much-favoured border pattern. *Surahani* rugs have a slightly higher pile than those of Baku. The vivid turquoise is almost exclusive to Surahani rugs, which often have such pale colouring that they look almost faded. Surahani rugs are usually made in small sizes and seldom use more than five different colours. Larger Surahani rugs have a honeycomb pattern composed of octagons, reminiscent of Turkoman *guls*.

Saliani rugs are very similar to those of Talish, but the magnificent cochineal reds and rich emerald greens are more typical of Karabagh colouring. Multicoloured boteh all facing the same way, feature frequently, and a quite individual double-headed boteh is often used in both field and border.

TYPICAL SPECIFICATIONS

Warp
Natural brown wool.

Weft
Natural wool; or cotton and wool mixed. Two shoots.

Pile
Wool. Low.
Surahani – medium.

Knot
Symmetrical.

Ends
Uncut top fringe, or a narrow band of plain weave and a white fringe at both ends.

Sides
One cord, overcast with white wool.

Handle
Soft and floppy.
Saliani – rich, densely knotted.

a. Opposite above *The shape of this rug is unusual for Chila carpets which tend to be longer and narrower. Second half of the nineteenth century.*
1.82m × 1.11m, 6′ × 3′8″.
Formerly in the Perez Collection

b. Opposite below *The outer border with a design of tiny flowers is characteristic of Chila work. Nineteenth century.*
3.50m × 1.44m, 11′6″ × 4′9″.
Formerly in the Perez Collection

c. Right *The stately composition of the field is created by rows of very decorative boteh. The main border features birds perched on branches. Chila, nineteenth century.*
3.80m × 1.55m, 12′5″ × 5′1″.

Daghestan including Lesghistan

In Daghestan and Lesghistan the population is predominantly Muslim and designs avoid any representations of cross-like ornament or human figures. Daghestan carpets have steeply stepped warps, a fairly high pile and are very tightly woven, making them extremely firm and stiff. The central field of Daghestan runners is often filled with multicoloured stepped polygons, or diagonal multicoloured stripes. Much use is made of cochineal red in this district. There is a large production of prayer rugs, many of them with formalized flowers geometrically arranged within a hexagonal or honeycomb pattern, or with flower-filled trellis patterns on a white ground.

The Daghestan district also produces some extremely fine soumaks and a unique flat weave known as 'sileh'. In these, the design consists of huge repetitive 'S' shapes in blocks of alternating colour. The two small comma-shaped feet on the bottom curve of each 'S' indicate that the design has evolved from a dragon shape, a supposition which is reinforced by the fact that some antique Daghestan soumaks are woven with ancient patterns of dragons.

Lesghistan is a more mountainous district so the rugs have a higher pile and the texture of the wool is more granular. The colours and designs are brighter and more simple than those of low-piled Daghestan rugs. A typical motif is the star, set like medallions down the field, or repeated in bright colours in wide borders on a white ground. The Lesghi are among the finest craftsmen in the Caucasus, both in their weaving and their skill in dyeing. Easily recognizable is a clear luminous yellow, a deep moss green, and a vivid blue. Lesghistan prayer rugs are distinguished by multiple borders filled with brightly coloured stars, a variation of the hooked diagonal 'S', or a calyx-and-leaf pattern. Fringes are often knotted in a flat trellis at both ends.

TYPICAL SPECIFICATIONS

Warp
Wool, natural white, or
brown and white.

Weft
Wool, natural white, or
brown and white.
Two shoots.

Pile
Wool. Long.

Knot
Symmetrical.
$1500–2200/dm^2(100–146)/sq.in.)$.

Ends
Cut fringe at both ends,
knotted in a flat trellis-
pattern.

Sides
One or two cords, overcast
with white or blue wool.

Handle
Extremely tight and rigid.
Lesghistan – granular and
stiff.

a. Opposite above *The field of
this Daghestan prayer rug is
entirely filled with a trellis and
flower pattern. Early
nineteenth century.*
1.75m × 1.27m, 5'9" × 4'2".

b. Opposite below *The direct
design and clear drawing in
this Lesghistan rug suggests
that it is early nineteenth-
century. The star-filled field is
typical of the region and the
border is derived from the
kufesque pattern.*
2.04m × 1.14m, 6'9" × 3'9".

c. Right *A flat weave known
as a 'sileh'. The S-shaped
motifs are highly stylized
dragons on which the head and
tails can still just be detected.
Nineteenth century.*
2.28m × 1.11m, 7'6" × 3'8".

PERSIA

One of the most stimulating aspects of the Persian carpet industry is the vitality with which it has always adapted to changing circumstances. This resilience is rooted in a long-established and basically uninterrupted history of textile manufacture, which reflects the importance of textiles in Persian life.

One such revival occurred during the nineteenth and twentieth centuries when the carpet industry had to balance demands for its products from both the domestic and export markets. Contrary to common belief this was not a period of decline and decadence. In the previous century Persia had been at the mercy of local rulers competing for power and little is known of carpet production during this period, but it is likely that production for local needs continued in villages and small workshops. It was this surviving workforce of skilled weavers that enabled the industry to recover and expand under the rule of Aga Muhammad Qajar, after the unification of Persia in 1787.

The rule of the Qajar Shahs (1787–1925) brought a long period of comparative internal stability to Persia, and this was naturally beneficial to the development of the carpet industry. Increased contact with Europe, aided by the establishment of permanent diplomatic, technical, and commercial representation, led to a renewed demand for carpets, to the benefit of Persia's export trade. The industry was supported by the Qajar government and flourished on many levels, the diverse products being gathered together by factories and merchants. As well as the town workshops, located in such cities as Tabriz, Meshed, Kerman, and Teheran with the larger ones supplying the Qajar court, there were village and tribal productions. A new feature in the industry was the presence of European capital and personnel, notably that of the Manchester-based firm of Ziegler and Co. They established their factory in Sultana-

bad (Arak) in 1883, using the existing network of local village weavers and determined to exercise firm quality control over the use of harsh and fugitive aniline dyes.

Knotted pile carpets and associated floor coverings were of great importance in Persian households. The traditional house, still being built in the nineteenth century, was planned as a series of rooms around courtyards. These rooms were flexible in function and had no furniture apart from storage chests, though European chairs and tables gradually came into use among the rich. The floor had to be well-carpeted to provide a comfortable surface for serving food, seating, and spreading out bedding. A family would build up its rug collection through bridal dowries, amassing an investment which could be converted into cash as needed. For everyday use, however, the floors were usually covered with locally-made felts, patterned in red and green, or blue and white, against a light brown or yellow ground. In more modest homes flat-woven gelims (kilims) also served as floor coverings. These were the work of tribal weavers who sold their surplus products in the bazaar for the local domestic market.

When the carpets were brought out and laid on top of the felts, they conformed to certain well-defined standards of taste and design. Early nineteenth-century pieces show a preference for graceful repeated floral motifs in well-balanced colours. Peony palmettes, for example, would be placed against a background of close-textured leaf scroll worked in dark blue, deep orange, and cream wools. Lattices of open-petalled flowers or vertical stripes of zigzag floral scroll were also popular. Large-scale pictorial designs, that could only be achieved by very fine knotting and skilled weaving, were introduced in the middle of the nineteenth century. These were inspired by Persian epic and romantic literature; as well as European prints, engrav-

a. Left *A Kurdish hamlet at the southern end of Lake Urmia in north-west Persia.*

ings, and photographs with their depictions of landscapes, buildings, and fashionably dressed women. European influence can also be seen in the bolder and more flamboyant style of the end of the century, when floral patterns were often woven with large bouquets of roses and peonies in colour schemes which included pinks and greens against a light beige ground. These pieces were not necessarily made for the export market and sometimes have inscriptions with the date and the name of a Persian patron.

The carpet industry has continued in the twentieth century, throughout Pahlavi rule (1925–79) and its revolutionary aftermath. In fact, Pahlavi rulers attempted to stimulate the industry by founding a government-owned carpet manufacturing company and later, when traditional crafts became associated with the national identity, they established cooperatives and other enterprises to provide additional outlets for the carpet weavers.

During the late 1960s and early 1970s, carpet production escalated to satisfy both the export market and the newly prosperous domestic sector. The women concentrated on weaving items for sale rather than for their own use and when questioned, said that they no longer made flat weaves as the market demanded knotted pile carpets. Designs multiplied from those based on traditional floral and medallion motifs, to the sophisticated creations of the professional designers employed by many carpet factories.

Kurdistan including Senneh and Bidjar

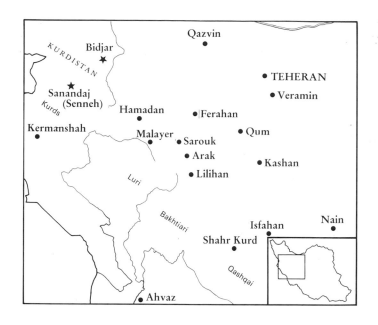

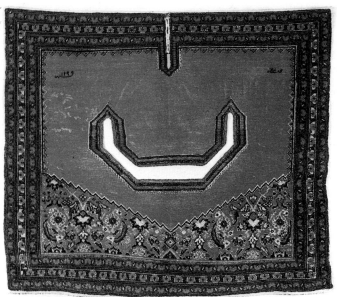

The Kurds, although related to the Persians both in language and religion, are a somewhat autonomous group, to be found in Iran, Iraq, and Turkey. The carpets of Kurdistan reflect the varied lifestyles of the weavers, who may be nomads or city and village dwellers.

The capital of the province, Sanandaj, has long been famous for its unusually fine weavings, which include both pile rugs and flat-woven kilims whose designs show mutual influence. Adapting the name of the city, these weavings are usually known as *Senneh* in the West. The kilims are among the finest of the Middle East, and their delicate designs are often achieved by the use of curved wefts. The colours are rich, deep, and disciplined, based on red, dark blue, ochre yellow, and beige. The most distinctive are superimposed geometrical shapes, usually hexagons, in contrasting colours, filled with interlacing floral motifs.

In *Bidjar* carpet weaving is a cottage industry, as looms can be found in the houses of both the town and its surrounding villages. There are shops in the town where the weaver can purchase the designs and the wool. The carpets are particularly hard-wearing, due to the manner in which the wefts are beaten into place: a long iron bar is inserted between the warps during the weaving and then hammered hard against the wefts. The designs are somewhat rectilinear and vary from small repeated floral sprigs, to large bouquets and medallions against a cream or rich red ground, or versions of the Herati pattern.

In the villages live many Kurdish tribal groups. Little is known about their weaving, and although it is often called 'Mosul', this name is too imprecise to be used with confidence. The designs can sometimes be distinguished from those of other Persian Kurds, and a particularly distinctive one in a soft shaggy pile is woven by the Zanjabi and Jaff Kurds. This is based on interlocking diamond motifs, filled with hooked borders, and can easily be

adapted to fit either floor covers or saddlebags. The Kurds also weave carpets in dark sober shades of red and blue, in designs based on the *mina khani* flower lattice. In some of the tribal carpets the knots are staggered along the rows, giving lines that are less steeply angled than usual.

TYPICAL SPECIFICATIONS

Warp
Senneh – natural white wool or cotton; sometimes silk, white or grouped in various colours. Bidjar – natural wool, white or brown; sometimes cotton; rarely silk. Village rugs – wool or cotton.

Weft
Senneh – wool, cotton, or silk; one shoot. Bidjar – wool, natural white or dyed in various colours; white cotton or yellow silk in later work; two to five shoots. Village rugs – undyed wool, or cotton; two shoots.

Pile
Senneh – wool, very low. Bidjar – fairly silky wool, medium height. Village rugs – soft wool; long.

Knot
Symmetrical. Senneh – 200–7500/dm^2 (133–500/sq. in.). Bidjar – 800–2500/dm^2 (53–166/sq. in.).

Ends
Senneh – plain weave, fringes often grouped and knotted. Bidjar – fringes, sometimes knotted. Village rugs – long shaggy fringes.

Sides
Two or more groups of cords, bound with wool.

Handle
Senneh – thin, floppy, and dry. Bidjar – compact and stiff.

a. Left above *A saddle cover with a design of peony palmettes and curved serrated leaves, inspired by town carpets, and a triple border of floral sprigs. Sanandaj, late nineteenth/century.*
1.80m × 1.20m, 6′ × 4′.

b. Left below *A wagireh or weaver's sampler with a vivid interpretation of the classic lotus and cloud scroll. The border has a stylized vine. Bidjar, late nineteenth or early twentieth century.*
0.61m × 0.69m, 2′ × 2′3″.

c. Right *A finely worked kilim from Sanandaj with a typical design of repeated floral cones and a floral scroll border. Late nineteenth century.*
1.80m × 1.20m, 6′ × 4′.

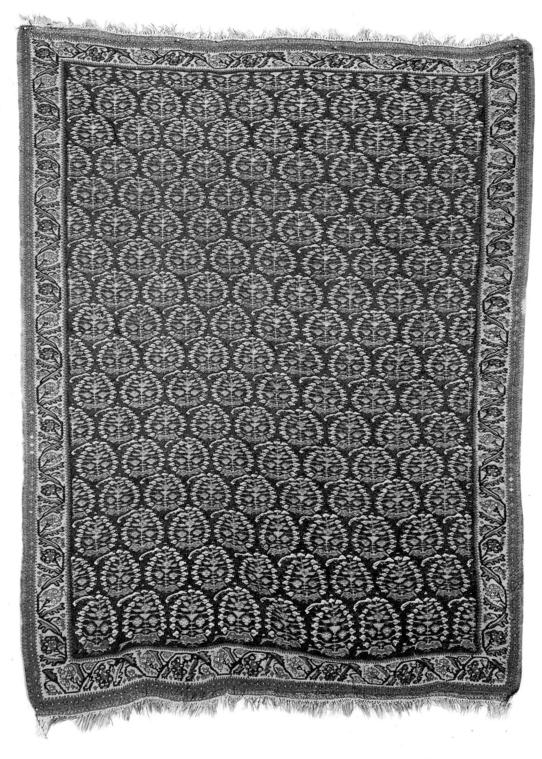

Tabriz including Heriz

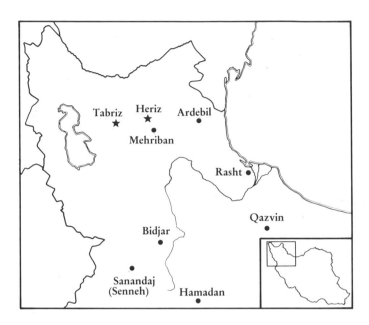

In carpet history Tabriz, a large city in the Turkish-speaking province of Azerbaijan, is famed for its part in the revival of the industry which took place through the energy and initiative of its merchants in the nineteenth century.

The industry is organized in factories located in the town and its suburbs. Factory sizes can vary from enterprises with about a hundred looms to more modest workshops with ten. The weaving concentrates exclusively on the commercial production of knotted pile carpets, in a wide range of sizes, designed according to the demands of the market. The carpets are woven in well-dyed wools which tend, however, to be somewhat harsh in colour. The colour range is rich with bright and deep reds, oranges, greens, and blues. The pile is usually wool but in luxurious items both silk and metallic thread may be used. Designs are accomplished and eclectic, as factory owners will happily borrow from other weaving areas any patterns which sell well. The best worked designs make imaginative use of the traditional medallion and corner pattern, repeated floral motifs, and pictorial compositions.

To the east of Tabriz is a group of villages which have been weaving carpets since at least the early nineteenth century. The most important of these are *Heriz*, Mehriban, and Asleh. Their carpets use clear brightly coloured wools. The designs are bold and angular and include an attractive repeated lattice of interlaced stems and curved feathery leaves, known as the Herati pattern and much copied in other carpet-weaving centres. The distinctive angularity of Heriz carpets is due to the weavers' great skill as copyists: they can reproduce the most complex classical designs without cartoons, but the result is somewhat idiosyncratic as they are incapable of weaving curves (see 238a and b).

TYPICAL SPECIFICATIONS

Warp
Tabriz – natural cotton. Heriz – white cotton, wool, or silk.

Weft
Tabriz – cotton, grey, white, red, or blue. Heriz – cotton or silk, often blue. Two shoots.

Pile
Tabriz – wool, occasionally silk. Heriz – wool, medium height, or silk and low.

Knot
Symmetrical.
Tabriz – 1000–2500/dm^2 (66–166/sq. in.).
Heriz – cotton – 500–1300/dm^2 (33–86/sq. in.); silk – 3000–8000/dm^2 (200–533/sq. in.).

Ends
Tabriz – plaited fringes or narrow bands of plain weave. Heriz – plaited fringe or flat-woven band.

Sides
Tabriz – groups of cords, bound with wool, cotton, or coloured silk. Heriz – two groups of cords, bound with coloured wool or blue or red silk.

Handle
Tabriz – fairly stiff. Heriz – stiff and heavy, but silk ones flexible and light.

a. Opposite above *A prayer rug with double columns framing lamps from which peony palmettes are suspended. Tabriz, nineteenth century.* 1.37m × 1.03m, 4′6″ × 3′4″.

b. Opposite below *A well-planned scheme of flowering medallions and cartouches against a plain ground. The border includes lotus, floral cone, and zigzag motifs. Tabriz, late nineteenth century.* 3.90m × 2.93m, 13′ × 9′9″.

c. Right *A silk carpet in a rich yet controlled colour scheme. The medallion design is made up of peony palmettes against a field of foliage and cloud scroll. Tabriz, nineteenth century.* 3.50m × 2.28m, 11′8″ × 7′7″.

Arak including Ziegler, Ferahan, Sarouk, and Lilihan

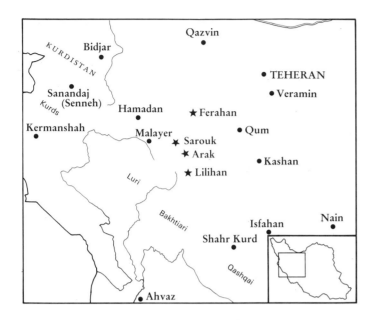

Arak is a small town in west Persia which has had a flourishing carpet-weaving industry since the nineteenth century. The production is entirely commercial and was stimulated by the activities of Tabriz merchants in the export markets. Their initiative was followed by the entry of European and American carpet companies, beginning with the Manchester-based firm of Ziegler and Co. in 1883. The companies maintained their premises in Arak until the late 1920s. They imported ready-dyed wools which they gave to the weavers together with charts of the required designs.

The industry was home-based, employing weavers both in the town and surrounding villages. Carpets woven under the aegis of the *Ziegler* company had designs based on small repeating floral patterns of Persian origin but adapted to European taste.

Arak also served as a collecting centre for the carpets woven in surrounding villages such as Ferahan, Meshkabad, Sarouk, and Lilihan. The finely woven carpets of *Ferahan* were distinguished for their excellent designs based on repeated floral-cone motifs arranged in hexagonal panels, or on meticulously worked versions of the Herati pattern. The products of Meshkabad are comparable to those of Ferahan but are in a coarser weave. *Sarouk* rugs are identifiable by their striking medallion compositions, while the products of *Lilihan* have soft fluent floral designs.

TYPICAL SPECIFICATIONS

Warp
Usually natural cotton, occasionally wool. Sarouk – depressed warp.

Weft
Usually natural cotton, sometimes blue or pink; occasionally wool. Two shoots.

Pile
Wool. Ferahan – low. Sarouk – medium height.

Knot
Asymmetrical, sometimes symmetrical.
$1000–7000/dm^2$ (66–466/sq. in.)

Ends
Narrow bands of plain weave, fringed.

Sides
Ferahan – three or four cords, bound with wool, usually red. Sarouk – two groups of two, three, or four cords bound with red or blue wool.

Handle
Ferahan – flexible and light. Sarouk – heavy, velvety, and stiff.

a. Opposite above *A striking design based on willow foliage and flowering shrubs with a rich floral border. Sarouk, nineteenth century.* 2.10m × 1.26m, 6'10" × 4'1".

b. Opposite below *This imaginative medallion design uses angular, stylized peony and lotus motifs. The border is a bold version of the Herati pattern. Ferahan, early twentieth century.* 2.10m × 1.35m, 7' × 4'6".

c. Right *The design for this carpet was supplied to the local weaver by the Ziegler Company. The flower and scroll motifs of the field and the garland border are both distinctive. Arak (Ziegler), late nineteenth century.* 3.50m × 2.83m, 11'8" × 9'5".

Veramin including Kurds, Lurs, and Teheran

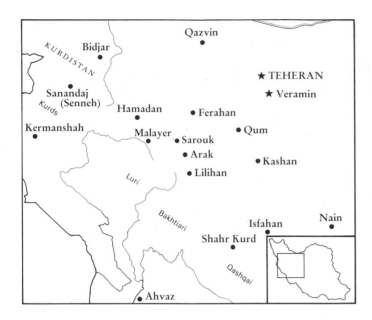

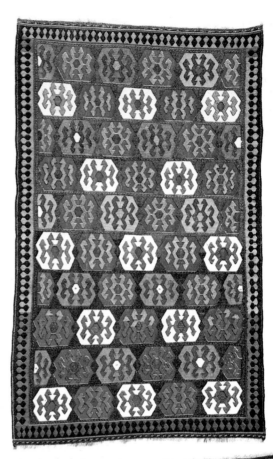

This small town, situated near Persia's capital Teheran, has an interesting and varied carpet production. Ethnically it is a lively place, as in addition to its settled Persian population, it is also a gathering centre for many tribal groups, such as Kurds, Lurs, Arabs, Shahsevan, Qashqai, and Turkoman.

Veramin's indigenous carpet industry only became established in the late nineteenth century and it now has a small but distinctive output. The dominant colours are dark blue, bright red, orange, and white, and the main design is a repeating interlaced daisy pattern, the so-called *mina khani*.

The tribal weaving of the Veramin area is extremely varied and often difficult to attribute correctly as so many influences are involved. Some kilims, for example, are woven with rosette patterns which may show the influence of town-carpet motifs. The *Kurds* weave knotted pile rugs with rosettes and hooked lozenge borders, as well as striking kilims with flame-like palmettes. The *Lurs* weave distinctive pieces, such as weft-wrapped saddlebags with repeated hexagon motifs containing hooked devices.

In *Teheran* itself, carpet weaving seems to have prospered only in the late nineteenth century. The designs were based on floral and medallion themes.

TYPICAL SPECIFICATIONS

Warp
Veramin and Teheran –
cotton. Tribal weavings –
brown wool.

Weft
Veramin – cotton, two shoots
alternating white and blue.
Tribal weavings – wool,
sometimes brown.

Pile
Wool.

Knot
Symmetrical. Asymmetrical in
Teheran rugs.

Ends
Tribal pieces have plain
weave, sometimes decorated
with rosettes.

a. Opposite above *A kilim
with a design of bands of
double hexagons enclosing
hooked motifs. The border
is a reciprocal trefoil. Lur,
twentieth century.*
2.80m × 1.65m, 9′2″ × 5′5″.

b. Opposite below *An
interlaced design on two levels
with bold, open flowers over
delicate, star-shaped flowers.
This is known as the* mina
khani *pattern. Veramin,
twentieth century.*
2.10m × 1.50m, 7′ × 5′.

c. Right *The repeated floral
cones of this design are usually
associated with the weavings
of Sanandaj. The border has
an oblique stripe and floral
scroll. Lur, twentieth century.*
2.03m × 1.38m, 6′9″ × 4′7″.

Qum and *Nain*

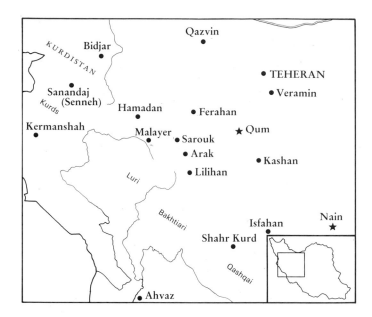

These cities only began to weave carpets in this century, but they have rapidly developed into important centres and are distinguished for the fine quality of their designs.

Qum attracts many pilgrims as it contains the shrine of Fatimeh Masumeh, the sister of the eighth Imam Reza. The carpet industry, established in the 1930s by merchants from Kashan, is entirely home-based and the weavers work from charted designs supplied by the contractor. As it is so recent and there is no earlier tradition of textile production, materials are imported from outside. In the past wools were brought in from Sabzawar and spun in the town, or were imported ready-spun from Tabriz.

Colours are rich yet restrained, with a dominant beige used for backgrounds. The designs are eclectic and show the influence of the repeated squares of Chahar Mahal and the elaborate floral compositions of Isfahan. There is also a preference for repeated ogee medallions, floral cones, lozenges, and oblique flower scrolls, all meticulously treated. Particularly interesting is the graceful and subtle treatment of Persian landscape compositions.

Nain is a small city on the fringes of the central desert, with a long history shown by the Friday mosque whose exquisite stucco decoration dates from the ninth century. It was traditionally a cloth-weaving town, making fabric for men's cloaks (*abas*). This industry declined when the cloaks started to go out of fashion and carpet weaving was established in its place in the 1930s.

The industry is a mixture of town-workshop and home-based looms. It concentrates on making extremely fine knotted pile carpets of rare quality, which are luxury commodities. They are worked in a palette of subtle restrained colours in which dark and light blue, crimson red, yellow, white, and beige dominate. The designs, created by professional designers, are immaculate compositions of star medallions and interlacing floral devices, often with peony scroll borders.

TYPICAL SPECIFICATIONS

Warp
Qum – cotton, occasionally silk.
Nain – silk or white cotton, on two levels.

Weft
Blue cotton. Sometimes silk in Qum.

Pile
Nain – wool.
Qum – wool, silk, or a mixture.

Knot
Asymmetrical.
4000–6200/dm² (266–400/sq. in.).

Ends
Plain weave. Fringes knotted or looped, or warps tied together.

Sides
Double cord overcast with red wool.

Handle
Very compact.

a. Opposite above *This disciplined composition has sharply-angled centre and corner medallions on a plain ground. The medallions are filled with a carefully detailed Herati pattern. Qum, mid-twentieth century.*
2.06m × 1.37m, 6′11″ × 4′5″.

b. Opposite below *An elaborate and fanciful prayer-niche design with columns entwined with flowers, a central tree in a frame, and birds and butterflies of Chinese inspiration fluttering around the lamp. Qum, mid-twentieth century.*
1.62m × 1.08m, 5′5″ × 3′7″.

c. Right *A typical Nain carpet with delicate foliage and peony-scroll borders. This design could only have been worked by an experienced weaver following a cartoon. Mid-twentieth century.*
3.23m × 2.24m, 10′6″ × 7′4″

Kashan

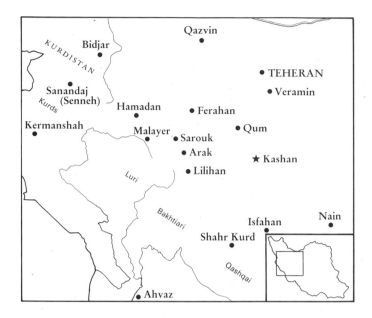

Kashan is a town on the fringes of the central desert which has long managed to preserve its traditional appearance created by the striking domed houses. It enjoyed an excellent reputation in the Safavid period for the variety and quality of its woven textiles, but like other centres such as Isfahan and Kerman, its carpet industry did not revive until the late nineteenth century. Initially, Australian merino wool was used, and this practice continued until the 1930s.

There are no carpet-weaving workshops in the town, as the industry relies for its products on home-based looms. These are distributed among households in both Kashan town and the surrounding villages. Knotted pile carpets only are woven, catering to both the home and export market and of the finest quality. A rich strong range of colours is used in which red, green, blue, black, and white dominate.

The designs are elegant and fluid, often based on elaborate medallions reserved on a red or blue field, which may be plain or filled with arabesque foliage motifs. The Kashan weavers also produce highly accomplished and sophisticated versions of Persian pictorial themes.

TYPICAL
SPECIFICATIONS

Warp
Natural cotton. Sometimes silk in white, yellow, or other colours. Warp fully or partially depressed.

Weft
Cotton, white or blue. Two shoots.

Pile
Velvety merino wool. Sometimes silk. Medium height.

Knot
Asymmetrical. $3000-8000/dm^2$ ($200-533$/sq. in.).

Ends
A narrow band of plain weave, with plaited fringes.

Sides
Four, sometimes two, cords, bound with coloured wool.

Handle
Compact, flexible, and velvety.

a. Opposite above *This interesting composition has a portrait of a dervish set against a fanciful interpretation of an Italianate palace on the horizon. Kashan, late nineteenth century.*
2.04m × 1.40m, 6′8″ × 4′.

b. Opposite below *A medallion carpet based on classical Safavid designs. Drop-shaped pendants radiate from a central star-shaped medallion against the rich floral ground. Kashan, nineteenth century.*
3.57m × 2.71m, 11′9″ × 8′11″.

c. Right *A sophisticated design in which medallions containing peony palmettes are reserved against a ground of carnation scroll. Peony and cloud-scroll border. Kashan, nineteenth century.*
2.18m × 1.20m, 7′3″ × 4′.

Isfahan

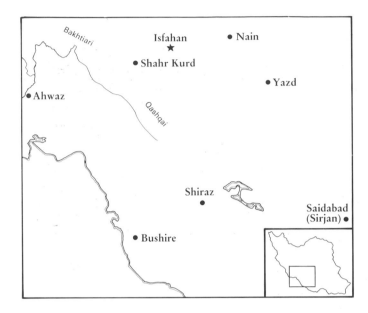

The beautiful city of Isfahan, Persia's capital from the late sixteenth to the early eighteenth century, was the centre of a flourishing carpet industry which supplied the Safavid court. This industry, however, declined after the Afghan invasion of 1722, and did not revive until the late nineteenth century.

At the beginning of this revival the industry depended on looms in the homes of weavers in the town. They either worked on their own account and sold their products in the bazaar, or contracted their labour to one of the merchants. Later, and this was a constant feature of Isfahan in the 1960s, the home weavers were supplemented by workers in small factories.

The colours are clear and evenly dyed – a range of blues, reds, crimsons, greens, oranges, yellows, beiges, and cream – and the elegant designs are mainly accomplished and meticulous interpretations of classical Safavid originals. Graceful medallions and corner motifs rest against fields of lotus, peony, and cloud scroll. Elaborate borders include floral scroll. Some carpets have repeated all-over designs of interlaced garlands and arabesque foliage scroll. One way designs include prayer niches and flowering trees. There are also distinctive and instantly recognizable pictorial compositions worked from cartoons based on Safavid miniatures, lovers reclining under flowering trees being a favourite motif. Other distinctive and immaculately worked designs are copied directly from the tile work of local Safavid buildings, such as the glowing mosaic of the early seventeenth-century mosque of Sheikh Lotfallah.

TYPICAL SPECIFICATIONS

Warp
Silk, in five strands, or cotton.
Warps slightly depressed.

Weft
Cotton, blue. Two shoots.

Pile
Wool.

Knot
Asymmetrical.
5000–9000/dm^2 (333–600/sq. in.).

Ends
Narrow bands of plain weave,
warps sometimes knotted
together.

Sides
Overcast with red or blue
wool.

a. Opposite above *An elaborate pictorial composition with a court reception in the centre and famous Persian monuments in each corner. Isfahan, early twentieth century.*
2.81m × 1.85m, 9'2" × 6'.

b. Opposite below *An accomplished medallion design in which flowering arabesque stems and tendrils are trained into trefoils and spiralling scrolls. Isfahan, late nineteenth century.*
3.60m × 2.74m, 12' × 9'.

c. Right *Two levels of arabesque foliage interlace, filled with peonies and carnations. The border is a bold arabesque scroll. Isfahan, nineteenth century.*
1.95m × 1.35m, 6'6" × 4'6".

Chahar Mahal

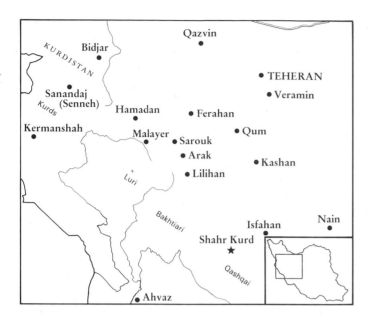

Chahar Mahal describes a region of villages of mixed Persian, Turkish, and Armenian population stretching west and south of Isfahan, whose main centre is Shahr Kurd. Many of the khans of the Bakhtiari tribes have long maintained permanent residences in these villages and have exercised suzerainty over them. Because of this Bakhtiari connection, the carpets produced in the villages have been erroneously given a Bakhtiari tribal attribution. They are in fact made by the long-settled inhabitants.

The organization is an excellent example of a village industry. The looms are in houses and of two types, and although most villagers prefer horizontal looms, the inhabitants of Shahr Kurd use the upright type. They work from charted designs weaving rugs and carpets of assorted sizes.

The colours are interesting and varied, including bright tones of red, green, blue, yellow, as well as soft greys and browns, but the effect is often spoilt by careless dyeing.

The designs are direct, attractive, and easily identifiable. There is a distinct preference for repeated motifs such as diamond shapes filled with floral devices, and square panels of contrasting colours containing floral cones, foliate sprays, and willow trees. Some carpets also have patterns based on central medallions.

TYPICAL SPECIFICATIONS

Warp
Natural cotton; or white or brown wool.

Weft
Cotton, natural or blue. Occasionally dark wool. One shoot, though occasionally two.

Pile
Wool, medium height.

Knot
Usually symmetrical. 800–4000/dm² (53–266/sq. in.)

Ends
A narrow strip of cotton plain weave, with one row of brocading.

Sides
Eight to ten cords in groups of four, bound with goat hair or dark wool.

Handle
Heavy and stiff.

a. Opposite above *A characteristic design of repeated lozenge motifs filled with alternating cypress trees and birds, with a strong lotus-scroll border. Chahar Mahal, twentieth century.* 2.13m × 1.57m, 6′11″ × 5′1″.

b. Opposite below *A graceful and sombre rug with a design of a flowering tree below the spandrels of a scalloped arch. The inscription records that it is Bakhtiari work. Chahar Mahal, twentieth century.* 2.18m × 1.63m, 7′1″ × 5′4″.

c. Right *The compartments of this carpet feature a variety of plant and palmette motifs and the border is composed of large white cartouches. Chahar Mahal, nineteenth century.* 2.18m × 1.47m, 7′2″ × 4′10″. *Victoria and Albert Museum, London*

Fars including Qashqai

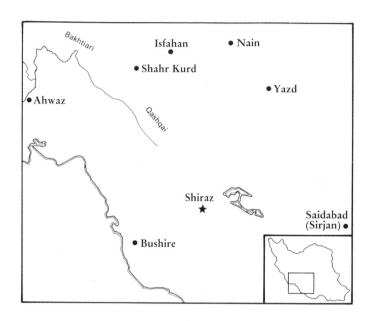

The capital city of Fars province, Shiraz, functions as a gathering centre for a variety of carpets and flat weaves. Typical village rugs are woven in brightly coloured wools – red, blue, yellow, and white. Designs tend to be bold and direct with hexagonal medallions reserved on a floral patterned ground. Sometimes the field is scattered with angular stylized animals and birds.

These village rugs show the influence of the designs of the *Qashqai*, a tribal federation whose annual migration routes encompass Fars province, and whose women have long had a reputation for the skill and vitality of their weaving. Their knotted pile carpets are woven in glossy wool in rich vibrant colours – red, yellow, green, blue, brown, and white. The wide design repertoire often incorporates adaptations of classical palmette scroll. The field may be filled with a range of lively motifs such as floral rosettes, floral cones, small animals, and birds. An interesting pictorial design found in Qashqai rugs is the lion motif, interpreted boldly and directly on a vibrant plain ground, or inserted into a typical Qashqai field of floral and animal motifs.

The Qashqai also weave magnificent kilims as well as saddlebags, storage bags, and animal trappings in wrapped-weft techniques embellished with tufting and knotting. In all these the designs are more stylized and geometric.

TYPICAL SPECIFICATIONS

Warp
Wool, usually cream, sometimes brown or mixed. Slightly depressed.

Weft
Wool, red or brown. Occasionally silk. Two shoots.

Pile
Wool. Medium height.

Knot
Village rugs – asymmetrical. Tribal rugs – symmetrical. 900–6000/dm² (60–400/sq. in.).

Ends
Warps cabled and plaited.

Sides
An additional cable inserted during weaving. The edge then bound with contrasting wool.

Handle
Heavy and flexible.

a. Opposite above *This is a tribal interpretation of the classic flowering-tree pattern popular in town workshops. The motifs are abstract and rather angular. Qashqai, twentieth century.*
2.10m × 1.20m, 7′ × 4′.

b. Opposite below *A kilim with sharply contrasted squares, grouped into a vertically aligned diamond pattern. The border has a bold zigzag. Qashqai, twentieth century.*
2.62m × 1.46m, 8′6″ × 4′11″.

c. Right *The field of this carpet is crowded with delightful floral and geometric motifs. The small stylized lions are a feature of Qashqai design. Early twentieth century.*
2.40m × 1.50m, 8′ × 5′.

Afshar

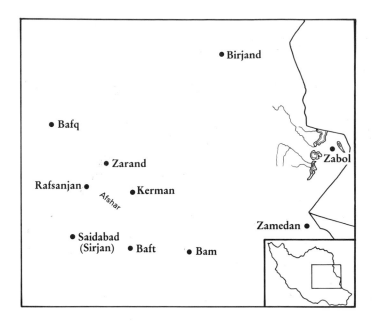

Apart from the thriving carpet industry in Kerman city and the surrounding villages, there are also the distinctive products of the Afshar tribes. These are Turkish-speaking people who came south from Azerbaijan, probably in the sixteenth century. They have long been settled around Sirjan, Rafsanjan, and Baft, though some are still nomadic and migrate between winter and summer pastures.

Their weaving, which appears frequently in the Kerman market, is easily identifiable by the boldness and directness of the designs, which are based on variations of hexagonal schemes and stylized flower and foliage motifs. Inevitably their designs have influenced those of their Persian neighbours in the villages so it is often difficult to distinguish between them.

Some nineteenth-century Afshar rugs are exceptionally large and have European-style floral designs. These factors, along with their asymmetrical knot, depressed warps, and cotton foundation suggest that they are the products of town workshops, although their colouring is distinctly 'Afshar'.

**TYPICAL
SPECIFICATIONS**

Warp
Light or dark wool; more
recently cotton.

Weft
Light or dark wool. Cotton
now more usual. Two shoots.

Pile
Wool. Medium.

Knot
Symmetrical and
asymmetrical. 930–3500/dm²
(60–225/sq. in.).

Ends
Plain weave, sometimes
striped or brocaded.

Sides
Overcast with variously
coloured wool.

a. Opposite above *The light-
coloured plain field is
patterned with stylized thistle
motifs and birds, contrasting
with the fluid scrolls of the
deep border. Afshar, late
nineteenth century.*
1.83m × 1.57m, 6′ × 5′2″.

b. Opposite below *A well-
balanced and strongly contrasted
design with a flower-filled
hexagon on a ground of rosettes
and serrated T-shaped motifs.
Afshar, late nineteenth century.*
1.32m × 1.15m, 4′ × 3′9″.

c. Right *The central medallion
is reserved against a striped
ground, the pattern of which is
derived from block-printed
fabrics. Afshar, late nineteenth
century.*
3.40m × 1.62m, 11′2″ × 5′4″.

Kerman

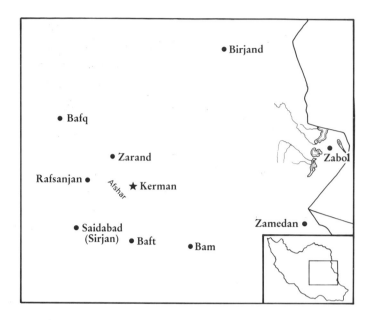

This large province of south-east Persia, which encroaches on the bleak terrain of the central desert, is one of the most important carpet-weaving areas with a consistently high reputation for technical quality and imaginative designs. The main city, Kerman, has a distinguished history to which its attractive surviving monuments bear witness. Although the carpet industry has existed since the sixteenth century, it has flourished especially during the late-nineteenth and twentieth centuries. A crucial factor in its success was the presence of skilled weavers and designers, who had worked on the production of fine multicoloured wool shawls woven in intricate, subtle, and colourful designs based on the floral-cone motif. As the shawl industry declined and the demand for carpets increased these craftsmen quickly learnt to adapt their skills.

The carpet industry is organized along the lines of town workshops and village production. Both home and foreign markets were served, particularly the American market during the 1920s. Indeed from about 1910 to the mid-1930s, American and British carpet companies had offices in Kerman, and in the late 1960s it was still possible to find a few offices and workshops run by Europeans.

The carpets were traditionally made of locally spun wool in a clear range of colours – a distinctive navy blue, light blue, red, orange, yellow, green, and beige. Many of these were obtained from natural dyes – madder, weld, indigo, and pomegranate rind.

Designs, always woven from a cartoon, are varied and of a very high standard. There are many variations of repeated floral-cone patterns derived from Kerman shawls, as well as floral medallion and corner motifs, flowering tree patterns, interpretations of classical Safavid carpets, elaborate pictorial compositions on Persian and European themes, and copies of Aubusson and Savonnerie carpets.

152

TYPICAL SPECIFICATIONS

Warp
Natural cotton.

Weft
Cotton, two shoots in white and one shoot in blue or pink.

Pile
Wool. Occasionally silk. Medium height.

Knot
Asymmetrical.
1200–5500/dm² (80–366/sq. in.).

Ends
A narrow band of plain weave with plaited fringes.

Sides
Two pairs of cords, bound with plaited wool, often blue.

Handle
Compact, soft, and fairly stiff.

a. Opposite above *A design of trees and flowers with peacocks, monkeys, and elephants. Some of the floral motifs are derived from nineteenth-century tilework in Kerman. Early twentieth century.*
2.24m × 1.47m, 7'3" × 4'11".

b. Opposite below *The design of this finely woven carpet is based on Antoine Watteau's* Les Fêtes Venetiennes *of 1718, and the border is derived from shawl designs. Kerman, around 1909.*
4.34m × 2.76m, 14'2" × 9'.

c. Right *A fine medallion design with a radiating rosette composition which integrates arabesque tendrils and floral cones. A linked cartouche border. Kerman, late nineteenth century.*
8.40m × 4.20m, 28' × 14'.

Meshed including Kurds

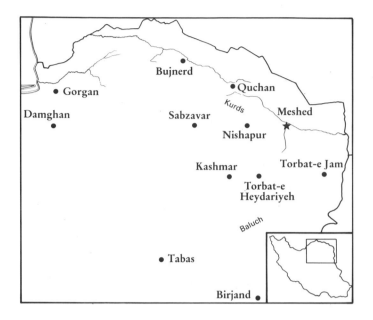

This is the major city of Khorasan province, famous for the holy shrine of the eighth Imam Reza. It functions both as a carpet-weaving centre and as a gathering place for the weavings of villages and tribes within its neighbourhood. Most of the town industry is organized in factories with about six to forty looms apiece. There are some home-based looms, but their work is of inferior quality to that of the supervised factory product.

Colour schemes are generally restrained, limited mainly to dark reds, blues, and beige. Designs are meticulously constructed with a preference for continuous intricate texture, both in the background and in the medallions. Equally accomplished designs commissioned, by town merchants, were woven in the villages of Birjand, Kashmar, Turshiz, and Doruksh.

Baluch and Kurd weavings are also to be found around Meshed. The *Kurds* now mainly inhabit Bujnerd, Quchan, and Kalat. Their work is lively and varied, incorporating knotted pile, kilim weaving, and weft wrapping. Their main products are flat-woven coverings, storage and saddle bags with designs based on hooked lozenges and octagons.

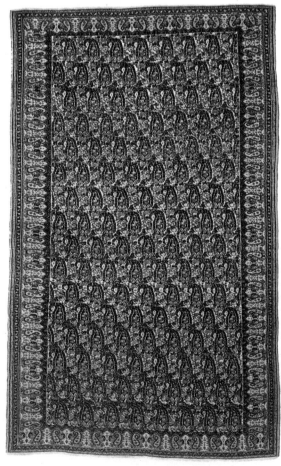

TYPICAL SPECIFICATIONS

Warp
Undyed cotton, sometimes natural wool.

Weft
Cotton, usually blue, sometimes natural white. Occasionally natural wool. Two shoots, but four shoots at intervals.

Pile
Soft, silky wool; medium to short.

Knot
Asymmetrical. Meshed carpets sometimes have jufti or symmetrical knots. 1500–4500/dm² (100–300/sq. in.).

Ends
Narrow band of plain weave. Fringes sometimes knotted.

Sides
Short lengths of reinforcing weft, often blue.

Handle
Compact and heavy.

a. Opposite above *A well-composed design based on a repeating peony lattice which is superimposed on a delicate floral ground. Meshed, early twentieth century.*
5.63m × 3.83m, 18′9″ × 12′9″.

b. Opposite below *This Doruksh carpet has an elegant design of boteh, or floral cones, which are used both in the border and the field. Meshed, late nineteenth century.*
2.18m × 1.27m. 7′2″ × 4′2″.

c. Right *A Kurdish kilim with repeated hexagons enclosing hooked motifs against a plain, dark ground. A hexagon and reciprocal trefoil border.*
3.30m × 1.69m, 11′ × 5′6″.

BALUCH

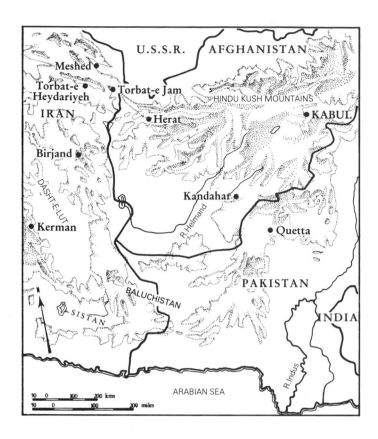

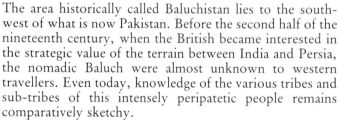

The area historically called Baluchistan lies to the south-west of what is now Pakistan. Before the second half of the nineteenth century, when the British became interested in the strategic value of the terrain between India and Persia, the nomadic Baluch were almost unknown to western travellers. Even today, knowledge of the various tribes and sub-tribes of this intensely peripatetic people remains comparatively sketchy.

One of the reasons for this obscurity is endemic to the majority of Central Asian tribal groups – a lack of written records, with only the vaguest hints and slightest mentions occurring from time to time in the work of Arab geographers. But the principal reason is probably to be found in the nomadism of the Baluch and the forbidding nature of the land called after them (not to mention the nature of the tribes themselves, who emerge from the sketchy historical records as one of the most warlike of their kind).

It should be realized immediately that in the context of weaving, the land once called Baluchistan has not, nor ever seems to have had, much relevance. What we know of 'Baluchistan', as opposed to 'Baluch' weaving, suggests that the tribes which inhabited Baluchistan itself were never great weavers. Their products seem confined to a narrow range of flat weaves and an equally narrow range of designs; such pieces are, to be blunt, dull and of ethnographic rather than aesthetic interest.

However, the Baluch have never been confined to Baluchistan itself. Groups of them are recorded in southern Persia in the area around Kerman in the tenth century, and

a. Opposite above *One face,
with knotted pile, from a
double saddlebag or* khordjin.
*Such weavings were produced
in large numbers by the
Baluch and this design, though
common, is one of the most
successful. Probably Khorasan,
circa 1900.*
0.95m × 0.79m, 3′2″ × 2′6″.

b. Opposite below *A splendid
Baluch camel-ground, tree-of-
life prayer rug. The various
border designs reflect the
influence of the Ersari-Beshir
Turkoman. The brocaded ends
are rich and intricate.
Probably from the Herat area,
circa 1900.*
1.52m × 0.86m, 3′6″ × 2′.

c. Right *A beautiful Baluch
rug, arguably one of the
oldest. The design is a highly
stylized* mina khani, *scattered
with a human figure and small
animals. The rare border
design seems to be a
formalized tree of life,
alternating with rosettes.
Probably Khorasan, mid to
late nineteenth century.*
2.18m × 1.09m, 7′ × 3′6″.

by at least the thirteenth century, large numbers were to be found wandering across the borders between Afghanistan and the south-east Persian province of Sistan. In the early eighteenth century, others were pushed northwards in forced migrations ordered by Nadir Shah to the Persian province of Khorasan; they were to be found in large numbers near the city of Meshed, in the regions of Torbat-e Jam and Torbat-e Heydariyeh, with the former becoming the main market place for their weavings. The finest Baluch rugs come from the large Afghani-Persian border region.

The anthropological complexity of this great area of land constitutes another of the apparently insuperable barriers standing in the way of a comprehensive classification of Baluch weaving. Arabs, Kurds, Turkoman, and the innumerable smaller Persian and Afghan tribal groups, such as the Timuri, Balhuri, Waziri, and Hazaras, all inhabit this same region and all produce, or produced, their own weavings. Some groups conquered others or intermarried; so the styles and techniques of their weavings, reflecting their distinctive cultural identities, became mingled with the different, although often similar, styles, and techniques of their now assimilated neighbours. The resulting confusion will probably never be unravelled by ethnographers and anthropologists.

Nevertheless, it is possible to recognize the styles and techniques of the principal group of Baluch weavings. This central core can then be expanded to include the work of more widely scattered members of the tribe, whose work has been influenced to a greater or lesser extent by that of their neighbours. Those pile rugs and other weavings which are usually considered to be the finest and most characteristic examples seem to come from north-east Iran and north-west Afghanistan, an area stretching from Meshed in the north to Herat in the south. In terms of the colours and designs of these most beautiful of Baluch weavings, it is probably no coincidence that a neat geographical triangle is formed if these two cities are joined up with a third, the Turkoman oasis settlement of Merv, for it is no denegration of the quality of the best Baluch work to suggest that its overall aesthetic seems to be derived from that of Turkoman tribal weaving. Indeed, it is probable that at some time in the past, the Turkoman taught their techniques and styles to the Baluch.

This 'northern' group of Baluch weaving is easily distinguished. The colours, in which deep tones of red and blue predominate, are rich and sombre, similar to those in Turkoman work. Also the wool used in these pieces is of an extraordinary quality, being long and so lustrous that the finest examples, despite the comparative coarseness of their knotting, have the texture and handle of silk velvet.

However, diversity is added to this group by the existence of one of the most famous and highly regarded Baluch designs: the small rectangular prayer rug with a *mihrab* field. This is often woven with natural camel hair and contains a tree-of-life motif, one of the most ubiquitous of Baluch patterns. The finest of these rugs have, despite their different palette, the same wonderfully lustrous appearance of their cousins.

TYPICAL SPECIFICATIONS

Warp
Natural undyed wool, ivory or white, sometimes with alternate warps depressed.

Weft
Dark or light brown wool. Two shoots.

Pile
Wool, occasionally with silk or goat hair. Medium height, but long and lustrous in the finest examples.

Knot
Asymmetrical, but often symmetrical.
600–2600/dm^2 (40–173/sq. in.).

Ends
Flat weave, sometimes with brocaded details. Warps may be grouped and knotted.

Sides
Two or three cords, overcast with dark brown goat hair.

Handle
Heavy, velvety, and flexible.

a. Opposite above *This type of prayer rug is usually attributed to the Baluch of the Adraskand valley, though some experts consider it to be Timuri work. The repeated octagons of the main border are similar to those in the saddlebag (see 157a).*
1.37m × 1.18m, 4′6″ × 3′10″.

b. Opposite below *An example of the large and somewhat amorphous group of East Persian–Afghani rugs which, on technique, are attributed to the Baluch. The archaic field designs probably represent a double-ended mihrab. Arab or Kurdish. Early twentieth century.*
1.9m × 1m, 6′4″ × 3′3″.

c. Right *Rugs of this group have a more naturalistic mina khani design. They are all very long and have a short dense pile. The border pattern is characteristic of the Baluch. Probably Khorasan, mid to late nineteenth century.*
2.42m × 1.15m, 8′ × 3′8″.

TURKOMAN

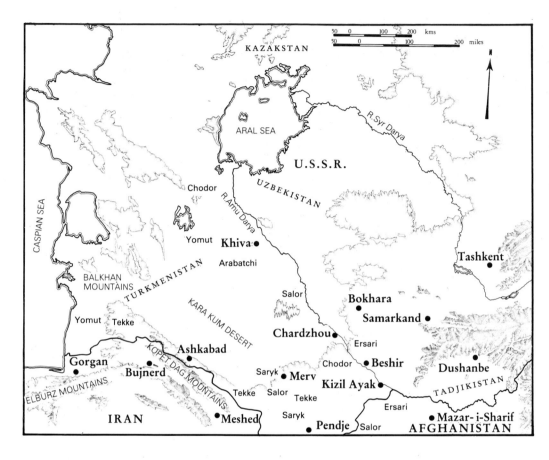

a. Opposite *An eighteenth-century Yomut main carpet. Yomut carpets can be found with a variety of* guls, *and this rare example with a spectacular tree skirt,* elem, *shows two of the most typical* gul *forms: the hexagonal motif filled with C's, erroneously known as the* ogujahli *motif and said to be derived from a phoenix; and the turreted* kepche gul *filled with small anchors. Both these ornaments are unique to Yomut weavings.*
Wher Collection, Switzerland

The Turkoman tribes are believed to have originated in the remote steppes of Asia at least two thousand years ago. Legend has it that Oguz, great grandson of Noah, founded the first tribe. He had six sons who in turn each had four sons, making the twenty-four clans or Turkoman tribes. The most important written records of these Indo-European nomads come from the 'tribal trees' of seventeenth-century Persian and Khivan chroniclers, for the Turkoman have no written history of their own. These 'tribal trees' mention the twenty-four tribes of Oguz and record the names of the Tekke, Yomut, Saryk, Ersari, and Khorasanian Salor.

The genealogy of the Turkoman tribes is important in attempting to understand what might loosely be called the 'heraldic' motifs of Turkoman carpets, known as *guls*, the interpretation of which presents many problems. It is rather as if modern scholars had to decipher a 'heraldic' tree of an ancient British family, with its crests, coats of arms, and armorials; but with no clues as to the origins of its symbolism, and no knowledge of the motifs signifying a second son or a marriage into a male line of an important family through the female.

The sons of Oguz are believed to have used the symbols of Sun, Moon, Star, Heaven, Mountain, and Sea. Each of their four sons are said to have borne the symbol of a totemic animal – dog, wolf, fox, sheep, stag, elk, bird – and it appears that tribes also split into pairs of 'black' and 'white'. Only two Turkoman dynasties have been recorded

with certainty: the 'Black Sheep' Turkoman (1389–1468) and the 'White Sheep' Turkoman (1378–1502). Through displacement and conquest, the ethnic mixture of the Turkoman people is largely Aryan with an intermingling of Turkomenized Arabs and a minority of Mongolian stock. By the ninth century there is some evidence that they had absorbed some Sunni Muslim beliefs, but in general the Turkoman did not have a recognizable culture, religion, or nation state. They shared a common set of traditions and rituals, and a common code of conduct, on to which they grafted the beliefs and customs of other indigenous people whose lands they passed through, conquered, or overran.

The history of the Turkoman tribes has always been one of movement – their culture overran the boundaries of Persia, Turkey, Afghanistan, and the Caucasus. In the distant past tribes from East Turkestan invaded and settled many remote and empty territories, becoming absorbed into the population over centuries. This is particularly true of Anatolia, where Turkoman tribes settled in considerable numbers from the eleventh century onwards, growing in numbers and becoming integrated into the population from the thirteenth century. Today a large proportion of Turkey's mixed and heterogenous population are descended from Turkoman antecedents. Turkoman patterns and designs form the basis of most indigenous Anatolian rugs and carpets, and one has only to look at the octagons of large-pattern Holbein rugs to see the clear similarity between them and the *guls* of the Salor. According to chronicles written in the eleventh and thirteenth centuries, the Salor at that time were considered to be the most noble and aristocratic of all the Turkoman tribes.

While the Turkoman are known to have ranged across the vast land mass which stretches from West Anatolia to the Chinese borders and beyond, it is in the contracted area bounded by the Caspian Sea and the Amu Darya river that the principal tribes of Saryk, Salor, Tekke, Chodor, Yomut, Arabatchi, Ersari, and Kizil Ayak have their homeland today. Weaving, jewellery, leatherwork, and carving have traditionally been the principle means of artistic expression to the Turkoman, and influences from far-distant cultures are still plainly visible in their patterns and designs.

Trading and barter between tribal communities and settled cultures developed through Bokhara, Merv, and Khiva. To these centres came caravans of nomads to barter meat, skins, wool, camels, and horses in exchange for cereals, tea, sugar, weapons, and ammunition. Wool products – in the form of trappings, rugs, and carpets – had a higher value in the market place than raw wool, and Turkoman tribes have been known for their carpet weaving from as early as the thirteenth century. But weaving was not primarily done in order to barter or sell: it was an essential part of their way of life, and every object had a vital function, from the woven bags which held clothes, bedding, salt, and cooking utensils to the prayer mats and carpets which added warmth and status to the household.

The Turkoman were a fierce warrior race, whose survival depended on water, fuel for their fires, and the availability of grazing for their animals. For these they fought ruthlessly, raiding and plundering, with many bitter blood feuds which were carried on from generation to generation. Historically, they formed alliances with other nations, seeking gain for themselves in the conquests of others. Even a small tribe needed about a hundred head of sheep to supply it with meat and wool, and thirty to forty camels and horses for herding, breeding, transport, raiding, and fighting. When the sparse grazing was demolished and the land around was stripped of fuel, they would be forced to move on, fighting the elements and each other for survival.

It is known that wells were dug, thirty to fifty metres deep, at isolated intervals on the barren plains but they yielded brackish water fit only for animals. So semi-nomadic settlements and villages (*auls*) could only exist where irrigation was carried out on the Persian system of underground conduits, or *ghanats*. Women, who were responsible for spinning, weaving, and felt-making, were a vital source of income as well as rearing children, so in the past many raiding parties carried off the women of the tribe along with the animals.

In the nineteenth century, Russia began to subjugate the tribes, who were a constant menace to caravans of merchandize crossing into Turkestan, and in 1885 they finally conquered the most powerful, the Tekke. Since the mid-nineteenth century the Russians had been building the Central Asian railway, which ran from the Caspian Sea through Askabad, Merv, Beshir, Bokhara, Samarkand, Tashkent, and Andishan, thus breaking into the traditional

trading centres for carpets and rugs of the Turkoman tribes. Apart from their value as barter, the Turkoman had no concept of value for their woven work, which was carried off in great quantities by the Russians for paltry sums, leaving almost nothing in the *auls* to show for the finest period of Turkoman weaving. In Russia, Turkoman carpets were cheaper to buy than commercially manufactured velvet, and there was a fashion for covering upholstered furniture with wonderful Turkoman work, mutilated and cut up to cover chairs and stools, a fact which today must be bitterly regretted.

a. Left *A Tekke tentband in which the design is formed in pile against a plain-weave ground. These long tent-bands held the framework of the tents firmly in place and were also highly decorative. Nineteenth century.*

With the coming of commercial values and the erosion of traditional ways, which continued throughout the nineteenth century, Turkoman work began to deteriorate. Many symbols of great antiquity and profound meaning were used merely as decorative motifs and once Russian policy had cut them off from Persia and India, severing the Turkoman's source of supply for beautiful natural dyes, the corruption of their culture was almost complete. Through the ever-encroaching commercialism and the swift transport of the railway, synthetic dyes quickly reached the Turkoman tribes. Little has survived of all the tribal work dating from before the nineteenth century; and it is significant that most of the weaving which was bartered in that disastrous period was the work of the Tekke, the first and greatest tribe to be subdued. In 1900, General Bogolubov, the Russian governor of Transcaspia, began to collect Turkoman carpets and other woven goods in an attempt to piece together the information contained in the *gul* patterns, and he later presented forty pieces of early Turkoman work to the Leningrad Museum.

Today the principal source of production and trade in Turkoman work is Ashkabad in the Soviet Republic of Turkmenistan. Great canals have been dug to take water to the waste lands, altering the traditional migrations of nomad Turkoman with their flocks and herds. Collective farms have absorbed some of the more settled tribes. Samarkand, Timur's fabulous city in the desert, is now the centre of a silk-spinning industry, where once the brocade manufactories produced gold-embroidered silks for Timur's pavilions and palaces. Tashkent, too, has long since lost its mystery and its links with China and the old Silk Road. Today it is the centre of cotton production and agricultural machinery. These changes have not left the Turkoman nomad tribes untouched. Even their breeds of sheep have changed, and with them the nature and texture of some of their work. In almost exactly a hundred years, the beautiful weavings of the Turkoman tribes have degenerated from a high tribal culture to airport art.

When Turkoman carpets, rugs, and other weavings first filtered out to the West, there was no knowledge of their complicated tribal communities, or any understanding of the apparently similar designs which were called by many ignorant traders 'elephant's foot'. Similarly, as was the custom of the day, the carpets were called collectively 'Bokhara' since it was from that location that merchants bought them and shipped them out to the West. Even the individual pieces were unidentified and their use was not known. Once the commercial value of this remarkably fine work was recognized, however, Western traders commissioned work regardless of its tribal origins, and the pre-viously unique and meaningful symbols became almost a cliché, copied by carpet-weaving centres with little connection to Turkoman tribes.

Fortunately, with increasing interest in Turkoman work and the growing number of collectors, anthropological and academic research has now led to a better understanding of this great tribal art. Over the last decade some tribal attributions have been reassessed, and museum acquisitions from specific tribes have reinforced academic theory and hypothesis. So today tribal attributions are made on a number of specific features, the combination of which determines the tribe or origin.

The Turkoman way of life was based principally on raising and herding fat-tailed sheep, goats, camels, and horses for sale or barter. Where there was an adequate supply of water they also engaged in subsistence agriculture in semi-nomadic communities. The feeding of their flocks and herds determined their movements from one seasonal pasture to the next. As with many other nomadic tribes, the entire community migrated, living in large, circular tents similar to the *yurts* of the Mongolians. Timber was scarce and wool was virtually the only material available for making all the necessities required in terms of storage, covering, and shelter. So the construction of these large round tents is remarkable for its ingenuity. The basic structure consisted of a trellis of cane, sapling, or heartwood, a series of roof poles to support the felt flaps, and a roof-wheel which locked the poles firmly in an umbrella-shape.

The felt, usually a whiteish grey when new, was made by the women, who laid layers of combed wool between cane mats, soaked it with water and rolled it, repeating the process until the wool finally felted together. The frame of the tent was held firm by girths of rope or long woven tent-bands, tied to one lintel post, encircling the trellis round the outside, and secured to the lintel post on the other side of the door opening. The roof poles slotted into the roof-

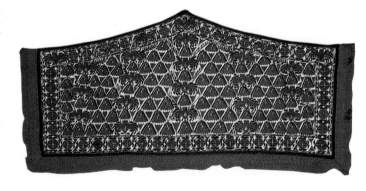

a. *Opposite below* A Tekke
animal trapping, asmalyk. *The
Tekke are renowned for their
embroidery and this piece
would have been made to
decorate the bride's camel
during a wedding procession.
Nineteenth century.*
0.85m × 1.25m, 2'9" × 4'1".

b. *Near right The most
important decorative motifs of
Turkoman carpets are the* guls
*or tribal emblems. This one is
specific to the Tekke tribe.*

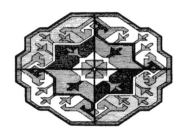

c. *Far right In the Turkoman
tribes all the weaving was
done by the women.*

wheel, which acted as a window providing ventilation and a smoke hole. In winter, when the extreme cold is almost unbearable, a wooden door filled the door-frame. In summer, to keep out dust, livestock, and insects, an *engsi* or special rug, was hung from a lintel pole.

Every piece of pile-woven work bears the symbols which identify the occupant's tribe. Everyday storage bags, floor coverings, and all the necessities for nomadic and semi-nomadic life were woven by the women of the tribe, used until they were worn out, and then replaced. In the event of a marriage, however, it is believed that a complete set of decorative trappings, tent bands, prayer rugs and storage bags of all sizes were woven by the bride and the bride's female relatives as a dowry, to show her worth and her skill. The marriage ceremony was a ritual, in which each finely woven piece had its particular place, which varied slightly from tribe to tribe. Only after the complete ritual of the marriage was completed were many of these pieces accorded a secondary, functional use.

These dowry pieces were a way of judging the wealth, skills, and ability of the bride-to-be, who was assessed on her execution of traditional patterns. It would seem that in many cases these have remained unchanged for generations, making them difficult to date without authentication. The older the weaving of individual tribes, the more common ground there appears to be between the patterns and *guls* of each one, which suggests a common ancestry for many Turkoman designs. A number of theories have been advanced as to how this could have arisen – from original tribal unity to warring alliances, cultural affinities, and geographical proximity – but none of them can be proved conclusively.

It seems that each tribe had its own main emblem which was used only on important pieces of pile-woven work; if a tribe was conquered or assimilated into another tribe, it could no longer use its own symbol, or *gul*, except on bags and smaller items – and the superior tribe then added that *gul* to its own on minor pieces, perhaps as evidence of its superiority. The great importance of the precise execution of a tribal *gul* in carpet-weaving is suggested by the unique

way that the inherent rigidity of the woven 'grid' is manipulated, often with the use of symmetrical, asymmetrical, and other completely original knots, in order to obtain a different angle on the diagonal to conform precisely to the drawing of the *gul*. Women's jewellery also bore the same tribal identification symbols.

The subtle use of barely distinguishable shades of red, from a purplish tone to a clear bright red, is quite remarkable in all Turkoman pile-woven work. Many pieces have a faint shadow, the result of the dyes used, which caused them to be called 'blue Bokharas' when they first filtered in to the West. Unlike any other carpets, the ground colour remains the same in both the border and the field, with the *guls* in well-spaced patterns down the centre.

The knotting is dense and fine, the pile medium or short, and the knot usually asymmetrical. The wool is always particularly lustrous, and the warp and weft are right-hand twisted, two-ply, undyed natural wool, or wool and goat hair. Cotton has been used in the pile for generations, since the sheep of many tribes had dark fleeces so natural white wool was hard to obtain. Where white wool is used, it has often been bleached in the sun. Silk, too, has been used in the pile, to give highlights and to show the wealth of the original dowry.

Although the designs and patterns distinctive to each tribe are different, the shape and size of the pieces seem to be much the same from tribe to tribe. *Engsis*, or door coverings, for instance bear a remarkable similarity from one tribe to the next. They are generally woven in a *hatchli* or door-frame pattern, which may have had shamanistic significance, or be related to the gardens of Paradise described in the Koran.

Weaving was done on a simple single-heddle horizontal ground loom which was set up inside the tent, or in a separate tent. It was always done by the women, with the smallest girl-child learning the techniques and patterns almost as she learned her language. Great pride was attached to the quality of the work, and it was not until the commercial values of the West seeped into the tribal communities that the quality of the workmanship declined.

163

Salor

The Salor are among the oldest-recorded Turkoman tribes, mentioned by Makmoud of Kashgaria in the eleventh century and by Rashid ad Din in the fourteenth century as one of the twenty-four tribes of the Oguz. By the fifteenth century part of the tribe had settled in Anatolia, and their early weavings form the foundation for pre-Ottoman Anatolian carpet designs. In Central Asia the Salor lost their pre-eminent position and were scattered after their defeat by the Persians in 1831. Having been further defeated within the Turkoman hierarchy when they were expelled from Merv around 1860, they moved to Pendje with the Saryk. At one time they were forced over the Afghanistan border and the tribe became split. Today there are some Salor on the Iranian border and some still on the Amu Darya, west of Bokhara.

Of all Turkoman weaving, the work of the Salor has the tightest, most dense knotting, so some carpets may split or crack if folded carelessly. Salor weaving has a hard, lustrous pile, which often includes a small amount of silk – more profuse use may indicate a later date. In common with early Tekke weavings, the Salor use an obscure red dye made from insects which appears not to be cochineal. The dye tends to corrode the wool, and has a dense matt appearance. Theirs is the widest colour spectrum of all Turkoman nomad work, using both cochineal and lac dye for reds, obtaining tones ranging from brilliant, clear scarlet to bluish red and brilliant crimson, with touches of magenta silk which in older work is almost violet. The field colour ranges from scarlet red to brownish red or purple red. Border colours may often be purple brown, orange tan, brick red, or dark aubergine.

Salor *guls* in older pieces show a family resemblance with the quartered *guls* of the Saryk, Tekke, and Ersari. After the defeat by the Saryk and later the Tekke, the Salor *gul* became what is sometimes called a 'dead' *gul* and was no longer used by the Salor. A gable-like motif seen in early Salor pile weaves appears later in most other Turkoman work. The main border design of Salor carpets is often seen in sixteenth-century Turkish carpets.

No cotton is used in the pile, since the Salor were able to use a natural white wool, nor is it found in the foundation. On the other hand, unlike most Turkoman, the Salor used a brown wool dyed with a corrosive black dye to outline designs and motifs.

Although the history of the Salor is relatively well-documented, very few examples of early Salor pile-woven work has survived to help clarify their migrations, flights, and apparent decline in the Turkoman hierarchy.

TYPICAL SPECIFICATIONS

Warp
Natural undyed ivory wool, stepped to give a ribbed back.

Weft
Natural brown wool. Two thin shoots.

Pile
Wool, sometimes with cotton or silk. Short.

Knot
Asymmetrical.
2000–5000/dm^2
(133–333/sq. in.).

Ends
Plain weave, warps grouped and knotted. Often extra dark blue fringes on tent bags and *asmalyks.*

Sides
Flat, multi-cord selvedge, wrapped in two-colour check, dark blue or blue green.

Handle
Hard, lustrous, stiff.

a. Opposite above *Hangings, often with a white ground, were woven to adorn the bridal tent and animals during weddings. This early nineteenth-century Salor example includes cochineal-dyed silk.*
0.48m × 1.4m, 1′7″ × 4′6″.

b. Opposite below *This* kejebe *panel is one of a pair woven to decorate the animal which carried the bride. Examples with one, two, or three medallions are much sought after by collectors. Salor, eighteenth century.*
0.73m × 1.88m, 2′5″ × 6′2″.
Victoria and Albert Museum, London

c. Right *This pattern is the only one found in Salor main carpets, although it has been copied by the Saryk. The minor* gul *is often seen on tent bags. The handle is generally quite firm and the wool is lustrous and shiny. The deep aubergine colour is typical of this tribe. Late eighteenth or early nineteenth century.*
3.13m × 2.39m, 10′4″ × 7′9″.
Hermann Collection, Munich

165

Saryk

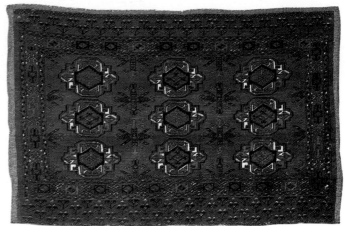

Early Saryk carpets are among the most beautiful of all Turkoman weaving. Until the first part of the nineteenth century, when their territory was far to the East around the Amu Darya, they retained a style that was very specific to their own tribe. Little remains to show for this early period, when their work was almost entirely of wool, with the occasional use of silk and white cotton for highlights. The designs were closely related to the Salor but had fairly specific features of their own. The clear soft red field colour is seldom found in other early Turkoman work.

By the middle of the century, they had drifted or been driven down to the area around Merv, which was mainly Tekke territory, and they began to adopt features of Tekke weaving. Their work became lighter in tone, with use of a light red brown and a slightly purple red; and a new richness was evident in the amount of silk used in large areas of crimson-red wool pile. White cotton was also used as highlights, in a repertoire of designs which, though more extravagant in terms of colour and material, had considerably diminished. By the end of the nineteenth century the Saryk had moved south to Pendje, almost on the borders of Turkmenia, with Persia to the west and Afghanistan to the east. It is believed that by this time the Saryk were almost completely dominated by the powerful Tekke tribe. The colour range tended to be more sombre, with deep purples and darker tones, such as a dark blue, and there was an even more extensive use of white cotton and cochineal-dyed silk. The composition of Saryk work had deteriorated however, and the carpets were far more crowded with a less well-spaced overall design. By the 1880s the Saryk were using synthetic dyes, which may have been obtained from the Russians.

All Saryk work was originally woven for their own use and examples prior to 1880 are extremely rare. Little is known about the history of the Saryk, one of the smaller tribes of Turkoman, but they appear not to have been powerful enough to resist outside pressures or those from more dominant tribes. As a result they seem to have moved frequently once they had left their original tribal homeland near the Amu Darya.

Distinctive in their weaving is the dark blue plain weave edge and fringe on bags, and the long plain weave kilim ends to main carpets. Saryk seldom used more than six colours, all rather sombre in tone in recent years. The field is a clear light red, red brown, purple red, dark brown, deep purple or dark brown. Other colours used are orange, tan crimson, dark blue, mid blue, blue green, and yellow.

The largest surviving group of early Saryk weaving is to be found in the Museum of Ethnography of the Peoples of the USSR in Leningrad.

TYPICAL SPECIFICATIONS

Warp
Fine natural undyed ivory wool, stepped in later carpets to give a ribbed back.

Weft
Undyed grey-brown or undyed ivory wool. Two shoots.

Pile
Wool, with cotton and silk. Short.

Knot
Symmetrical, occasionally asymmetrical. 2000–4000/dm^2 (133–266/sq. in.).

Ends
Long plain weave ends. Dark blue plain weave edge and fringe to bags.

Sides
Flat multi-cord selvedge wrapped with wool in two-colour check. On smaller pieces, single overcast selvedge cord.

Handle
Lustrous wool, stiff, generally coarser than Tekke or Salor.

a. Opposite *This tent bag, or chuval, has some of the most typical designs found in Saryk weaving: the minor border composed of small triangles and the small flowers found in the panels at each end. Chuvals can be found with either this gul or the octagonal Salor chuval gul. Early nineteenth century.*
0.85m × 1.35m, 2'8" × 4'6".

b. Right above *This panel has the small version of the* kejebe *design which is also found on Salor weavings. Typical of Saryk is the pek-kan border and the double lines at the top edge. The blue plaited rope on the sides would have been much longer originally and was used to tie the trapping around the animal. Early nineteenth century.*

c. Right below *Saryk main carpets are generally found with one of two principal gul forms, the rare octagonal* temirchen gul, *and a version of the old chuval gul, which is more common and is seen in this example. This carpet is one of the most typical. The major and minor borders are only found on Saryk weaving and can be seen on both large and small pieces. First half of the nineteenth century.*
2.31m × 2.23m, 7'7" × 7'3".
Wher Collection, Switzerland

Tekke

The Tekke became the most powerful Turkoman tribe by allying themselves with the khans of Khiva to gain control over the Yomut and the Chodor, but in turn they were subdued by the superior forces of the Russians in 1885. Probably because of this defeat, the largest group of Turkoman weaving which has survived from the nineteenth century is that of the Tekke. It is also the most widely recognized and copied. In spite of their migrations and alliances, the Tekke remained most consistent in their *gul* design. The exception is the design of their border patterns, which up to the mid-nineteenth century tended to be simple, but in later work became extremely detailed and far more complex. The once-powerful Tekke are now more or less confined to an area in the south of Turkmenistan on the borders of Iran, curving round to the border with Afghanistan. Among the many woven pieces made by the Tekke are large storage bags similar to those made by the Ersari, whose territory is close to Tekke tribes. A second group of Tekke are grouped in the mountains on the Iranian border towards the Caspian Sea.

Tekke camel-flank panels (*asmalyk*) have designs which are clearly related to the border patterns in eighteenth-century Caucasian carpets – a wedge-shaped leaf, a comb or feather, and a curled leaf meander. Tekke work provides a rich field for research, since so much of their work has survived, but many of the deteriorating, crumbling motifs have become hard to identify in their degenerate forms. Some still recognizable motifs of ancient tribal origin are the 'finger', 'ram's horn', and 'camel's teeth'; a symbol representing an amulet and a talisman, and a tree form, possibly derived from the shamanistic 'tree of life'.

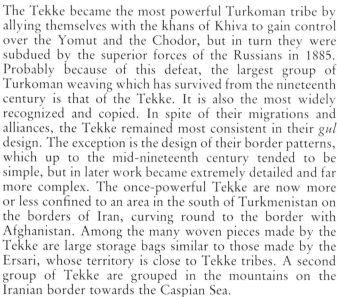

In early Tekke work, the *guls* quartering the field are joined in a geometric pattern, seemingly of ancient origin and recognizable in some fifteenth-century Anatolian Holbein carpets. Like the Salor, the Tekke seldom used white cotton in the pile, since natural white wool was available. Unlike the Salor, the dark outline of patterns is in a natural dark brown wool, often undyed, which fades to a lighter

brown. In smaller pieces, the Tekke used brilliant cochineal-dyed magenta silk as highlights, and both synthetic and cochineal-dyed wool can be found together from about 1880. A particularly recognizable feature of some Tekke main carpets is the wide kilim end, in the same colour as the field, with triple blue horizontal lines. Sometimes this pattern is used as an end panel in the pile.

TYPICAL SPECIFICATIONS

Warp
Natural undyed ivory wool. Later work slightly stepped, possibly due to Salor influence.

Weft
Wool, undyed ivory, grey, or brown. Two thin shoots, one in more densely knotted pieces.

Pile
Wool, with silk and occasionally cotton. Short to medium.

Knot
Asymmetrical, some symmetrical at edges. $3000–6000/dm^2$ (200–400/sq. in.).

Ends
Plain weave ends and edges, same colour as the field, often with triple blue line.

Sides
Overcast in blue, or sometimes red, wool.

Handle
Silky, hard, and smooth.

a. Opposite above *Door hangings,* kapunuk, *were used to decorate tents for special occasions. This rare early nineteenth-century example has a white ground.*
0.77m × 1.18m, 1'9" × 2'6".

b. Opposite below *A variety of ornaments can be found on Tekke tent bags. This pattern is typical, as are the border designs. But the skirt,* elem, *is somewhat unusual in this example. The motif used here is usually found on Tekke carpets. This particular* chuval *contains a large amount of cochineal-dyed silk pile. Early nineteenth century.*

c. Right *An early nineteenth-century Tekke main carpet, illustrating the characteristics of Tekke weaving. The border has a varied yet ordered design, and the main gul is simple and sophisticated. The three projections in each quarter appear often in Turkoman guls, but in the Tekke they appear as three arrows.*
2.25m × 1.85m, 7'4" × 6'1".
Wher Collection, Switzerland

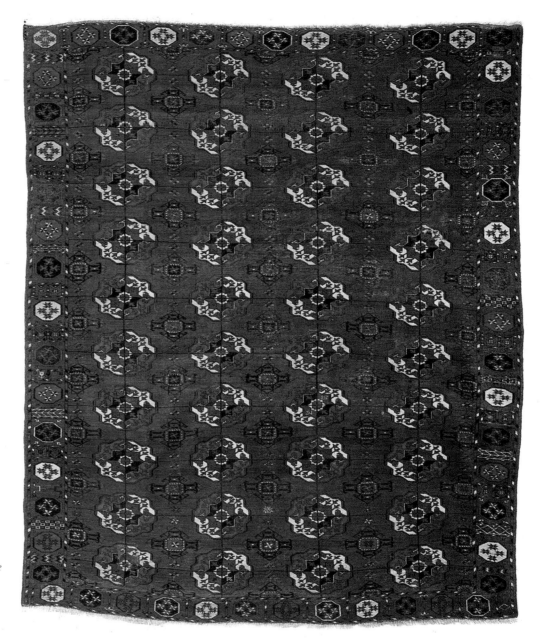

Yomut including Arabatchi

Today the Yomut are the largest, most widely scattered of all Turkoman tribes, living a mainly nomadic life in an area stretching west to the shore of the Caspian Sea, right across Turkmenistan through the Balkhan Mountains, into the Kara Kum desert and almost to the shores of the Aral Sea. At one time, allied to the Chodor, the Yomut caused the khans of Khiva considerable trouble, raiding and harassing the population, so that help from the Tekke was sought to help subdue them.

Alone among the Turkomans, they used their tribal *gul* almost as a decorative pattern (see 160a), embellishing it with edges of serrated vine-leaf pattern or a curled-edge palmette, more like small medallions than the well-spaced Turkoman *gul* pattern. Several different *guls* were used, either by sub-tribes who are as yet unidentified, or as variations on the Yomut main *gul*. A bird motif, like a flying eagle, is common, and in nineteenth-century border patterns there is also a 'running dog' motif, known to the Yomut as a 'married woman's finger'. Yomut weaving has much more blue than most other Turkoman work – and for a short period a vivid green was also used. Yomut *guls* are often worked in several colours, unlike archetypal Turkoman *gul* patterns, with a symmetrical use of different coloured *guls* to achieve a diagonal pattern.

It is clear that different groups of Yomut had different weaving techniques with common features, which may account for the Yomut use of the 'Tauk Noska' *gul* with four pairs of animals. These carpets are generally woven with a symmetrical knot, on a deep purple-red field. Storage bags of all shapes and sizes are made, all with differing designs, but in general all have plain undecorated ends to the pile weave. Yomut tribesmen also had saddle cloths which were remarkably beautiful, with multiple stripes each worked in a different pattern – and it is said that the Yomut often showed more attachment to their horses than they did to their women.

Ceremonial *asmalyk* camel-flank panels, woven as part of a bride's dowry, frequently feature a white field. Among the diverse pieces made by the Yomut and not found in any other tribe are finely decorated woven pouches of envelope form. These were used to carry the ceremonial marriage bread, possibly symbolic of fertility and the provision of food. The enormous variety of pieces made by the Yomut are tantalizingly thought-provoking, since few of the same objects by other Turkoman tribes have survived.

The work of the *Arabatchi* has only recently been identified in the West, confirmed by pieces in the museums of Central Asia acquired directly from the tribes. The Arabatchi lived south of Khiva, between the Yomut, Chodor, and Salor and their work has features of all three. It contains the 'Tauk Noska' *gul*, and so-called 'Khiva' carpets have been attributed by the use of this *gul* to the Yomut, the Chodor, and the Kizil Ayak. The colours are usually a reddish brown for the field, with small areas of bright sugar pink and bright green which are not synthetic. In general, Arabatchi work is the ugly duckling among Turkoman pieces, but occasionally there is a swan among it – probably the best examples are the earliest.

One distinguishing feature of main carpets is the extra narrow border between the main border and the field. On *engsis*, a pictorial representation of camel caravans is found, related to both Chodor and Salor versions. The Arabatchi produce *engsis* with a repeating design of stemmed flowers in the field and the standard cross-design. The stemmed-flower pattern is also used in the skirts of tent bags and animal trappings.

TYPICAL SPECIFICATIONS

Warp
Heavy two-ply wool, undyed natural ivory to brown.

Weft
Yomut – undyed brown wool, sometimes with goat hair. Arabatchi – cotton and goat hair mixed. Two shoots.

Pile
Wool. Yomut – short to medium. Arabatchi – long.

Knot
Symmetrical and asymmetrical. 1800 2800/dm^2 (120–186/sq. in.).

Ends
Plain weave.

Sides
One or two warp cords, bound with red, blue, or aubergine wool.

Handle
Firm, dense, grainy.

a. Opposite *The Arabatchi wove two distinctly different forms of door rugs. The most famous show a design of ascending flowerheads, as seen here. In the alternative version the field is divided into four by a cross-shaped form. Typical of both types is the animal caravan at the base. Each animal carries a wedding litter and has a triangular amulet hanging from its flank. Nineteenth century.*
1.28m × 0.85m, 4'2" × 2'8".

b. Right above *An early nineteenth-century Arabatchi chuval. This tribe tend to use an archaic gul, and the sugar pink colour and flowered skirt are also typical. This bag would have originally have had a back. It was woven to decorate a wedding tent, then used as a storage bag, and finally became a rug in a Western house.*

c. Right below *A large Yomut tent bag or chuval. This is a typical example of one of the most commonly found tent bags, but it is particularly beautiful and is one of a pair. Early nineteenth century.*
0.95m × 1.14m, 3'2" × 3'8".
Wher Collection, Switzerland

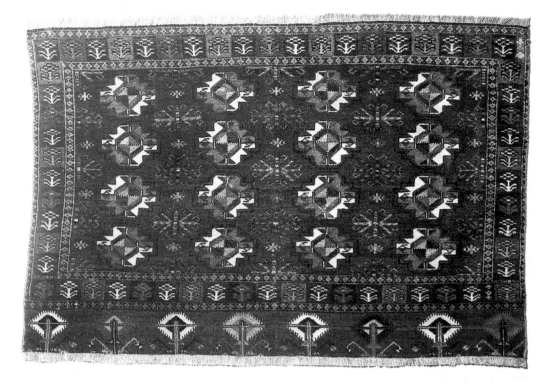

Chodor

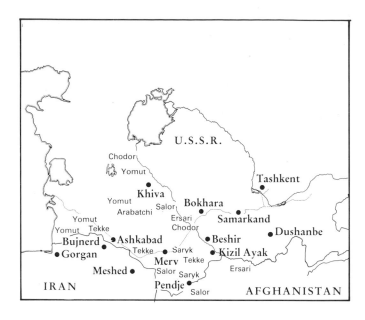

The early territory of the Chodor was in the north of Kazakstan on the Caspian Sea, from where they began to migrate in small groups, moving down to the khanate of Khiva in a steady trickle from the sixteenth century. Finally the whole Chodor tribe was located in Khiva by the eighteenth century. From that time, through their warring history and their alliance with the Yomut, the Chodor dwindled in numbers and few remain today. These live in two small pockets, isolated from each other by hundreds of miles. One group of Chodor is to be found in the north near Khiva, with the Yomut as neighbours, the second live among the Salor and Ersari, far to the south near the town of Beshir.

As testament to their greater numbers in earlier days, a large amount of Chodor weaving has survived. Earlier weaving was of a more positive, deep red, compared with later pieces which are muddier in tone. In the latter a soft light red and a purplish brown are the most common field colours. Recent work tends to be coarse, with a considerable amount of cotton, both in the pile and weft. It is a sad decline from eighteenth-century Chodor weaving which was full of style, of high quality and with great imagination deployed to design top and bottom panels with completely different patterns. By the nineteenth century the Chodor were producing great quantities of weaving of indifferent quality compared with this rare early work. Today, Chodor work is poorly made, with unevenly stretched warp and weft resulting in lumps and wrinkles, and undistinguished ends.

The Chodor use two principal *guls*. One is the 'Tauk Noska' *gul* with four pairs of stylized animals, like the *gul* of both their northern and southern neighbours, the Yomut and the Ersari. The other, and most common, is the 'ertman' *gul*, used in a diagonal trellis arrangement which is very far removed from Turkoman tribal traditions. The Chodor also employ a different treatment of *guls* in the field pattern, interlocking them to form an allover pattern. The *chuvals* (storage bags) and camel trappings show the half *gul* or 'ertman' *gul*, sometimes almost in a tile pattern with the *guls* worked in a vivid blue and not the typical Turkoman spectrum of reds.

Many Chodor have apparently married into other tribes, an unusual occurrence for Turkoman people, but this has almost certainly been done for survival. There are some links with the Khirghiz, evident in Chodor patterns and designs which are very similar to Khirghiz work originally executed in felt appliqué. Most recent weaving is loose, in a similar technique to the Ersari, with little left to show for the fine craftsmanship that was once characteristic of this fragmented tribe.

TYPICAL SPECIFICATIONS

Warp
Natural brown wool, slightly displaced.

Weft
Thick cotton, or part cotton and wool. Two shoots.

Pile
Wool, coarse and long.

Knot
Asymmetrical.
1800–2500/dm²
(120–166/sq. in.).

Ends
Plain weave, some pieces only have a fringe.

Sides
Flat, four-warp cord, overcast with goat hair or wool in two-colour check; or brown wool wrapped around two pairs of warps.

Handle
Dry, harsh, floppy.

a. Opposite *A nineteenth-century Chodor bridal camel trapping,* kejebe, *showing typical Chodor colouration. The design of the main border is possibly derived from appliqué work. Early nineteenth century.*
0.5m × 1.75m, 1′6″ × 5′8″.

b. Right *This typical Chodor main carpet shows the* ertman gul *in a diagonal repeat. This particular ornament can first be seen on a fifteenth-century carpet from Anatolia. One often finds a wavy line separating the* guls. *The borders of this carpet are closely related to Yomut designs. Early nineteenth century.*

Ersari including Kizil Ayak

The Ersari are probably the most numerous of all Turkoman tribes, and did not suffer the losses so damaging to many other tribes during the unrest in the nineteenth century. Originally their territory was on the north-eastern shore of the Caspian Sea, where the Chodor also lived. But like them, they began to migrate south and today the Ersari are mainly to be found down the southern reaches of the Amu Darya, with some in Uzbekistan and the majority on the Turkmenistan border with Afghanistan.

With such a large and well-spread territory, it is clear that sub-tribes formed and underwent separate development, and of these the Beshir are among the most important, having developed certain weaving characteristics specific to them. Indeed, until recent research clarified the situation, Beshir weaving was classified as 'Bokharan' and not related directly to the Ersari tribe at all. There is some excuse for this, since Beshir work has a very distinctive appearance. Their designs have been considerably influenced by the textiles woven in Bokhara, and many of the motifs found in Beshir weaving owe their origins to Persia and China. The Beshir Ersari were settled, and lived in domed mud-brick houses, which perhaps explains the lack of surviving *engsis* which were an essential part of tent trappings. Instead, it is believed that they may have made rugs of similar design to *engsis*, but without the long 'skirt' panel at the bottom, and with equal kilim ends top and bottom. On the other hand, camel trappings are common.

Some classic tribal weaving of the Ersari survives from the end of the eighteenth century and the beginning of the nineteenth century, in some of which the *gul* shape is integrated into an all-over repeating pattern. The use of a clear green is also evident in these pieces. Other designs which occur frequently are flower heads arranged in traditional Turkoman *gul* patterns in the field, within a typical tribal format. The Ersari made storage bags of a similar design to those of the Tekke, with horizontal stripes and decorative top and bottom panels.

Quite unlike other Turkoman work are the large Ersari rugs which use a particular version of the Herati pattern as well as the well-known *mina khani* motif, which is also often used on other weavings. Ersari rugs contain far more yellow than any other Turkoman work and, unusually, their use of silk in the pile is not confined to the cochineal-dyed magenta silk, but extends to yellow and blue as well. In all these rugs, the Ersari show little awareness of tribal traditions.

The work of the *Kizil Ayak* is most closely related to that of the Ersari, of whom they form a sub-group. However, their *engsis* contain 'ertman' panels from the Chodor and their main carpets almost invariably feature a 'Tauk Noska' *gul* from the Yomut.

TYPICAL SPECIFICATIONS

Warp
Black or brown wool, sometimes incorporating goat hair in old Beshir pieces. Also grey, greyish brown, natural undyed ivory or light tan wool. Kizil Ayak – not depressed.

Weft
Natural dark brown wool, thick, two shoots. Tan and ivory more rare. Cotton unusual. Kizil Ayak – two shoots of red wool.

Pile
Wool, glossy, long, and soft.

Knot
Asymmetrical in all variants, with symmetrical knots at edges. 800–1400/dm² (53–93/sq. in.).

Sides
Dark brown goat hair as side finish. Two to three pairs of warps in selvedge, overcast in red wool, occasionally two-colour check. Kizil Ayak – two pairs of warps, wrapped with red or brown wool or goat hair.

Ends
Dark brown goat hair as side finish. Plain weave in red with blue stripe.

Handle
Firm, glossy, soft.

a. Opposite *The most desirable of all Ersari weavings are the prayer rugs, often attributed to the town of Beshir. The designs come in several variations, and although this example is one of the most typical, it is also one of the most beautiful. The Ersari tend to use large areas of natural brown wool, which is highly lustrous, in combination with deep blues, greens, and pinky reds, against an ivory background which gives a spectacular effect. Early nineteenth century.*
1.90m × 1m, 6'3" × 3'3".
Wher Collection, Switzerland

b. Right *The Ersari wove spectacular main carpets, often influenced by textile designs and Persian carpet patterns. Their bright colourful designs make them some of the most attractive carpets produced in Central Asia. First half of the nineteenth century.*
4.50m × 2m, 14'8" × 6'6".

175

EAST TURKESTAN

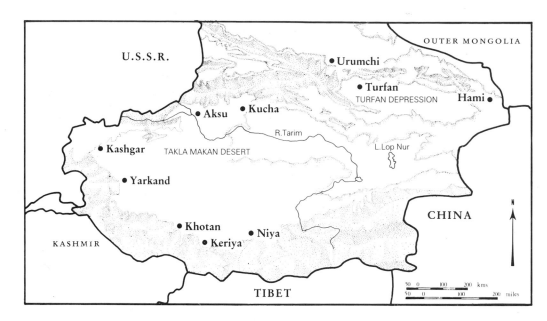

a. Opposite *This bold design represents the peak of East Turkestan production. The traditional three-medallion pattern is probably of Buddhist origin and is harmoniously balanced by the reciprocal trefoil border. Late eighteenth century.*
3.75m × 1.38m, 12'4" × 4'5".
Wher Collection, Switzerland

East or Central Turkestan, in the heart of Central Asia, is a desolate region largely occupied by the Takla Makan desert. Known as the Tarim Basin from the name of its main river, it is only inhabited in the oases bordering the desert. These oases – Kashgar, Aksu, Kucha, and Turfan in the north, Yarkand, Khotan, Keriya, and Niya to the south – are all connected with the Silk Route, which has acted as a commercial and cultural link between East and West since antiquity. The Tarim Basin contains many archaeological sites from which carpet and textile fragments, sculpture, paintings, and manuscripts have been unearthed, testifying the great economic and cultural richness of this region in the first millenium of our era.

A considerable number of carpet fragments have been discovered, so it is reasonable to suppose that carpets were widely known and marketed at least since the third century AD. Structural analysis has revealed a number of different weaving techniques: symmetrical knotting, cut-loop weaving, and Spanish knotting. It is surprising, though, that no fragment has yet appeared with the asymmetrical knot, which is common to carpets of this region from the eighteenth century onwards. As local weaving techniques rarely change (unless new designs require technical innovations), it may be doubted whether these fragments truly represent the local tradition. They may instead be imported goods. The few designs that are still decipherable are fragmentary and common to different weaving areas, so they hardly indicate a local production. Literary sources, however, show that carpets were produced in the region, and the Buddhist pilgrim, Yuanzhuang, confirms the existence of carpet manufacture in the seventh century in the oases of Jiansha (Kashgar) and Juson Dana (Khotan). Later literary evidence is scant, but it is probable that carpets were knotted under the Mongol domination of Turkestan in the thirteenth and fourteenth centuries, and later on under the Chinese.

Very few carpets from East Turkestan can be given a date

earlier than 1800, but the number and quality of nineteenth and twentieth-century pieces suggest that a highly organized production had existed for many centuries. This supposition is confirmed by the unique character of these carpets and their highly individual designs, which are mostly of pre-Islamic origin.

The carpets are often known in the West as 'Samarkand', from the name of the city in West Turkestan where they were sold for export to Europe and America at the end of the nineteenth century. In dating these carpets, two facts must be taken into consideration: the gradual deterioration and ornateness of the designs, and the changes in colouration. The latter is especially evident after the 1870s with the massive introduction of chemical dyes. The bright and intense colours of the early carpets were replaced by poor fugitive dyes, which gave the lighter shades of violet, pink, grey, green, and yellow which were then so fashionable in the West. Such carpets are still sold as seventeenth and eighteenth-century specimens by unscrupulous dealers.

Most of the extensive production of East Turkestan was concentrated in the oases of Kashgar, Yarkand, and Khotan. These large fertile areas are dotted with villages with inhabited by people of Turkic origin – Turanians, Kirghiz, Kazaks – and various Mongol and Chinese groups. In the oases, carpets were woven in private workshops or small factories, under the patronage of the local administration and supervised by masters of the craft. The latter were also in charge of buying wool in the bazaar, having it dyed by professional dyers, and contracting the weavers, the majority of whom were men. Both horizontal and vertical looms were used, and the designs, in reality quite few, were taken from other carpet specimens and dictated knot by knot to the weavers.

The format of the carpets was dictated by the dimensions of the mud or wooden heated platform which occupied the middle of the room. The carpets were laid on this platform, singly or in pairs, and frequently covered with felt since

people slept and assembled on them. The dimensions of the rugs vary between 1 by 2 metres (3½ by 6½ feet) and 2 by 4 metres (6½ by 13 feet). Only at the beginning of the twentieth century were much larger and sometimes squarer carpets produced to meet western demands. Small cushions, horse blankets and saddle rugs (usually oval) are rare. Long runners with multiple prayer niches (*safs*) become common under the rule of Jakub Beg (1865–78), a religious but despotic ruler, but no single niche prayer rugs are known.

East Turkestan was subject to a number of foreign rulers, and therefore was brought into contac with many stylistic and cultural influences, but despite this the carpet designs maintained their character. Many of their forms and symbolism derive from the ancient shamanistic and Buddhist beliefs of the first Turkic inhabitants.

The most traditional if not the most common design is the pomegranate tree stemming from a vase, an ancient symbol of fertility in the Far East in which the vase represents Mother Earth and the pomegranate is significant for its many fruit. The design which occurs most frequently is probably of Buddhist origin and features three, round superimposed medallions, representing the Buddha, Sakyamuni, flanked by his two acolytes. In later examples many variants are known. Sometimes one single medallion appears in the centre, frequently accompanied by four quarter-medallions in the corners. Rare examples show eight to ten medallions in two rows enclosed in a square lattice. Another motif is a hooked *gul* containing a rosette, either imported from West Turkestan or developed autonomously in East Turkestan.

Less common are designs of Persian origin (like the schematic rendering of the 'Herati' pattern) and of Chinese origin, such as the cloud-collar lattice design or large peonies derived from Chinese silks. A few rare examples show a Mughal lattice scheme, imported from India in the course of trade. Twentieth-century carpets often have pictorial designs.

The motifs of the main borders are numerous and highly original. The most fascinating is composed of large bold trefoils derived from Chinese cloud-collar iconography, which in later examples is rendered with narrow multi-coloured stripes symbolizing clouds, mountains, and water. Eight-petalled rosettes and geometric bunches of three flowers are also common. Minor borders have meandering vines, swastikas, the greek key and T-shapes.

East Turkestan carpets have a cotton foundation. The wool of the pile is lustrous, but hard and not very durable it is unusual to find a piece in good condition. Silk and metal thread were used especially in the productions of Kashgar and Yarkand. Dyes were mainly imported from neighbouring provinces. Until the third quarter of the nineteenth century, the field was usually brick red, dark or light blue, or more rarely ivory or yellow. Red, blue, light blue, blue green, white, yellow, and brown were common for the designs.

Kashgar and Yarkand

Situated in the extreme west of East Turkestan, *Kashgar* was the most famous, rich, and cosmopolitan of the three oases. It is well known for its crafts, but produced fewer carpets than Yarkand and Khotan, with no peculiar technical differences to distinguish them from other productions. Carpets are attributed to Kashgar because of their generally finer weave and the presence of many designs of foreign influence. These include the Persian Herati pattern and Chinese floral motifs. Silk carpets with details of metal thread come mainly from Kashgar. The palette is generally more delicate, favouring pastel shades such as salmon reds, light blues, yellows, jade green, and also a strong bluish red obtained from lac. Few late examples are known and most

of the production is generally assigned to the end of the eighteenth and the first half of the nineteenth century.

The *Yarkand* oasis was a major caravan centre not only for the east-west Silk Route but also for commercial and cultural contacts with India. The carpet production was mainly in wool, but included a few silk rugs characterized by clearly defined, sharp designs which tend to be less crowded than those of other areas. The vase-and-pomegranate and three-medallion designs are the most common, and *guls* were also popular. A number of *safs* are known. Colours tend to be more intense and contrasted than in the rest of Turkestan. Yarkand carpets are usually distinguishable by their thick, light-blue wefts.

TYPICAL SPECIFICATIONS

Warp
Undyed white cotton, occasionally light blue or yellow. Machine-spun from the 1850s.

Weft
Yarkand – Light blue cotton, rarely white or light yellow, sometimes machine-spun. Also silk. Two or three shoots. Kashgar – undyed white cotton, sometimes silk, or with soumak details in metal thread. Two shoots.

Pile
Wool, hard and glossy; or silk. Short.

Knot
Asymmetrical. 500–1400/dm^2 (33–93/sq. in.)

Ends
Lower – warp loops. Upper – short flat weave; fringes sometimes knotted in groups of eight to ten warps.

Sides
Double overcast of brick red wool.

Handle
Thin, stiff and granular.

a. Opposite left *The pastel colours and delicate ornament are typical of Kashgar production. Hooked guls alternating with small rosettes also appear regularly in Khotan carpets. Late eighteenth century.*
3.25m × 1.68m, 10′7″ × 5′6″.
Wher Collection, Switzerland

b. Opposite right *The vase and pomegranate pattern is probably the most typical East Turkestan design. It is a very ancient motif connected with fertility rites. Yarkand, early nineteenth century.*
4m × 2.12m, 13′2″ × 7′.

c. Right *Clearly defined designs and intense colours are characteristic of Yarkand carpets. This rare example with a plain ground is particularly successful. Early nineteenth century.*
3.84m × 1.83m, 12′7″ × 6′.
Wher Collection, Switzerland

Khotan

Khotan, the largest of the East Turkestan oases, had the most extensive production of carpets, especially at the end of the nineteenth century in response to the demands of the Western market. In fact, most of the late aniline-dyed examples are generally attributed to Khotan. Most of the carpets are of wool and feature the three-medallion pattern, followed by the *gul* design, the vase and pomegranate, and other motifs of foreign influence. Khotan carpets have a warmer palette and are also distinguishable by a looser weave and brown wefts, which tend to be in three, rather than the more usual two, rows between the knots.

Carpets were also woven in other parts of East Turkestan but for the time being attribution to definite places or tribal groups is still premature.

TYPICAL SPECIFICATIONS

Warp
Undyed white cotton, occasionally light blue or yellow. Machine-spun from the 1850s.

Weft
Brown wool in older pieces, then undyed white cotton. Also silk. Two or three shoots.

Pile
Wool, hard and glossy; or silk. Short.

Knot
Asymmetrical. Wool –
500–1000/dm² (33–66/sq. in.)
Silk – 3500–4500/dm² (233–300/sq. in.).

Ends
Lower – warp loops. Upper – short flat weave; fringes sometimes knotted in groups of eight to ten warps.

Sides
Double overcast of brick red wool.

Handle
Fairly loose.

a. Opposite left *The design of this Khotan carpet is very unusual and no other similar examples are known. The warm colours are characteristic of early Khotan examples. Early nineteenth century.*
3.25m × 1.50m, 10′8″ × 4′10″.

b. Opposite right *This saddle rug belongs to a small, well-defined group which features brick red grounds, central medallions sometimes substituted with Fo dogs, and a decorative motif based on short parallel lines. Khotan, first half of the nineteenth century.*
0.95m × 1.70m, 3′ × 5′6″.

c. Right *A balanced, archaic design composed around the three-medallion scheme. In later examples the composition tends to be more crowded and the palette is weakened by pale, fugitive aniline dyes. Khotan, first half of the nineteenth century.*
1.70m × 0.95m, 5′6″ × 3′1″.

TIBET

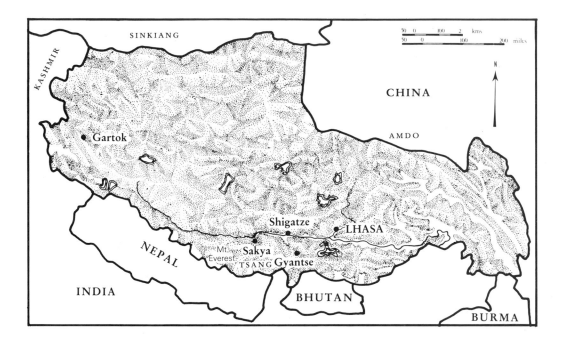

Tibet, now perforce part of the Chinese Republic, covers a very large area extending from the northern ranges of the Himalayas to the Central Asian steppes; bordering Nepal and India to the south, and China to the north and east. The southern provinces, surmounted by the glaciers and peaks of the Himalayas, harbour green valleys with salt lakes, and the central and eastern regions enjoy a relatively mild climate. In western Tibet the high plateau and desert, interrupted by gorges and isolated oases, allow little human settlement, and in the north, towards Central Asia, the steppes are boundless and empty. Tibet has one of the lowest population densities in the world, but in it live a vast number of different ethnic groups, generally related to the Chinese. Practically isolated from external interference until the 1950s, the people were concentrated in a few urban settlements which were mainly inhabited by high officials, merchants, and monks. The rest of the population was either scattered in the numerous villages and monasteries and lived on agriculture, or else led a very precarious nomadic life, rearing sheep, goats, and yaks or attacking the numerous caravans of merchants, pilgrims, and monks which crossed Tibet during the brief summer months.

It is likely that carpet weaving in Tibet has a very long history, but for the time being proof of this rests on logical suppositions rather than substantial evidence. The actual origin and development of this production remains obscure.

It is obvious that the largely nomadic lifestyle of the Tibetans and the very harsh climate of this mountainous region are perfectly suited to the use of carpets. Also, Tibet is a wool-producing region and its inhabitants knew of carpets through their close links with East Turkestan and China, where carpet weaving was well-established.

Reliable archaeological evidence shows that weaving was practised in Tibet from very early times and the antiquity

of this tradition is confirmed by the unusual knotting technique still used by Tibetan weavers (see 18b). This knot is not only extremely old (it is found in carpet fragments excavated in Syria, dated to the third century AD), but it is totally different from the asymmetrical one used in neighbouring countries. The sophisticated nature of nineteenth-century Tibetan carpets, with their use of additional knotting for particular motifs and their varied design repertoire, offer further proof that the industry is of considerable age. Finally, a fertile background for the development of carpets would have been provided by the rich and early artistic heritage of Tibet, which includes painting, sculpture, silver, jewellery, and textiles.

Despite all this, no surviving Tibetan carpet can be safely dated to before the end of the nineteenth century. This cannot be explained by claiming that the early carpets have worn to threads and have disappeared, for the temples and monasteries have acted as safe depositories where carpets were stored carefully and used as cushions or pillar rugs. Yet the only rugs of any age that have been found in these places tend to be Chinese, of the Ningxia group but frequently decorated with Tibetan motifs, or from Eastern Turkestan.

Nor are carpets depicted in the early frescoes or the many surviving *thangka* (religious paintings). In the photographs taken by the early Western travellers to the region, most of the carpets are again either from China or East Turkestan, perhaps because they were more highly valued than the local products. The early travel literature rarely mentions rugs, and when it does the information is either inaccurate or imprecise, failing to specify whether the floor covering is a felt or a carpet, or whether it is a local or imported product. It seems, too, that carpet weaving in Tibet first developed among city dwellers which would suggest that it was not a native craft. The carpets them-

a. Right *A* khaden *depicting, with typically Tibetan exuberance, a version of the ancient dragon and phoenix design. These carpets are usually backed and bordered with red cloth. Early twentieth century.*
1.80m × 0.90m, 5′10″ × 2′.

selves show a marked dependence on Chinese and East Turkestan models, rather than reflecting the specifically Tibetan styles which are to be found in the other art forms.

With only these facts at our disposal, the development of early Tibetan weaving will remain a mystery until a genuinely old piece becomes available.

The only known Tibetan carpets are limited in number and dateable only from the end of the nineteenth century. These pieces, though not great art, have a strong personality and their bold colours and designs convey something of the magic and power of the high plateaux.

The production of rugs, known in Tibetan as *drumze*, was not a tribal craft but was concentrated in towns and villages. The cities of Shigatse and Gyantse in the southern province of Tsang were particularly notable for their high quality output. Lower-grade rugs were also knotted in Kampa Dzong near the Nepal border. Rug weaving also took place in the central province of Ü, mainly in Lhasa and its vicinity; and in the eastern provinces of Amdo and Kham in the towns of Minyag and Derge.

Rugs were knotted for local use or for commercial purposes in small-scale cottage industries or as a domestic craft. Usually men and women from the lower classes were employed by aristocrats to weave either in factories or in their households. The women did the weaving, on vertical looms, while men took care of the finishing. Dyed wool was purchased in the market or from professional dyers. The rugs produced under the patronage of landlords were usually of better quality and showed more variety of design because the weavers had access to imported textiles and carpets. With the opening of stable commercial relations with the West at the end of the nineteenth century, production underwent a prodigious development and it continues in the Tibetan refugee camps of Nepal and India.

Rugs were used mainly in the houses of the aristocracy, in monasteries, or as trappings for horses and mules. The farmers and nomads were generally too poor to own rugs, and often used felts, rough woollen textiles, or animal skins instead. The late nineteenth and early twentieth-century production generally consisted of rugs for sitting and sleeping, known as *khaden*, and small, squarish fringed mats, called *khagangma*, which were placed on top of the *khaden* as sitting rugs for people of high rank. The former measured approximately 0.8 by 1.7 metres (2½ by 5½ feet), and the latter 0.75 by 0.85 metres (2½ by 2¾ feet).

Rugs were also made exclusively for monastic use. These included long runners, decorated with repeated identical squares, used to cover the narrow platforms on which monks assembled for ceremonies; and seat covers and backrests, with a scalloped upper-edge, usually made in a set to decorate head lamas' thrones. A large part of the production consisted of saddle rugs which were used, and frequently made, in sets of two. Those rugs made to go under the wooden saddle, or *makden*, were traditionally oval, rectangular, butterfly-shaped, or oblong with two notched corners, while those meant to go on top were rectangular. Small pile weavings of different shapes were woven to decorate horses and mules. Larger carpets known as *saden*, were

woven on special commission and used as floor coverings, door hangings or to wrap columns in monasteries.

Tibetan rugs are easily identifiable by their technical, stylistic, and chromatic features. They are characterized by the cut-loop technique which, in nineteenth and twentieth century production, is common only to Tibetan rugs. The foundation is generally all wool and the pile is cut high, giving a heavy and thick handle. Rugs from Tibet are usually backed and bordered by red cloth.

The designs are strongly reminiscent of Chinese and East Turkestan models, but are characterized by an exuberance and a naturalism which is very different from their prototypes. The most common scheme in *khaden* rugs is composed of three superimposed round medallions; more rare are two medallions, or a central one accompanied by floral elements. The main border is traditionally decorated with swastikas, T-shapes or naturalistically drawn flowers. Common to all are pictorial subjects, such as dragons (frequently paired with phoenixes), cranes, bats, lions, and vases with flowers, all derived from Chinese iconography and having symbolic meaning. The eight Buddhist symbols of happy augury commonly appear, sometimes singly. Other popular motifs include lively, floral arabesques, large peonies or lotus flowers, reminiscent of Chinese brocades, and tiger stripes. The rarest and probably oldest design schemes are those with repeating geometric motifs. The designs do not always include borders.

The colours are strong and vivid. Aniline dyes were introduced in the last decade of the nineteenth century and appear together with vegetable dyes. Ground colours are usually blue, black, red, and orange, rarely yellow and ivory; while designs are in red, orange, pink, yellow, beige, blue, light blue, green, and white.

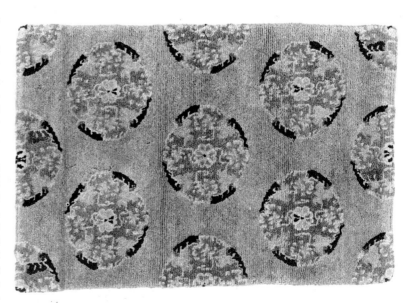

TYPICAL SPECIFICATIONS

Warp
Undyed white and/or brown wool. White cotton in later examples, hand or machine spun. Sometimes wool and cotton combined; very rarely wool and silk.

Weft
Undyed white and/or brown wool. Two shoots.

Pile
Soft, matt wool. Medium to long. Sometimes with contouring around the motifs.

Knot
Cut asymmetrical knot. 400–1400/dm² (26–93/sq. in.).

Ends
Short plain weave, generally turned and hemmed, sometimes with extra, coloured, thick wefts. Warps often looped. Generally protected by red cloth binding.

Sides
Two or more terminal warps cabled together by weft, frequently reinforced by additional selvedge. Red cloth binding. Sometimes a fringe is added to the sides.

Handle
Thick, heavy, frequently backed by cloth.

a. Opposite *A small mat, used as a cushion by wealthy people and lamas of high rank, with a repeating flower medallion design of Chinese derivation. This motif is found on Chinese brocades of earlier date. Late nineteenth century.*
0.53m × 0.76m, 1′9″ × 2′5″.
The Textile Museum, Washington

b. Right *This lively set of saddle rugs is composed of the traditional rectangular mat to go over the saddle and the makden to go underneath, in a butterfly shape copied from saddle cloths in British India. Late nineteenth century.*
0.91m × 0.63m, 2′10″ × 2′.
0.76m × 1.27m, 2′5″ × 4′1″.
Dr and Mrs Murray Eiland, Jr. Collection

CHINA

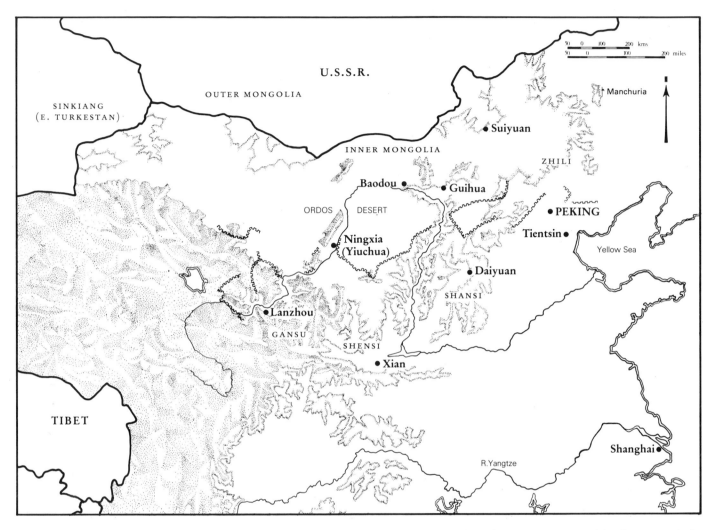

Although carpet weaving is a very old tradition in China, carpets are not as widespread as the other decorative arts and it is only fairly recently that they began to incorporate the official style required by the Chinese court. There are many reasons for this. Wool was not widely available except in the north-western provinces, and in the Chinese climate and way of life carpets do not play such a prominent role as they do in other eastern countries.

In addition to these practical reasons there are also aesthetic ones. Scholars of Chinese art have seen carpets as peripheral to the great official arts of dynastic China, partly because the medium is not suited to those qualities of precision and perfection that are so integral to Chinese art. These are found instead in other textiles, such as embroidery and very fine silk-tapestry weaving (*kossu*). Also, carpets are disparaged by some Chinese as 'barbarian' art as they are associated with the Central Asian hordes that have threatened China throughout history. Western carpet experts, on the other hand, have overlooked them precisely because they are not close enough to the aesthetics of Central Asian and Islamic art.

These attitudes, and the lack of early examples of Chinese carpet weaving, have encouraged the general public to identify Chinese carpets with the twentieth-century production made for export. Woven in large workshops, which are frequently organized by foreign firms, these carpets are usually a decadent and sterile interpretation of the Chinese ornamental tradition.

Paintings and literary sources indicate, however, that carpets have a long history in China and were known at the time of the Han and Tang dynasties (206 BC–220 AD, and 618–906 AD). The famous Wenji paintings of the twelfth century show a caravan of Khitans, a tribe of Turkic origin. The carpets in this scene are drawn with great care and show definite Central Asian characteristics. Despite this, carpets are not mentioned in the detailed imperial annals of the period, nor do they feature in paintings of Chinese life.

It appears that the weaving of carpets first started, at a very early date, in those regions such as Ningxia whose cultural links were closer to the Central Asian heritage than to the imperial China of the eastern provinces. The weavers of the well-known Ningxia carpets were Muslim, their ancestors having been converted to Islam by the Arabs in the ninth century. They were linked, therefore, to the people of East Turkestan who had woven carpets for centuries. Carpet weaving may, in fact, have begun in

a. Right *The austere design, the colouration, and the corroded brown border date this carpet to the eighteenth century. The dragons symbolize the powers that dominate the world and thus represent the emperor. Ningxia.*
3.07m × 1.80m, 10' × 5'10".

Ningxia at the time of this conversion, but the designs of the early carpets remain a mystery.

Later, Father Jerbillon, a Jesuit priest who accompanied the Emperor Kangxi to Ningxia in 1696, describes how the emperor was interested in the carpets and insisted on watching how they were made. It is not impossible that this visit resulted in carpets being made for the imperial court.

The story of this early carpet weaving is still obscure and very few carpets have survived that can be dated, even tentatively, to the seventeenth century. A small and little known group can be ascribed to the eighteenth and nineteenth centuries, and these can be compared with the highest forms of Chinese art. They are close in style to Chinese court art, but appear to have had a slower artistic evolution than other art forms of the period. Characterized by a limited but effective polychromy, the austere and delicate designs convey, as is common in China, philosophical, religious, and social concepts. The eighteenth-century pieces are usually coarser in weave and have uncluttered compositions, usually with geometric designs. The outer edges are brown and tend to be corroded, whereas in the later examples they are blue.

Unfortunately, the dating and origin of these pieces is still problematic. But it is clear that this production developed outside the Chinese artistic and cultural sphere, and that its aesthetic principles were grafted on to a preexisting and ancient tradition of which no traces now survive.

Despite the superficial homogeneity of Chinese carpets, different groupings do exist. The production is concentrated in northern China but attribution to precise locations is usually speculative.

Ningxia

In the vicinity of the Great Wall in north-western China is situated the important trading centre of Ningxia, capital of the province of the same name which extended from Inner Mongolia down to Lanzhou and later became part of the great Gansu province. It was inhabited by Chinese and Mongolian groups mostly of Muslim faith. Due to the old and great reputation of Ningxia as a carpet-producing centre, this term has become associated with Chinese carpets of quality and age. As such it has frequently been abused by dealers and is generally employed to differentiate the old production from the commercial goods produced from the end of the nineteenth century onwards.

Carpets were not only woven in Ningxia, which acted as a trading centre, but also in the surrounding region where weaving was organized as a small cottage-industry or a domestic craft. Carpets were woven in the towns of Xinig, Daiyuan, Lanzhou, Sinig, and Suzhou where wool was plentiful and trade with Tibet, Mongolia, and the rest of China was well established. Ningxia carpets are characterized by a low knot-density, floppy handle, cotton foundation, and soft silky wool.

Designs are numerous but easily recognizable. While in Islamic carpets they are interdependent and intermingle to form a whole composition, in Chinese carpets the decorative elements seem to float, static and isolated, on the surface of the carpet. The central medallion design is the most common. It is generally rounded and looks like a concentration of single motifs such as foliate dragons, stylized flowers, or geometric frets. The medallion or its components are generally repeated in the corners, on a ground that is usually plain but is sometimes adorned with neatly drawn arabesques.

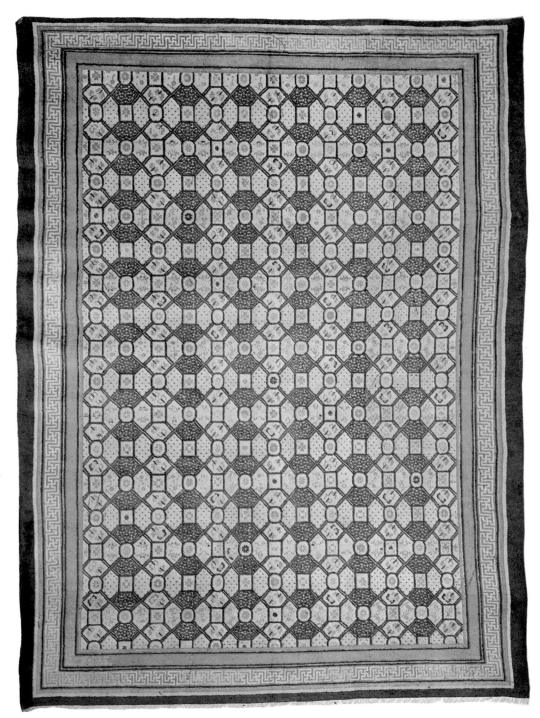

a. Opposite left *The somewhat stiff composition and the drawing of the bats and dragons suggest that this carpet dates from the nineteenth century. Ningxia.*
3m × 2.08m, 9′9″ × 6′9″.

b. Opposite right *A minute motif known as the 'rice' pattern appears regularly on carpets of this period, usually on a yellow but sometimes on a white ground. A five medallion scheme is often superimposed on this background. Ningxia, mid-nineteenth century.*
3.32m × 1.88m, 10′6″ × 6′2″.

c. Right *The geometric lattice pattern of this unusual carpet is similar to the architectural elements that adorn Chinese houses. Flowers and small butterflies symbolic of conjugal happiness are recognizable in the lattice. Ningxia, mid-nineteenth century.*
4.07m × 3m, 13′4″ × 9′10″.

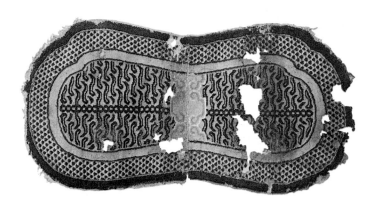

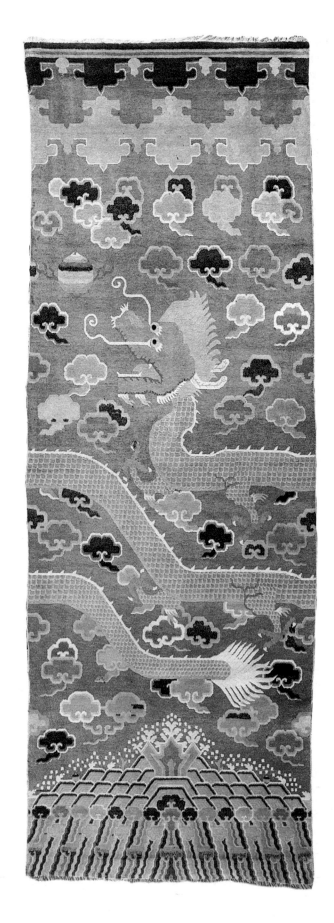

The second group of designs includes different types of lattice motifs, such as repeating swastikas, a very stylized version of the cloud collar, small lozenges, and octagons alternating with squares. A third group is characterized by floral elements such as the peony or the lotus, geometrically arranged and accompanied by elegant scrolling leaves.

The borders are traditionally composed of two main elements: geometric patterns such as repeating swastikas symbolizing infinite luck, the greek key, and T-shapes, or the so-called pearl border. Minor borders are usually bands of plain colour.

A very peculiar group of Ningxia rugs consists of pieces especially woven for Buddhist monasteries in China, Tibet, and Mongolia. These rugs are designed to wrap around columns and depict coiling dragons, the eight symbols of happy augury, or in later examples naturalistically drawn lamas. Cushions and chair backs are also common, together with long runners with repeating squares used by monks during ceremonies. The numerous saddle rugs were generally oval or rectangular with notches in the corners. They were also made for Tibet and Mongolia with a vast number of motifs.

In older pieces the field is generally a light walnut, while in nineteenth-century examples light colours from white, ivory, and beige to yellow or different shades of pink, apricot, and peach were frequent. Blue grounds are extremely rare and generally late. The designs are in various tones of blue, white, and pink, and there is a very wide variety of formats including large and small carpets, runners, saddle rugs, and cushions. Very few round carpets are known.

TYPICAL SPECIFICATIONS

Warp
Undyed white cotton, occasionally wool, or wool and cotton; machine-spun in later examples. Silk in silk carpets.

Weft
As above. Two shoots, four in older examples.

Pile
Wool, soft and silky. Rarely silk.

Knot
Asymmetrical.
400–900/dm^2 (26–60/sq. in.).

Ends
Short flat weave with fringes, sometimes loops in the lower ends.

Sides
Two warps cabled together by weft.

Handle
Floppy, light, soft.

a. Opposite left *For a long time saddle rugs of this design and construction were attributed to Mongolia. A closer analysis confirmed that they belong to the Ningxia group and were woven for the domestic and export markets. Early nineteenth century.*
0.65m × 1.25m, 2'2" × 4'2".
Wher Collection, Switzerland

b. Opposite right *This was woven in the Ningxia region, to be wrapped around the columns of Buddhist monasteries in China, Tibet, and Mongolia. The design is devised in such a way as to show a coiling dragon once the rug is in place. Nineteenth century.*
4.04m × 1.09m, 13'3" × 3'7".

c. Right *This Ningxia carpet is decorated with scrolling peonies symbolic of wealth and respectability. The light red field is more common in mid-nineteenth century specimens, but in this case the carpet dates from the early part of the century.*
3.20m × 1.80m, 10'4" × 5'10".

Baodou, Gansu, Peking, and Mongolia

One easily distinguishable group of carpets was probably woven in the province of *Gansu* or in Inner Mongolia. Their designs are clearly of East Turkestan derivation and frequently present a round central medallion in tomato red, on a dark blue ground spotted by small roundels in red, white, and light blue known as the *bulo* design. They have a cotton foundation and are slightly finer than the Ningxia group. The wool of the pile is high, silky, and soft, and the carpets are elongated in shape like those of East Turkestan.

Another identifiable group was knotted in the oasis of *Baodou* on the border of the Ordos desert. It is an important trading centre which comprises *Suiyuan* and *Guihua* and other small villages in which carpets were woven. The majority of the known pieces date from the late nineteenth century and are distinguishable from Ningxia carpets by a tighter weave and a more opaque wool. They are quite small, averaging 0.8 by 1.6 metres (2½ by 5 feet). Dark blue is common as a ground colour in Suiyuan rugs, while in Baodou ivory, beige, and various shades of brownish red are more usual. Designs are in blue, yellow, and white, or strong red in older examples. They are very varied and include stylized flowers, lattices, and realistically drawn stags, horses, birds, human figures, sceneries, and vases on tables.

According to many writers, an organized carpet industry was started in *Peking* under imperial patronage in the 1860s by a Tibetan monk and his assistants. But although the great majority of early Peking rugs are attributable to the second half of the nineteenth century, an earlier production could have existed on a small scale.

Peking carpets are much more compact than those of the Ningxia group because of a tighter weave which averages between 900 and 1300 knots per square decimetre (60 to 86 per square inch). The wool is shinier but not as soft, the foundation is always cotton, and the handle is less pliable. Formats are usually large in response to local and especially foreign demand.

Older Peking carpets have designs resembling the Ningxia-group examples, but by the end of the century motifs were simplified for easier weaving and to satisfy the Western market. Plain grounds of blue, beige, or white are spotted with realistic bunches of flowers and a great number of Taoist symbols such as the One Hundred Antiquities, the attributes of the Eight Taoist Genii, the Eight Precious Things, and the Four Gentlemanly Accomplishments.

At the beginning of the twentieth century the Art Nouveau style was adapted to the Chinese tradition, sometimes quite successfully. Production boomed in the first decades of the new century to satisfy the ever-growing demand and a semi-industrial production was established in Tientsin and other cities. New colours such as light green, pink, wine red, and grey were introduced with unfortunate results.

Carpets were woven in other centres of the Gansu, Zhili, Shensi, and Shansi provinces but their production has not yet been identified.

Any discussion of carpet production in *Mongolia* should be considered purely speculative. The environmental, social, economic, and artistic conditions for a local production certainly exist: Mongolia is a very high, dry plateau inhabited by pastoral tribes of Mongol and Turkic origin, and similar groups in other areas are known to weave carpets. Yet no existing piece of any significant age can safely be classified as Mongolian, nor is there any literary or archaeological evidence for carpet production. Moreover, most of the so-called Mongolian saddle bags are now being more accurately attributed to Ningxia. They, together with pieces for monasteries, were exported to Mongolia in great numbers as indicated by the numerous Ningxia column rugs with Mongolian inscriptions. A small group of weaves is nonetheless currently attributed to Mongolia in the trade and, without any valid proof, by a few writers. It consists of carpets with a cotton foundation, long fleecy pile, floppy handle, asymmetrical knotting open to the left (400 to 800 knots per square decimetre/26 to 53 per square inch), and two to three shoots of weft. They are usually large and slightly wider than long. A group of smaller pieces (approximately 1.3 by 2 metres/4 by 6½ feet) of tighter weave are also called Mongolian. The designs are of Chinese derivation, drawn in a simpler and bolder style. Central geometric round medallions are common, frequently accompanied by stylized flowers or realistic bats, butterflies, dragons, and ideograms. Borders are extremely simple with repeating swastikas or the greek key. Colours favour ivory, beige, and camel fields, and designs in brown, black, violet, blue, turquoise, and light green.

a. Opposite above *The carpets usually attributed to Gansu province are characterized by designs of East Turkestan derivation and colouration. The red dots in the field are known as the* bulo *pattern.* 3.70m × 2.10m, 12'2" × 6'9". *Wher Collection, Switzerland*

b. Opposite below *A carpet made in Peking for the Western market. The quality of the wool and weaving are high but the design has been simplified and standardized. The field is decorated with the One Hundred Antiquities. Late nineteenth century.* 3.87m × 2.77m, 12'7" × 9'1".

c. Right *This Suiyuan carpet is unusual for its early date and handsome design of flying bats, instead of the more common pictorial designs. Late nineteenth century.* 3.35m × 1.40m, 10'10" × 4'6".

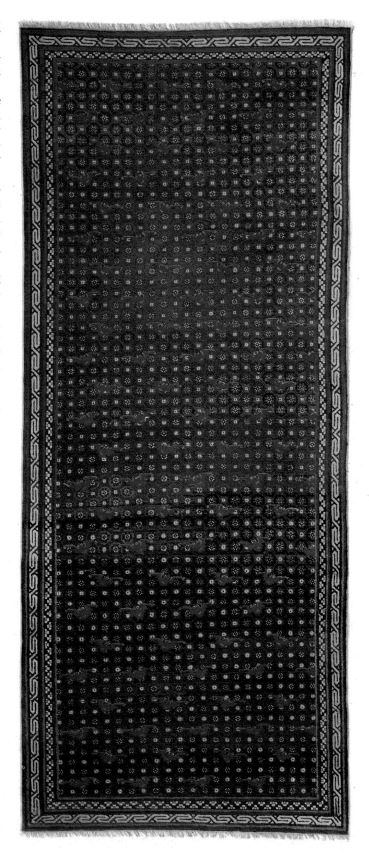

INDIA

In contrast with other oriental countries, the production of knotted pile carpets may not be indigenous to India due to the climate and the relative lack of suitable wool. Instead, flat-woven cotton dhurries have a longer recorded history and are far more common in Indian homes. The art of weaving pile carpets may have only been introduced in the sixteenth century by the Mughal rulers, who originally came from Central Asia, and under their rule carpet weaving flourished. By the beginning of the eighteenth century, however, Mughal influence had declined. In 1739 Nadir Shah, a Persian, invaded North India and sacked Delhi. A century of unrest and fragmentation followed. The Deccan was consolidated in 1724 by a Mughal general who established the independent rule of the Nizams of Hyderabad, other provinces broke away from central Mughal authority, and the Sikhs had captured Lahore and the rest of the Punjab by 1799. Meanwhile the British had

been expanding their control of former Mughal and Deccani territory and, having established fortified commercial bases in Calcutta, Madras, and Bombay, they gained effective control over most of the former Mughal empire by 1818.

With the loss of Mughal authority came a decline in court patronage that eventually had a profoundly adverse effect on carpet weaving in India. All the same, weaving did continue and fine carpets were still produced in the eighteenth and early nineteenth century. Some were destined for export but the best examples were undoubtedly woven to adorn the palaces of the emerging regional rulers. Efforts were made to encourage carpet weavers to emigrate to the new capitals and to maintain traditional standards of design, but these attempts were not particularly successful and carpet weaving steadily decreased. Finally, with the exceptions of Warangal in Hyderabad State, Kashmir, and the private workshops that had opened in the north-eastern provinces, all important carpet weaving had ceased by the middle of the nineteenth century. This was due to the lack of markets, the lack of interest from the British rulers in local crafts, and the changing tastes of regional rulers, who now preferred European and Persian carpets for their palaces. Despite this rather dismal situation some fine carpets were still being made in Kashmir and Warangal. When these were exhibited in the 1851 Great Exhibition in London their popularity was such that it prompted a dramatic attempt to revive the industry. Factories were established at Srinagar, Amritsar, Mirzapur, and Agra while many of the central jails organized carpet weaving in their workshops as an activity for long-term prisoners and as a possible source of revenue. Old carpets were collected and copied and new patterns invented. It was hoped that Europe and America would now become the major markets for Indian carpets, but unfortunately the first result of this new organization was a flood of poorly constructed, poorly dyed, and poorly designed carpets which temporarily subdued foreign interest. Most of the smaller private firms closed and only the jail workshops, which did not necessarily require profits, survived. The only commercial firms to continue production were those which were able to drastically reduce their operating costs by lowering the quality of materials and further depressing the wages of their desperate workers.

By the end of the nineteenth century, carpets which were entirely designed, dyed, and constructed in the 'traditional' manner were no longer being woven in India, though some well-produced copies of Persian and Mughal carpets, which shared both traditional and modern materials, were still being made in limited quantities in prisons such Agra and Yaravda central jails. Most of these carpets were personally requistioned by government officials or were used for furnishing public buildings. They are eagerly collected today.

Commercial production did continue in the present century and even, in a sense, flourished after independance in 1947, for India and Pakistan are now the largest exporters of carpets in the world. But this quantity is generally unmatched by its quality and these modern carpets have a poor reputation. As basic floor coverings, though, they do offer a relative value for money as the prices are remarkably low – a reflection, unfortunately, of the wages of the weavers.

In the design of Indian carpets there is no abrupt, dramatic difference between those which were woven at the end of the seventeenth century, the classical Mughal period, and those which might date from the beginning of the eighteenth century. Carpet weavers are naturally conservative and as long as their patrons remain content with the classical patterns, the weavers prefer to repeat or to further refine earlier models. That refinement (or possibly over-refinement) is the most characteristic trend in Indian carpet design of both the eighteenth and nineteenth centuries. It was generally produced by reducing the size of each classical design element and multiplying their numbers within the same space.

a. Above *An eighteenth-century Indian carpet with the millefleurs design that became so popular in the nineteenth century. This developed out of the classical Herati or Indo-Isfahan pattern, the elements decreasing in size and increasing in number until the entire ground was covered. 2.51m × 1.85m, 8'3" × 6'1". The Textile Museum, Washington*

Two basic carpet patterns became increasingly widespread in the eighteenth and nineteenth centuries. The first originated in the classical Mughal design of a large single naturalistic plant enclosed by a graceful ogival arch. This became transformed into tiny complex systems of either identical plants or alternating systems of massed floral elements, both of which were surrounded by rigid lattices. The second pattern was provided by the classical 'Herati' or 'Indo-Isfahan' design. In this, the number of palmettes, rosettes, and leaves increased until most of the ground was covered. Next, each element became smaller, allowing an additional number of palmettes, rosettes, and leaves to appear. This created the popular 'millefleurs' carpets which became common in the early nineteenth century. Parallel to the development of both new types of carpets was a growing complexity of the basic leaf-and-blossom meander border. The number of elements increased, the size of each element decreased, and the border began to resemble the ground patterns.

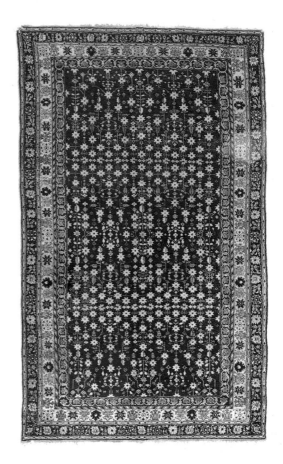

Apart from these typically Indian designs, many carpets of the nineteenth century are based on Persian models, which were either adapted or copied directly. These, though totally derivative in design, are sometimes successful and the trend has continued up to the present day. Since the 1940s Indian weavers have taken their designs from a wide range of sources, copying European, Chinese, and Turkoman motifs.

All Indian carpets are made in commercial workshops and there is no tribal and very little small-scale cottage industry manufacture. This is reflected in the designs, which are taken either from a cartoon or are written in a code known as a 'talim'. Ever since the Mughal period the traditional Indian designs, with their splendid asymmetric positioning and their radical use of open space to frame the elements of the pictorial and plant carpets, have demanded close cooperation between professional artists and carpet weavers. The sizes of Indian carpets, too, reflect their workshop origins. They are not based on traditional requirements but simply follow the demands of the market, some being enormously large, up to seventy feet in length.

Cotton is widely used in Indian carpets, for the warp, weft, and, even in certain nineteenth-century examples, for the pile. The cheaper and more modern carpets also use other cellulose fibres, jute and hemp. Silk had been used by the Mughals to some extent, but by the nineteenth century it was confined to the Deccan and southern India, and is now used only in Kashmir, for fine carpets. Wool is sometimes used in the warps of fine carpets, but is generally confined to the pile. It varies in quality and unfortunately dead *chunan* wool, which tends to loose its lustre when removed from the carcase with caustic soda, is often used.

Indian carpets of the Mughal period had a high reputation for their colours and dyes. The most characteristic colour was a blueish red, derived from lac, but in the nineteenth century the use of cochineal became widespread. Browner reds obtained with madder also became popular at this time. Other favourite colours included light

TYPICAL SPECIFICATIONS

Warp
Usually white or off-white cotton. Machine-spun and plied cotton introduced in third quarter of nineteenth century and now most common. The Deccan – pink, beige and white cotton. Multi-coloured silk warps used for finest quality nineteenth and twentieth-century wool and silk pile carpets. Warps heavily depressed, except in some Deccan examples which are slightly depressed.

Weft
White cotton. Coloured silk in silk carpets. Two or three shoots.

Pile
Wool, silk, or cotton.

Knot
Asymmetrical, except in some twentieth-century carpets from Gwalior which use the symmetrical knot.

Ends
A narrow strip of plain weave, alternate warps may be braided and knotted together.

Sides
First and last pairs of warps overcast. Modern carpets tend to have additional heavily plied cables inserted, to be overcast with the side warps.

a. Opposite above *A fairly typical example of an Indian millefleurs carpet. The ground is covered with an intricate system of tiny massed elements in which no single motif dominates. Middle to late nineteenth century.*
2.51m × 1.47m, 8'3" × 4'10".

b. Opposite below *Few commercially designed carpets of this period combine such disparate motifs so successfully. The border pattern is originally derived from Mannerist Europe and the field of naturalistic plants from Mughal silks. Late nineteenth or early twentieth century.*
3.98m × 3.04m, 13'1" × 10'.

c. Right *This outstanding rug is a faithful copy, reduced by one third, of a mid-seventeenth-century carpet now in the Metropolitan Museum of Art, which was first illustrated in 1929. Twentieth century.*
4.46m × 3.09m, 14'8" × 10'2".

a. Left *Although the major border is somewhat awkward, this silk pile carpet from Hyderabad is typical of the fine drawing and graceful proportions which characterized the best mid-nineteenth-century Deccani carpets. The palmettes that dominated the Herati prototype have been replaced here by symmetric white rosettes and by branched clusters of leaves. Detail. Mid-nineteenth century.* (2.35m × 1.35m, 7'7" × 4'5".) *Victoria and Albert Museum, London*

b. Opposite *This workshop creation combines the tiny multiple blossoms and intricate stemwork of Indian millefleurs carpets with major Harshang-style Caucasian palmettes and slanted minor palmettes associated with South Persian Vase carpets. Late nineteenth to early twentieth century.* 4.74m × 3.36m, 15'6" × 11'1".

and dark green and burnt orange. Aniline dyes were not widely adopted in India for long and instead the natural dyes were replaced by chrome dyes.

The production of carpets in India, unlike that of either Persia or Turkey, does not easily accommodate the general format of a gazetteer. Lists of traditional geographic centres, traditional weaving groups, or regional structural peculiarities are neither useful nor relevant to the Indian situation. The structure of most Indian carpets is fairly uniform, and although accounts and documentary sources point to particular areas of carpet production, it is rarely possible to identify specific carpets from these areas.

One area that can be discussed in some detail is the Deccan which still maintained a successful carpet making industry in the eighteenth and nineteenth centuries. These carpets exhibit colours and motifs which are not normally associated with North Indian Mughal carpets and may be explained by the Deccan's close economic, cultural, and

religious ties with Persia, Egypt, North Africa, and Turkey. Warangal, in particular, preserved its reputation into the nineteenth century and was famous for its silk pile carpets.

In the Punjab, Lahore had been recognized as a carpet-weaving centre since the seventeenth century but production subsequently declined, though there are a few references to good-quality jail carpets being made in the mid-nineteenth century. Amritsar, also in the Punjab, only began to produce carpets after the 1840s when Kashmiri refugees, fleeing from famine and the decline in the shawl-weaving industry, set up looms. By the end of the century this production was fairly successful. In Kashmir itself there may have been some carpet weaving at the beginning of the nineteenth century and gradually this replaced the shawl weaving, becoming well established by the end of the century. At this time carpets were also produced in Mirzapur and, on a smaller scale, in Rajasthan.

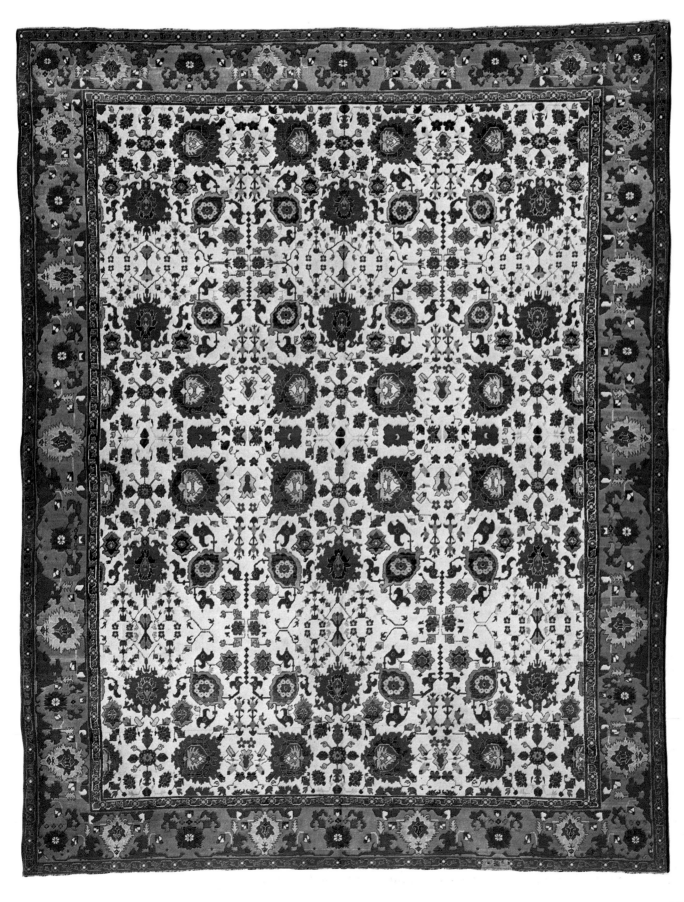

Dhurries

Ironically, it was the cloistered, uncommercial atmosphere of the Indian prison workshops which nurtured and promoted the renaissance of the other traditional Indian carpet, the dhurrie. In this environment, the technically unsurpassed pictorial dhurries were woven, and they so captured public attention at the Delhi International Exhibition of 1903–4 that new standards were set and the basis for today's modern industry was created. Although these flat-woven cotton carpets were mentioned at least as early as the fifteenth century, in a South Indian land grant, and were cited in the same Mughal chronical, the 'Ain-i-Akbari, which is the first record of the production of pile carpets in India, it must be assumed that dhurrie weaving is much older than any of our records and is one of the most ancient forms of floor covering.

These simple, weft-faced flat weaves have been woven in every part of India by all of the castes and religious groups traditionally associated with weaving. They are used by all of the major communities – Hindu, Muslim, and Sikh – and are common in both rural and urban areas. Dhurries perform a number of functions, which are indicated by their size. Small ones, approximately 1 by 2 metres (3 by 6 feet) are used as bed dhurries, covering the stretched rope base of the 'charpoy' bed, to be followed by the mattress, sheets, and blankets. These small, personal dhurries, though rarely seen by non-family members, may receive the most attention and be finely woven and lavishly decorated. Long narrow dhurries, sometimes up to 10 metres (35 feet) in length, are woven to be used as communal prayer carpets in mosques. They are normally decorated with individual niches and further embellished with all of the symbols normally associated with knotted-pile prayer carpets. Some of the communal prayer dhurries, or *safs*, found in mosques in the Deccan appear to date from the eighteenth century and are our oldest surviving examples. The individual niches are not necessarily required for prayer carpets, and other large, beautiful dhurries are also woven for that purpose. These large dhurries, however, are not restricted to use in mosques. Traditionally, they were used for all gatherings, weddings, or feasts and were always to be found spread under the huge canopied tents. Dhurries were also appropriate in more formal circumstances and some of the enormous *darbar* dhurries, woven for use in the palaces of Rajasthan and Punjab, are among the largest carpets ever made. These could reach widths of 8 metres (25 feet) and lengths of up to 18 metres (60 feet). They are still widely made and may be hand or machine loomed, and dyed with chemical or natural dyes. Although much of this production is for local use, there is also a flourishing export trade as dhurries are now very popular in the West.

Although dhurrie weaving may involve a number of different techniques, all Indian cotton dhurries are woven in the same weft-faced simple tabby weave that is used in kilims. The coloured patterns of the most common design, simple stripes, are produced by warp-sharing techniques such as dovetailing and double interlocking. Small vertical designs may utilize slit-tapestry weaving and the more complicated curvilinear elements of the pictorial dhurries even use 'eccentric' wefting which curves around the motifs.

a. Opposite above *A very fine bed dhurrie made in Bikaner central jail between 1900 and 1920. The designs are characteristic of Rajasthan but show a mixed Hindu-Muslim origin, the flowering shrubs being seen in Bikaner shawls, and the decanters in the centre and the tiny horizontal cypress trees being Mughal in origin.* 2.31m × 1.35m, 7'7" × 4'3".

b. Opposite below *An inscription on this striking pictorial dhurrie records that it was woven in Sabarmati jail, Ahmedabad in 1917. Such pieces would have been made as samples to show prospective clients, who would then order a copy without the inscription. The weaving of this one is extremely fine, comparable to many European tapestries.*

c. Right *A South Indian room dhurrie, which was probably placed in the courtyard of a mosque. The pastel colours are similar to those in multiple-niche prayer dhurries. Early twentieth century.* 3.30m × 2.36m, 10'10" × 7'9".

MOROCCO

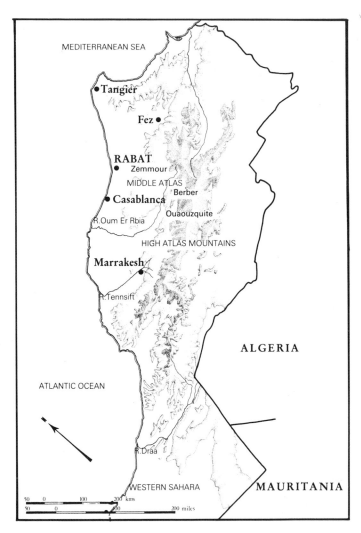

Morocco has a mixed Arab and Berber population of some six hundred tribes, each with their own traditions of weaving and design. Because of their indiscriminate love of colour, most of them have sadly succumbed to the bright allure of aniline dyes which has brought their weaving into very low repute. Nevertheless some tribes have managed to keep their integrity, and in recent years the government has instigated a system of quality control to encourage rural tribes to revert to traditional colours, patterns, and dyes.

In the high mountains of the Middle Atlas live Berber tribes whose flat weaves have a definite tribal authenticity, particularly the tent bands for their black goat-hair tents, the *hanbels* (blankets), and the herdsmen's cloaks, all of which retain traditional patterns of intricately interlocked diamonds. Their shaggy, long-piled rugs are woven with an instinctive eye for harmony in yellows, oranges, and shades of madder red. East of Rabat, the Zemmour weave saddle rugs using both pile and flat weaves together in a patchwork of rectangles with a central knotted panel under the saddle. Their saddle bags are intricate and showy, with long tasselled fringes, and their *hanbels* very large, woven on a traditional deep red ground with narrow stripes of tiny

geometric patterns. The Berbers of the High Atlas weave *glaoua*, or black pile rugs, in lustrous wool with stripes of flat weave. The Ouaouzguites have their own variation of these, in which the black pile is overlaid with a red and white trellis, and the back displays brilliant warp and weft threads, woven in broad bands of yellow and madder reds.

The settled Arab tribes of the Tennsift River weave *gtifa*, descendants of the traditional 'Rug of Kings'. These are thick red pile rugs with long bright aprons in typical Moroccan colours of chestnut, white, madder red, black, blue, and yellow. In the cities, the *gtifa* developed into 'Rabati' carpets. These are among the few Moroccan rugs with a disciplined formality approaching those of Anatolia, but they suffered a decline with ruinous use of aniline dyes in meaningless motifs. In 1936 the French established a model dyeing workshop for 'tapis de Chichaoua' to revive traditional red-ground Rabati rugs, and recently the government instigated a system of quality control to encourage rural tribes to use traditional patterns and dyes.

It is interesting that Moroccan patterns, built up from small squares of different-coloured pile, seem to owe more to Moorish tile and mosaic designs than any textile tradition.

TYPICAL SPECIFICATIONS

Warp
Middle Atlas – wool, sometimes with goat hair. High Atlas – wool, several colours. Gtifa – black goat hair. Rabati – red or red-brown wool.

Weft
Middle Atlas – wool, or wool and goat hair. High Atlas – several colours. Gtifa – black goat hair. Rabati – red or red-brown wool.

Pile
Wool. Middle Atlas – long, shaggy and coarse. High Atlas – medium, soft and silky. Rabati and Gtifa – medium to short.

Knot
Symmetrical, except for Middle Atlas rugs which also have asymmetrical and Berber knots.

Ends
Middle Atlas – plain weave with braided fringes. High Atlas – plain top fringe and plain or decorated end-apron. Gtifa – long, striped, plain weave aprons. Rabati – decorative flat weave.

Sides
Middle Atlas – overcast with blue wool. High Atlas – banded in several colours. Gtifa – overcast with black goat hair in saw-tooth pattern. Rabati – overcast with red or red-brown wool.

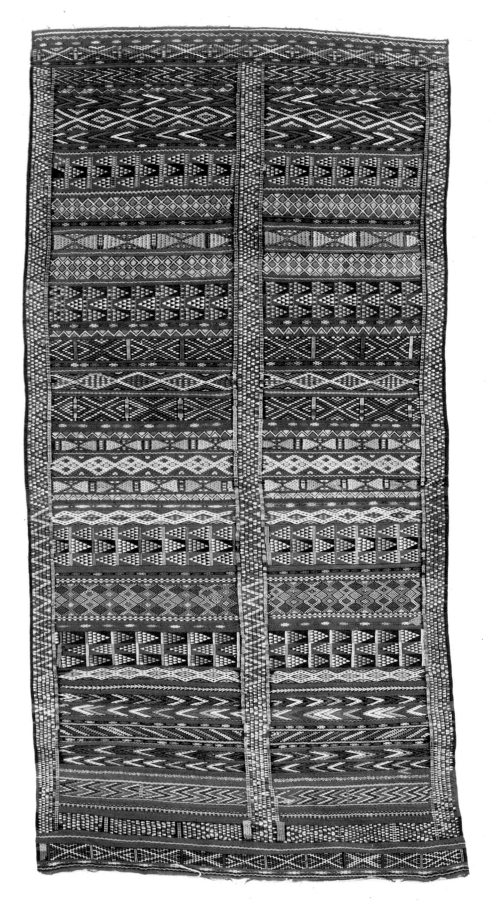

a. Opposite *A Rabati carpet with a number of features derived from Turkish rugs. These include the central medallion and the paired tulips in the outer border. Rabat, early twentieth century.* 2.40m × 1.83m, 7'10" × 6'. *W. Russell Pickering Collection*

b. Right *An unusual Zemmour* hanbel *with vertical stripes superimposed on horizontal bands of intricate patterning. Mid twentieth century.* 3.30m × 1.67m, 10'10" × 5'6". *W. Russell Pickering Collection*

EUROPE

Even the toughest and most durable carpets are fragile and although some may be treasured and cared for by each generation they seldom survive more than a few centuries. Consequently, with little information available, the history of early European carpets can be discussed only in general terms – based mainly on supposition and inference. It is generally agreed that the art of carpet knotting is a product of the East, brought to Spain in the Middle Ages and to north-western Europe by the fifteenth century. In Spain it is possible to see how eastern models were first copied and then adapted, sometimes subtly, sometimes dramatically, until the designs became totally European and only the technique was alien. In England almost exact copies of Turkish carpets were made, with English colouring, in the late sixteenth century; presumably domestic copies were cheaper than imported originals. In time the technique was adopted in every European country; wool was plentiful and carpets were admirably suited to the cold winter weather. Yet carpet knotting has never been uniformly successful in Europe: in Scandinavia, production was on a domestic basis and carpet knotting became a folk art; in France, it flourished in great workshops but only when protected and patronized by the monarch; elsewhere – and England is a typical example – it was finally left to architects and artists to commission carpets, almost as works of art, to complement their grand interiors, and it is therefore fitting that many later carpets are signed and dated – as works of art.

a. Opposite *This is probably the earliest surviving Spanish carpet, and is known as the Synagogue carpet since its design may represent the Ark of the Law. Fourteenth century.*
3.03m × 0.94m, 10′ × 3′.
Staatliche Museen zu Berlin, Islamisches Museum

Spain – the first European carpets

In the Middle Ages the Iberian peninsula formed a physical and cultural bridge between Christian Europe and the Islamic world, and Spain has often been described as the 'gateway' through which the oriental art of carpet knotting was Europeanized. The first known reference to carpets being woven in Spain is contained in a Latin poem of the eleventh century, and documents of the twelfth and thirteenth centuries indicate that carpet weaving was a well-developed industry in the provinces of Murcia and Andalusia, especially in the towns of Alcaraz and Letur. The Arab geographer El Idrisi, praising the woollen carpets made in Chinchilla, said it would be impossible for others to imitate them. Indeed, there is evidence that carpets were exported from Andalusia to Egypt, and it is known that they were used at the court of the Caliph in Cairo in 1124.

All surviving Spanish carpets made before the seventeenth century were woven with a single-warp knot, sometimes called the Spanish knot (see 18a). It is considered to be a characteristic peculiar to Spanish carpets, although fragments of similar technique have been found in Central Asia and are dated to between the third and sixth centuries. It may never be possible to indicate what, if any, connection there was between Central Asia and Spain, but it is agreed that the technique of weaving a knotted pile must have been introduced to Europe through the Eastern Mediterranean. It may be that the Coptic method of producing a looped pile fabric using a similar knot provided the inspiration for Spanish weavers, and it is known that Coptic weavers were employed in Spain in the tenth century.

After the Islamic conquest of Egypt in 642AD, the Arab armies moved steadily westwards and settled over the whole coastal area of North Africa. Extending the spread of Islam, they moved north by way of Gibraltar and, between 710 and 716, began to establish a political and cultural domination of Spain that was to last until the end of the fifteenth century. They brought with them craftsmen, skilled in building, wood carving, silk weaving, pottery, and metalwork, and introduced not only new designs but also new techniques from the Near East. Their first great capital was at Cordoba in Andalusia. It was established in 756 and was second only to Constantinople in size. It quickly rivalled Baghdad, the capital of the Eastern Caliphate, in wealth and culture. Several tenth-century accounts of diplomatic missions to Cordoba have survived, in which ambassadors marvel at the wonders of the palace, filled with beautiful mosaics, tapestries, and luxurious carpets, although there is no evidence that these carpets were knotted.

With the end of the tenth century came political intrigue and disunity. The Muslim states fell, one by one, to a Christian counter-attack, until only the province of Granada in the very south of Spain was left in Muslim hands. Consequently, the carpet-weaving areas referred to in medieval texts were within the newly re-conquered Christian areas. However, it is thought that the weavers were Muslim, or 'Mudéjar' as Muslims who had chosen to remain in Christian provinces were called. Although Spain was politically and religiously divided, the art of the Christian provinces could not remain isolated from three

centuries of Islamic tradition, nor could the cultural magnificence of Granada be ignored. The legacy is to be seen in later Spanish carpets which combine perfectly Islamic and Christian elements.

The exportation of carpets from Spain, which, it has been noted, was documented in the twelfth century, continued. When Eleanor of Castile arrived in London in 1255 to marry Prince Edward, she brought with her textiles and carpets from Spain to decorate her rooms in Westminster – it would seem, though, that the display of such wealth made her the target of much sarcasm. So well-developed was the carpet industry that Pope John XXII (1249–1334) could order carpets to be woven in Spain for his palace in Avignon, and Spanish carpets are listed in the inventories of many other European palaces. If Spanish carpets were known in Western Europe, it is not inconceivable that attempts were made to copy the technique. Parts of a large decorative hanging, woven with a single-warp knot, have survived in East Germany. The hanging was made by nuns in Quedlinburg in the Harz Mountains under Abbess Agnes sometime between 1186 and 1203. It is possible that the nuns discovered this knot independently, but it seems more reasonable to assume they were copying the technique from other pieces woven either in Spain or in the Near East. Throughout the Middle Ages, silk textiles from the East were brought to Western Europe by merchants and returning crusaders; knotted carpets were certainly among the goods carried but the numbers involved must have been small, for several hundred years were to pass before they had a real impact on any European country except Spain.

In Spain there was a flourishing carpet industry, but apart from some fragments excavated in Egypt, none of the Spanish carpets once counted as treasures and listed in medieval inventories has survived. What is thought to be the earliest surviving Spanish carpet is now in the Islamisches Museum in East Berlin (see 204a) and is usually dated to the fourteenth century. In attempts to explain the pattern, scholars have drawn analogies with silk designs in Central Asia and Persia and, perhaps more convincingly, with decorative features in a mid-fourteenth-century synagogue in Toledo; because of this, it is sometimes called the Synagogue carpet and it has been suggested that the design represents the Ark of the Law. It is unique, and the lack of comparable material makes it a mysterious and frustrating piece.

Fortunately enough examples of Spanish carpets have survived from the following centuries to show how the alien technique of carpet knotting was successfully adapted to express Spain's native style. By the second half of the fifteenth century Anatolian carpets were being exported to Spain, where they were copied using a single-warp knot. The carpets produced were not slavish imitations: changes were always made to the designs. Large-pattern Holbein carpets were copied and appear in inventories as 'wheel' carpets from Alcaraz. There is a wonderful example in the Textile Museum in Washington (see 207a) which shows how the Turkish design was adapted to Spanish taste. The detailed drawing and interlacing of the stars owes more to Moorish art than to Turkish, and similar designs can be found on Hispano-Moresque silks and architectural panels.

b. Left *The octagonal motifs in vertical rows of this Spanish carpet are based on a Turkish large-pattern Holbein rug. Sixteenth century.*
4.57m × 2.08m, 15′ × 6′10″.
Victoria and Albert Museum, London

a. Opposite *A 'wheel' carpet from Alcaraz, Spain. The design is derived from Turkish large-pattern Holbein rugs. Second half of the fifteenth century.*
1.85m × 0.93m, 6′1″ × 3′1″.
The Textile Museum, Washington

c. Above *Christian traditions are evident in this carpet, in the coats of arms and the figurative motifs of the borders. Spain, possibly Letur, fifteenth century.*
3.97m × 2.24m, 13′ × 7′4″
The Textile Museum, Washington

a. Above left *A handsome Spanish carpet with a field design of pomegranates, or lobed leaves, derived from contemporary silks. The border combines Christian and Islamic motifs. 1450–1500. 2.34m × 1.65m, 7′8″ × 5′4″. The Textile Museum, Washington*

b. Above right *A rather coarse copy of an Ottoman court carpet. The double-headed eagles in the border are symbols of the Hapsburg dynasty. Spanish, early seventeenth century. 4.11m × 2.36m, 13′6″ × 7′9″. Victoria and Albert Museum, London*

c. Opposite *A thoroughly European design with a field based on silk patterns. The monogram and skulls indicate that the carpet was woven for use in church. Spain, 1575–1625. 2.96m × 1.85m, 9′9″ × 6′1″. Victoria and Albert Museum, London*

The additional border at the top and bottom is decorated in this instance with an undulating pattern, but in many other Spanish carpets the decoration consists of non-Islamic motifs – human figures, birds, and animals – probably derived from Iberian folk art.

Another type of Spanish carpet displays an octagonal motif repeated in several vertical rows (see 207b). This is a variant of a large-patterned Holbein for which no complete Turkish prototype now exists. A fifteenth-century fragment of similar pattern, made with a symmetrical knot, is in the Archaeological Museum in Madrid and comparable carpets, thought to be Turkish, are depicted in European paintings. So .it is possible that these Spanish carpets provide the only real clue to a Turkish design which has not survived elsewhere.

Christian artistic tradition is evident in an important group of fifteenth-century armorial carpets, which are thought to have been woven in Letur. The coats of arms indicate for whom and approximately when they were woven. One carpet (see 207c) contains the arms of King Alfonso of Aragon and Queen Maria of Castile, so must have been woven at some time between their marriage in

1415 and their deaths in 1458. Many of these carpets are extremely long in relation to their width and were probably made for the long corridors of large Spanish houses. The small geometric field is thought to have been inspired by the type of tiled floor found in Christian houses, while the borders display a combination of Christian figurative motifs and traditional Islamic decoration, the men and animals being interlaced with a ribbon-like band originally derived from kufesque patterns. Similar borders, combining the two artistic styles, are found in another carpet (see 208a), one of several in which the design of pomegranates, or lobed leaves, is copied from contemporary Italian and Spanish silks. Such patterns, with fine, curving lines, made great demands on the skill of the carpet weaver.

In 1492 the forces of King Ferdinand and Queen Isabella finally expelled the Moors from Granada. Spain was then united under Catholic monarchs and turned increasingly away from Islamic art, looking towards Renaissance Europe for inspiration. However, Turkish carpets continued to be copied in Spain, the model on one occasion being a late-sixteenth-century Ottoman court carpet (see 208b). The ground is a reasonably faithful rendering of the original design, but it is badly drawn and woven to European taste using blue and yellow, instead of red with a hint of blue and green. The double-headed eagles in the border were the symbol of the Hapsburg dynasty. Of similar date, but thoroughly European, is a carpet (see 208c) with a border of conventional Renaissance design and a field reminiscent of contemporary silk patterns. The use of the monogram IHS (*Iesus Hominum Salvator*) and the four skulls indicates that the carpet was woven for church use, either at funerals or during Holy Week – it also reflects the near-obsession with death that prevailed in the Spanish church during the Inquisition.

Some Mudéjar craftsmen had remained in Spain under asylum until they were banished in 1609, and from that date all practical links with Spain's Islamic past seem to have been severed. During the seventeenth century the carpet weaving industry moved to Cuenca in the north and the symmetrical knot gradually replaced the Spanish – which had always been more difficult to tie, but which had enabled the weavers to produce their delicate curving lines. The designs generally followed the main European fashions. Philip V (1683–1746) established a Royal Factory for carpet weaving in Madrid under the direction of a Flemish master. Although extremely fine carpets were woven here, they were designed in a French style, often indistinguishable from the products of the Savonnerie factory in France. From the middle of the eighteenth century onwards Spanish weavers continued to produce knotted carpets, but the inspiration for the designs came not from Iberian art but from France.

England – early carpets

The arrival in England of Spanish carpets with Eleanor of Castile in 1255 seems to have had no lasting effect; rushes continued to be scattered on floors of even State Apartments and as late as 1598 it was reported that Queen Elizabeth's chambers were strewn with hay. This is despite the fact that some Turkish carpets had been imported into England, via Venice, in the early sixteenth century. Cardi-

a. Left *An English carpet,
dated 1585. The field is a copy
of Turkish Star Ushak designs.*
2.74m × 1.83m, 9′ × 6′.
*His Grace the Duke of
Buccleuch and Queensberry*

b. Below *A fragment of an
English carpet in which the
royal coat of arms is
surrounded by stylized flowers.
Dated 1600.*
0.53m × 1.06m, 1′10″ × 3′6″.
*Victoria and Albert Museum,
London*

c. Opposite above *A French
Savonnerie carpet, woven
between 1673 and 1681 for
Louis XIV.*
*The Metropolitan Museum,
New York. Gift of the H.
Samuel Kress Foundation*

d. Opposite below *Knotted
carpets made in England were
known as Turkey work. The
smaller panels were used for
chair upholstery or cushions.
Early seventeenth century.*
0.48m × 0.60m, 1′7″ × 2′.
*Victoria and Albert Museum,
London*

nal Wolsey had received sixty carpets in 1520, although it had taken him (one of the most powerful men in England) over two years to negotiate for them. When he fell from favour in 1528 his possessions were forfeited to the Crown, and presumably the carpets were added to those already owned by Henry VIII. When Henry died in 1547, his inventories listed over four hundred carpets of "Turkey making", which is generally understood to refer to knotted pile carpets. The King is usually depicted standing on a carpet, and so detailed and accurate are the portraits by Hans Holbein that it is possible to identify these carpets with confidence as imports from Turkey. Other contemporary Tudor portraits display curious features in the carpets, which could be due to artistic inaccuracy, or the artists could be faithfully depicting English-made copies of Turkish carpets. There are three matching Star Ushak carpets at Boughton House in Northamptonshire which were made in England, possibly in Norwich: one is undated, one bears the date 1584, and one 1585 (see 210a); they all contain the arms of Montagu and Harrington woven into the border on each side. As in Spain, the English nobility often commissioned weavers to include heraldic devices in the designs (see 210b).

The English were not slow to adapt the technique of carpet knotting to local artistic traditions and carpet weavers developed their own style, based on the common flowers to be found in every English garden. Roses, honeysuckle, and oak leaves were among the motifs incorporated into carpet designs (see 210d). All knotted carpets made in England were called 'Turkey work', and as large carpets were very expensive, smaller panels were made in sizes suitable for chair upholstery or cushion covers. These were popular throughout the seventeenth century and production did not decline until the 1680s, when importation of Turkish and other Eastern carpets increased. By the middle of the seventeenth century both the Turkey Company and the East India Company were shipping carpets from the East to England, indicating not only the extensive network of trade established by England, but also the extent of the nation's wealth. Almost all commercial attempts at carpet knotting in England seem to have died as a consequence of the number of Eastern imports on the market. When the industry was revived in the middle of the eighteenth century, with help from France, it was looked upon as something new and not connected with the Turkey work of the previous generation.

France

Although copies of Turkish carpets must have been woven in the sixteenth century, the real beginnings of carpet weaving in France can be dated to the opening years of the seventeenth century. In 1601 Henri IV convened a Commission to establish new trade and manufacture in the kingdom, to which, in 1604, Jean Fortier proposed the establishment of a factory to weave carpets in the manner of the Turks. The same suggestion was made by Pierre Dupont in 1605, and in 1608 Dupont was granted a licence to use a workshop in the Louvre. From the beginning, designs were commissioned from artists of repute and the carpets were woven in the style of contemporary decorative art. In 1627 Dupont and a pupil of his, called Simon

Lourdet, also acquired premises near the Colline de Chaillot which had formerly been a soap factory. It is from this that the name Savonnerie originated, and it is applied to all the products of the factory – carpets, panels, and wall-hangings – which were woven exclusively for the court. From its establishment the factory was given royal patronage and protection: a law was passed temporarily forbidding the importation of carpets from the East into France, and the Savonnerie workshops were granted a monopoly for the production of knotted pile carpets. At the same time, another law decreed that a certain number of poor children had to be apprenticed each year.

The carpets were totally European in design. In 1663 Colbert, one of Louis XIV's ministers, conferred a new constitution on the Savonnerie workshop, which stated that a painter from the Royal Academy had to inspect the designs produced for the carpets and had to teach drawing to the staff every month. Initially the painter Charles Le Brun was responsible for the designs woven for the Tuileries and the Louvre; they included landscapes and classical and allegorical scenes, set among acanthus leaves, scrolls, and naturalistic flowers (see 210c). In 1682 the court moved to the palace of Versailles and the riches and power of the Sun King soon became known throughout Europe.

However, many Protestant craftsmen had been leaving France because of increasing persecution, culminating in 1685 in the Revocation of the Edict of Nantes which had previously guaranteed freedom of worship in France. It is estimated that at least sixty thousand fled to England alone. The loss of skilled artisans, plus the financial crises arising from the wars in the latter part of the reign of Louis XIV, meant that by the end of the century many looms at Savonnerie were idle. Because their carpets were woven only to furnish royal palaces or to be given as gifts by the king, the fortune of the factory fluctuated with the size of the royal purse. But after this period of little activity work did start in 1711 on a series of carpets for the chapels and smaller rooms of Versailles and Fontainebleau, and it was not until the end of the eighteenth century that some looms were again idle.

The style of Savonnerie carpets did, of course, evolve in the course of these two centuries, but the changes were often slight and generally speaking the designers showed extreme conservatism. It was not unknown for old designs to be re-woven, and in the late 1780s reproductions were made of carpets originally designed and woven in the 1660s. The practice of using an artist to control the designs continued, and those involved included Belin de Fontenay, Pierre Josse Perrot and François Boucher. The magnificent mid-seventeenth-century allegorical scenes and classical ornamentation gave way to graceful, curvilinear, rococo patterns in the eighteenth century. The informal atmosphere of the age was reflected in the royal palaces: at both the Louvre and Versailles the large rooms were sub-divided into more intimate areas and the decoration of the walls, the furniture, and the furnishings reflected the prevailing tendency to turn away from the rigid classical forms of the previous century. The carpet designs became a little less crowded; more floral elements in the form of garlands and wreaths were introduced, and the colours became lighter,

a. Above *Towards the end of the eighteenth-century, styles became lighter and more informal. This French Savonnerie carpet has naturalistic swags of flowers and fruit. (Cut and rejoined.) 2.20m × 1.80m, 7'3" × 5'11". Victoria and Albert Museum, London*

b. Opposite *This design is inspired by the inlaid wooden floors made during this period. Aubusson, France, First Empire period, 1804–14. 5.80m × 7.10m, 19' × 23'. Musée Nissim de Camondo, Paris*

with pink, yellow, and pale blue replacing the browns and black which had been used as ground colours (see 212a). Financial problems again beset Savonnerie towards the end of the century and attempts were made to keep down costs by using a coarser warp and weft and by weaving designs which contained fewer curved lines. In an effort to raise money Savonnerie carpets were offered for sale to the public, but with little success for the lesser nobility preferred the excellent, but cheaper, products of the carpet looms at Aubusson.

Aubusson, on the banks of the River Creuse, was well known for the tapestries which had been woven there for several centuries. In 1743 the King's Council decided to establish carpet weaving at Aubusson to meet a growing demand for knotted carpets, which could not be satisfied by the importation of expensive Turkish and Persian ones. Vertical looms and samples of Turkish carpets were sent from Paris and for the first three years the venture was financed by the Crown. In 1746 two Paris merchants, Pierre Mage and Jacques Dessarteaux, took over the workshops as a private enterprise. Jean-Joseph Dumons, who had been a designer of tapestries at Aubusson, was

appointed to design carpets, but for several years his designs were direct copies of various Turkish carpets then being imported. Although a government inspector reported that these copies were equal to any work produced in Turkey, an Aubusson carpet made in 1745 for Cardinal de Rohan is a very inadequate interpretation of the Smyrna model. Aubusson designs were much less complex than those of Savonnerie; their carpets were also cheaper and less exclusive, although inventories from Versailles show that a considerable number were used in the less important rooms.

By 1750 it was becoming apparent that customers were no longer happy with copies of oriental carpets and attempts were made to create new designs. Perrot, who had designed carpets for Savonnerie, was consulted and the king sent Savonnerie carpets to Aubusson to be used as models. Then, in 1753, a new style was created when the painter Le Lorrain designed a carpet which he called *à grande mosaïque* – referring to the central medallion of flowers. It was a purely French style, composed of garlands, rosettes, and scattered flowers, in some ways similar to contemporary Savonneries but simpler. This developed

a. Left *Detail of a carpet made in Exeter by Claude Passavant in 1757. The basic design is Savonnerie but the inclusion of the dog is an English feature. (4.57m × 3.81m, 15' × 12'6".) Victoria and Albert Museum, London*

in the last two decades of the eighteenth century into a more linear style, in keeping with the fashion for Greek and Roman ornament. The ground of the carpets was often woven in shades of one colour – *en camaïeu*, giving the effect of a cameo – to create wonderful effects (see 212b). Two types of carpet were made at Aubusson: knotted pile carpets woven on vertical looms, and later in the eighteenth century, flat-woven carpets produced on horizontal looms in the manner of traditional tapestries. To a certain extent the same designs could be woven in either technique, and as the fashion for tapestries declined during the First Empire, it was the carpet production that kept Aubusson in business.

The Revolution of 1789 proved a trying time for France, but with the Proclamation of the Empire in 1804 an era of great prosperity for the Savonnerie and Aubusson weavers opened. Carpets were ordered in vast numbers from both workshops to replace those destroyed or damaged during the Revolution. Two architects, Percier and Fontaine, created an Empire style, basing it on Etruscan and Roman ornament. They supervised the design of carpets in order to achieve total unity in interior decoration. The carpets for the palaces were enormous, and were covered with classical war-like motifs – shields, helmets, lances, and trophies. The floral tradition survived however. Several carpets of the period seem to mirror formal gardens, with flower-beds and pathways. Others retain the popular garlands and

add either classical figures such as Muses, or birds such as peacocks or swans. Although the use of carpets was becoming more commonplace, hand-knotted carpets were still expensive and from the mid-eighteenth century their limited market was gradually reduced by the increasing production of machine-woven carpets which were eventually manufactured on power-looms in the mid-nineteenth century.

England – the eighteenth century

Less than one century earlier it had been the French who had reintroduced the art of carpet knotting into England. In 1750 two disgruntled craftsmen from Savonnerie took rooms in Westminster and began to make carpets. Although they succeeded in obtaining some form of patronage from the Duke of Cumberland and made a carpet for him to present to the Princess of Wales, their venture was doomed to financial failure. They moved to Fulham in 1753 to share a friend's tapestry weaving studio but were forced to sell the entire factory in 1755; their looms and designs were purchased at auction by a Swiss emigré, Claude Passavant, who took them to Exeter. Two early English carpets have survived from Passavant's factory, one dated 1757 (see 214a) and one dated 1759. Although the inclusion of a dog in the middle of the 1757 one is completely English, the basic designs owe a great deal to Savonnerie carpets and it is possible that they are based on models brought over by the two French weavers.

The early Georgian period (1714–1760) was a time of elegance, prosperity, and expanding trade. In 1756, in an attempt to improve the design and quality of British products, the Royal Society of Arts offered annual premiums for, among other things, the making of carpets in the Turkish and Persian manner. It was not solely artistic interest that prompted such an offer; the Society estimated that £16,000 per year were spent importing oriental carpets. If they could be made in England it would not only create employment, but would also create a demand for large quantities of English wool. The first recipient was Thomas Moore of Chiswell Street, London, who shared the premium with Thomas Whitty, a woollen-cloth manufacturer of Axminster. The following year, 1758, Thomas Whitty shared the premium with Claude Passavant. Whitty, founder of the Axminster Carpet Company, had been inspired to copy some Turkish carpets imported by a friend, and the first one he made was purchased by Lady Shaftesbury. Within only a few years the Axminster factory was thriving, although as no mark was woven into the carpets it is often impossible to recognize its early products. Initially oriental models were copied, but soon new designs were used which followed contemporary styles in the decorative arts.

It was the age of great houses and great architects, and fashion demanded that the pattern of the carpet reflected that of the ceiling decoration (see 217a). Several architects took great pains to achieve this unity of design and Robert Adam often designed carpets, to be woven by Thomas Moore of Chiswell Street, for specific rooms in houses which he had built or enlarged. The carpet in the Red Drawing Room at Syon House, near London, was designed by Adam and bears the name Thomas Moore with the date 1769 in the border. Several carpets designed by Adam and woven by Moore are at Osterley Park House. Thomas Chippendale, the furniture maker, seems however to have preferred to recommend Thomas Whitty of Axminster to his clients. Under the influence of Adam, designs became more classical in feeling, some even incorporating Etruscan and Pompeian motifs.

A totally different style became fashionable at the beginning of the nineteenth century, when the Prince Regent commissioned the Axminster factory to weave three carpets for the Royal Pavilion at Brighton. They were made for the Music Room, the North Drawing Room, and the Banqueting Room. One measured 18½ by 12 metres (61 by 40 feet), weighed 772 kilos (1,700 pounds), and was the largest carpet in the country. The other two were designed by Robert Jones; one was circular and the other was made with end-pieces specially designed to fit into alcoves. The designs show the Chinese influence so apparent in the decoration of the Pavilion, with gold stars, birds, insects, dragons, and lotus blossoms. These were certainly the largest and probably the most exotic carpets woven by the Axminster looms, but activity in the factory was decreasing. Thomas Moore's prosperity had declined after the death of Adam in 1792 and his factory was sold in 1795. Thomas Whitty's factory at Axminster lasted longer, but was finally sold in 1836 to a Mr Blackmore who took the

looms and weavers to Wilton and continued production there. He was relatively successful, was commissioned to weave carpets for Windsor Castle, and exhibited at the Great Exhibition of 1851. His carpets were typically mid-Victorian extravagances of flowers, depicted in a variety of styles – French, Italian, and Persian.

The first half of the nineteenth century was not an easy time for the weavers of hand-knotted carpets. The prolonged war with France had drained the economies of both France and England and the rich were no longer able to spend as freely as they had once done, although tremendous prosperity awaited England once the inventions of the Industrial Revolution bore fruit. The development of power-driven looms enabled manufacturers to produce cloth, and carpets, faster and cheaper than ever before and made attractive furnishings available to a wide market. Machine-woven carpets were now within the budget of most middle-class families. These carpets were made in many centres: Kidderminster, Halifax, Wilton, Axminster, Edinburgh, and Kilmarnock. It is estimated that in 1850 there were over four thousand power-looms in Kidderminster alone. How could hand weavers compete?

Scandinavia and other European countries

It is in the non-industrialized countries of nineteenth-century Europe that the tradition of hand-knotting continued. The fact that Anatolian carpets existed in Scandinavia by the fifteenth century is attested by the Marby rug (see 49b) and by the appearance of Turkish carpet motifs in Scandinavian embroideries. The making of pile carpets using the symmetrical knot probably dates back several centuries in Finland, and it is a matter of debate whether this technique was borrowed, as it was elsewhere in Europe, or whether it developed independently.

Until 1809 Finland was a province of Sweden and it is therefore almost impossible to separate the two artistic traditions; however, the knotted *ryijy* (rya) carpets of Finland have survived in larger numbers and are better documented. The word *ryijy* comes from a Scandinavian dialect, and means rough and shaggy; the earliest *ryijy* rugs probably had a long woollen pile, perhaps resembling a sheep's fleece. When mentioned in sixteenth-century inventories they are described by colour, and it is commonly held that they were undecorated. The colours listed are white, black, and grey (perhaps all undyed wool), and occasionally yellow and red. An inventory dated 1558 from Uppland Castle included white *ryijys* with black borders. The fact that the early rugs were so plain may indicate that they were not copied from Turkish imports. As Turkish carpets are listed in a 1563 inventory, Finnish weavers certainly had the opportunity to copy patterns and may not have chosen to do so because they already had a long-established tradition of plain pile carpets. A book on military science by Peder Månsson, published in 1552, suggested that *ryijy* rugs ought to be used to repair any breaches made in a defensive wall, which seems to indicate that they were in plentiful supply. Indeed, they were not the luxury products of Spanish, English, or French looms; they were essential household articles used as bed-coverings.

215

a. Opposite *The pattern of this carpet is designed to reflect that of the ceiling decoration. Its lightness and elegance is characteristic of the neo-classical period. Axminster, England, late eighteenth century.*
6.85m × 5m, 22'6" × 16'3".
Victoria and Albert Museum, London

b. Right above *A Finnish* ryijy *rug, dated 1799 with the initials MLT. This could have been woven as a bed covering or as a decorative hanging, and it has long tufts of white wool on the reverse side to give extra warmth.*
1.75m × 1.21m, 5'9" × 4'.
Victoria and Albert Museum, London

c. Right below *This flat-woven rug is known as a* röllakan *and was probably used as a cover for beds or chests. Norway, late eighteenth or early nineteenth century.*
1.52m × 1.21m, 5' × 4'.
Victoria and Albert Museum, London

Plain rugs, woven for warmth and not decoration, are more easily made if the rows of knots are spaced and if the pile is left long; it is only when the pattern becomes important that the pile must be dense and short. The surviving *ryijy* rugs which are patterned date only from the eighteenth century onwards. They are woven with a symmetrical knot, although it is sometimes tied around four or even six warp threads. In some rugs only two shoots of weft separate the rows of knots, but in others there is a centimetre (half an inch) or so of plain weave. *Ryijys* are usually woven with the pile on both sides. Many incorporate dates and initials in their designs and are said to be bridal rugs, woven to commemorate a marriage, then used in the home as bed-coverings or decorative hangings (see 217b). Several variations of certain designs exist; were they the products of the same workshop, which offered clients a choice of design (and date and initial), or were patterns available for domestic production? By the middle of the nineteenth century designs had become more rigid, and because of the inevitable influence of industrialization the production of *ryijy* rugs declined.

There is no evidence that Europeans were producing decorated flat-woven carpets before the eighteenth century. Although woollen covers have survived from several countries (see 217c), there is nothing to indicate that they were used as floor coverings; they are not hard-wearing textiles and although they may have been placed on the floor to decorate the house on special occasions, it is more probable that they were used to cover beds, chests, and coffins. It is really only towards the end of the nineteenth century, in the Balkans, that flat-woven carpets were produced in any great numbers. The influence of Turkish techniques and designs is apparent in the early pieces, which are often indistinguishable from Anatolian kilims;

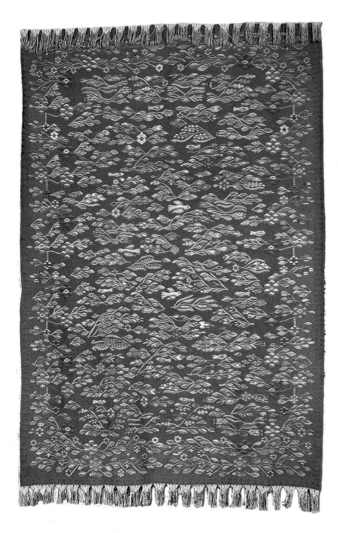

but a strong nationalistic feeling, following the overthrow of the Ottoman yoke in the latter part of the nineteenth century, resulted in a more European style reminiscent of traditional tapestry hangings (see 218a).

England – William Morris

Several societies were founded in the second half of the nineteenth century in an attempt to call attention to the poor standard of artistic design. The carpets and carpet designs which had been exhibited in the Great Exhibition of 1851 were pastiches of many styles, both national and historical, and were based on naturalistic flowers, shaded to give the impression of a third dimension. These were condemned by many critics, including William Morris who had strong views on carpet design. Morris had an extensive knowledge of Persian, Turkish, and Chinese carpets and, as an Art Referee, advised the South Kensington Museum (now the Victoria and Albert Museum) on the acquisition of oriental carpets. Two of the Museum's finest Persian carpets, the Ardebil (see 37d) and the Chelsea, were acquired on his recommendation. It is interesting to note that he used only oriental carpets in his own house and there is no evidence that he ever used the products of his own looms. If he condemned English carpets, he also condemned the imported Eastern ones of his time, criticizing their indiscriminate use of aniline dyes and their

a. Above left *Flat-woven rugs were made in Eastern Europe. When Ottoman rule of these regions came to an end in the late nineteenth century, the designs became more European. Rumania, 1920s.* 3.37m × 2.34m, 11'1" × 7'8". *Victoria and Albert Museum, London*

b. Above right *The Bullerswood carpet, woven in 1899 by Morris & Co. The directional quality of the design reflects Morris's interest in Persian Vase carpets.* 7.64m × 4m, 25'1" × 13'1". *Victoria and Albert Museum, London*

a. Above *This carpet was designed by Duncan Grant and displayed in the Ideal Home Exhibition of 1913. The work of the Omega Workshop was influenced by new movements in design and painting in Europe.*
2.74m × 2.26m, 9′ × 7′6″.
Victoria and Albert Museum, London

b. Right *The British designer Betty Joel had her carpets woven in China. The close knotting and method of clipping a groove around outlines was particularly suited to her designs. 1935–7.*
2.71m × 1.82m, 8′10″ × 6′.
Victoria and Albert Museum, London

westernized designs, which were frequently copied from English machine-woven carpets.

His first hand-knotted carpet was made in 1878 and the following year the coach-house and adjoining stable at Kelmscott House, his home in Hammersmith on the banks of the Thames, were converted into weaving sheds. The carpets produced were small in size and the early ones bear the Hammersmith mark – the letter 'M' with a hammer and waves to indicate the Thames. He was determined that the design should lie "absolutely flat upon the ground" with no attempt to create a three-dimensional effect. Many of his designs are based on Persian models, but they were never copies; he was selective in his approach and seemed concerned with the meaning behind the designs. Morris did not expect his inexperienced weavers to create fine lines and details, so he gave them reasonably bold designs. From 1883 to 1889 he adopted a classical format for his carpets, with a central medallion and quartered medallions in the four corners. These are his most traditional designs, in which Persian influence is easily discerned. From 1887 onwards a number of carpets were woven by Morris & Co. with directional patterns, with a definite top and bottom. This is partly due to Morris's interest at that time in the Persian 'Vase' carpets (see 70c), which have a directional bias, and partly due to the increasing involvement of Henry Dearle in the administration of the firm and the designing of its products. The 'Bullerswood' carpet (see 218b) was

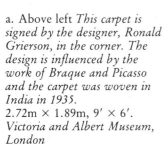

a. Above left *This carpet is signed by the designer, Ronald Grierson, in the corner. The design is influenced by the work of Braque and Picasso and the carpet was woven in India in 1935.*
2.72m × 1.89m, 9′ × 6′.
Victoria and Albert Museum, London

b. Above right *Contemporary designers are also making carpets. This was made in England by Helen Yardley in 1984.*
1.85m × 1.20m, 6′ × 4′.

woven in 1889 for the Sanderson family and is probably the company's most famous carpet. It was designed partly by Dearle who, unlike Morris, expected the weavers to reproduce extremely intricate details and to weave fine, graceful lines. Often the results were less graceful than he expected, and scholars have seen the correcting hand of Morris in the Bullerswood design, trying to compensate for Dearle's over-attention to detail. 'Bullerswood' is the last carpet that Morris had any part in designing and from 1890 Henry Dearle was solely responsible for the design of all new carpets.

Small rugs, more characteristic of the Morris style, were woven in the early twentieth century, but in 1912 the carpet looms were transferred to the Wilton Royal Carpet Company. Financial problems dictated that carpet designs should be only those most acceptable to the market and one design, dated 1917, for the Library of Australia House in London, is almost a straight copy of an Adam design from the late eighteenth century. In time, the economic turmoil created by the First World War brought a slow death to Morris & Co.

The Swan Song?

The Great War brought a swifter demise to less well-established companies. Several English artists had consciously rejected both the stuffiness of Victorian design and the wholesomeness of the Arts and Crafts Movement, and were seeking to create a new style worthy of the twentieth century. The most interesting group was the Omega Workshop, established in Bloomsbury by Roger Fry in 1913. He was greatly influenced by Continental design – especially the work of the Wiener Werkstätte in Austria and Paul Poiret's Studio Martine in Paris – and by the work of the Post-Impressionist painters. Fry considered that British design since Morris had once more become a pastiche of many different styles. The artists he gathered under the informal umbrella of the Omega Workshop worked mainly as designers, delegating the actual production to others. They would accept commissions to design furniture and furnishings for specific houses and employed contemporary artists to design original pieces. The textiles and carpets produced by the short-lived workshop (see 219a) used strong abstract designs, in complete contrast to the uninspired decoration common at the time.

It is strange that the Great War should have precipitated the end of several ventures in Britain, and yet have encouraged the growth of the Bauhaus movement in Germany after 1919. Under the leadership of Walter Gropius, its aim was to train artists and craftsmen to design for modern technology and mass production. Some knot-ted carpets were produced, but more attention was paid to the textures and patterns that could be achieved with a flat weave. It was really the Cubist painters of France who had the greatest effect on carpet designs. The Exposition des Arts Décoratifs in Paris in 1925, from which the term Art Deco is derived, was a statement of France's total supremacy in the decorative arts. Modern interiors were pale and streamlined, and textiles – curtains and carpets – were used to introduce abstract splashes of colour. British artists responded well to the challenge laid down by France and the 1930s witnessed a renaissance in carpet design. Most of the mechanized carpet factories were reluctant to move away from their tried-and-tested patterns that guaranteed an income. However, the Wilton Royal Carpet Company and the Edinburgh Weavers were willing to make efforts to produce the type of carpet which would be suited to modernistic architecture and interior design. Marion Dorn and E. McKnight Kauffer were among the first to design carpets to the high artistic standards set by France, and sold their products to luxury hotels, ocean liners, and individual clients.

The European knotted carpet may seem to have travelled along a divergent path, away from Eastern carpets, but the 1930s saw a remarkable swing back towards the source as several artists discovered the technical limitations of European weavers. Betty Joel had carpets woven at Tientsin in China to her designs because she required a finer pile than was being achieved in Britain using a jute warp and a symmetrical knot. The Chinese method of using the asymmetrical knot on a cotton warp and of clipping a groove around each motif was specially suited to her very precise designs (see 219b). For similar reasons, Ronald Grierson sent his designs to be woven in India (see 220a).

It is difficult to anticipate the future of hand-knotted carpet weaving in Europe. Nothing particularly new has been created since the Second World War, and it is still a slow, therefore expensive, way of producing a floor covering. The social and economic face of Europe has changed: the few Royal Houses and noble families which remain are not commissioning carpets; governments have more pressing concerns; the rich are husbanding their resources in these times of economic depression. Few commercial firms are knotting carpets by hand, although several artists and craftsmen are willing to accept commissions for small rugs (see 220b); and it seems improbable that the situation will change – although fashion, by its very nature, is cyclical. As carpet production increases in many parts of the Near and Far East, and imported carpets are more numerous and less expensive, the vogue in Europe is once more for oriental carpets.

NORTH AMERICA

Considering the use of carpets in American domestic interiors in 1850, Andrew Jackson Downing remarked, "The floors of the better cottages in this country – at least, in the Northern States are universally covered with carpet or matting." His observation reflected a striking change which had recently occurred, as a direct result of changing taste and technological evolution. Floor coverings had not been commonly used in the earliest American homes of the seventeenth century; indeed, it was not until the very end of the colonial period that rugs and carpets began to be used on floors, even in the homes of the wealthy. Many of the carpets first used were imported, and these became the design sources for the first American-made rugs and carpets.

The first half of the nineteenth century saw the coexistence of large quantities of home-produced goods, increasing output of high quality factory-made goods, and the development of handmade products of great individuality and beauty. Rug making, like quilt making, became a form of artistic expression in which the individual objects transcend utility to become art objects in their own right.

At the beginning of the nineteenth century, many rural American women were skilled in textile making and those with a certain amount of leisure time were able to employ these skills in making floor coverings. Some of these women even sought to imitate imported straw matting or painted floor cloths. Writing in 1877, Mary A. Beach remembered her childhood home, saying, "As far back as I can remember, there were no carpets in the house. Very soon, however, Mother herself cut flags in the marshy places and having colored linen blue, red, yellow for warp, wove some homemade matting. This was for the best room, which was the north front room, the place for company." This remarkable woman made a painted carpet for another room in her home, first weaving a linen ground-cloth and nailing it to the side of the barn to be painted in oils. Her daughter stated that "It did not cover the south room entirely, but it did almost and saved scrubbing."

Lyman Beecher also recalled his mother's unusual efforts to create a painted carpet for their home, saying:

"We had no carpets; there was not a carpet from end to end of the town. All had sanded floors, some of them worn through. Your mother introduced the first carpet. Uncle Lot gave me some money, and I had an itch to spend it. Went to a vendue and bought a bale of cotton. She spun it, and had it woven; then she laid it down, sized it and painted it in oils, with a border all around it, and bunches of roses and other flowers over the centre. She sent to New York for her colors and ground and mixed them herself. The carpet was nailed down on the garret floor and she used to go up there and paint."

Woven rush mats and freehand-painted floorcloths were fragile things which have seldom survived to be studied, yet they certainly added colour to the rooms in which they were used and must have been sources of pride to their creators.

Handwoven carpets

The desire to provide colourful floor coverings in early America was more often expressed in handwoven carpets. These were fabricated in strips ranging from 68 to 100 centimetres (27 to 40 inches) wide which were then sewn together to form room-sized carpets. Most carpets of this type were flat-woven, without pile. Some were made at home, but most people employed local professional weavers. Plain tabby-woven carpets were made with striped or neutral warps and a filling of colourful rags. Sometimes rag carpets were made in carefully controlled colour patterns, but often the rags were simply used as they came. In such cases the carpets were referred to as 'hit or miss'. The earliest rag-filled carpets have homespun linen warps (see 223a), but at least from the second quarter of the nineteenth century, factory-spun cotton warps were pre-ferred. Late in the nineteenth century, the Shakers brought rag carpet making to perfection and became widely known for the durability of their products, as well as for the beauty of their colour arrangements which sometimes featured dramatic chevron patterns achieved by twisting two coloured wefts together as the work progressed (see 223b).

Warp-faced carpets with colourful lengthwise stripes were widely used in stairhalls. These imitated imported striped carpets, called in newspaper advertisements "Venetian carpets", and were used in the late eighteenth and throughout the nineteenth century. Indeed, striped carpets were so popular that they were even imitated in painted floorcloths and painted floors. In 1830, a New England minister's wife, Ruth Henshaw Bascom, recorded painting her parlour floor in stripes of blue, yellow, purple, red, and green in a pattern that simulated a striped carpet.

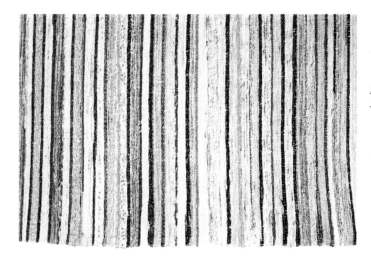

a. Left *The earliest rag carpets used random rag strips and a handspun linen warp. This thrifty recycling of wornout textiles appealed to many people and provided colourful floor coverings. New England, 1800–30. Detail. (1.93m × 2.08m, 6'4" × 6'9".) Old Sturbridge Village, Massachusetts.*

b. Above left and right *Although similar to those produced by other professional weavers, Shaker rugs are renowned for their attractive colours and durability. Details. Late nineteenth century. Hancock Shaker Village, Pittsfield, Massachusetts*

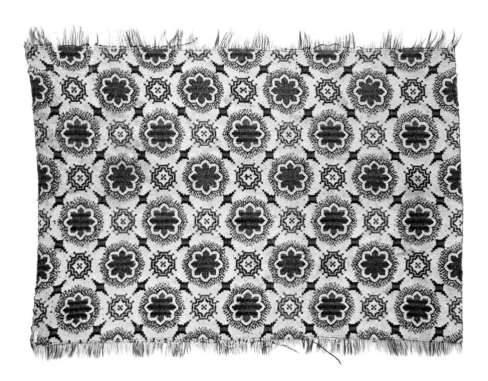

a. Left *A flat-woven carpet in a block design, woven by a resident of Sturbridge and used as a parlour carpet for many years. The warp is of homespun wool, coloured with natural dyes. Circa 1830. 0.60m × 0.88m, 2' × 3'. Old Sturbridge Village, Massachusetts*

b. Above *A carpet made in the early nineteenth century by the Copp family, who were professional weavers. It is made of wool and is reversible. Detail. The National Museum of American History, Washington*

Other types of flat-woven carpets employed more complex techniques and produced reversible goods with geometric 'block' (see 224a) or 'bird's-eye' designs. There are many patterns for these in early nineteenth-century professional weavers' manuals and collections of manuscript drafts. An excellent surviving example is that in the collection of textiles from the Copp family of Stonington, Connecticut, now in the National Museum of American History in Washington (see 224b).

Needlemade carpets

Certainly the most creative carpets made by American women are those made with the needle, rather than the loom. Few room-sized examples of these survive, with the notable exception of the Caswell Carpet in the Metropolitan Museum of Art (see 225a). The maker of this carpet, Zeruah Higley Gurnsey, worked on it for two years, finally finishing it in 1835, ten years before she became Mrs Caswell. The carpet is made of homespun and handwoven linen squares which are entirely covered with colourful woollen embroidery. Each square was placed in a frame and the embroidery done with a tambour hook which produced a continuous chain of wool on the surface. No two squares are alike, but there is remarkable colour harmony in the overall carpet. Most of the motifs are naturalistic, with fruit and flowers predominating. In some squares there are birds or butterflies. Some of the motifs are highly original, but others are clearly based on quilt squares. Three of the squares show cats or dogs curled up on striped, or Venetian, carpeting. One section of the carpet is removable, since it was intended to serve as a hearth rug. In this area the overall design is larger, with a basket of fruit and flowers between two arborescent vines. On three sides there is a Van Dyck border of triangles, its name derived from the clothing of portrait subjects by this painter.

a. Above *This embroidered carpet has a removable section, with a basket of flowers, for use as a hearth rug. 1832–35. 4.06m × 3.73m, 13'4" × 12'3". The Metropolitan Museum, New York, Gift of Katherine Keyes, 1938, in memory of her father, Homer Eaton Keyes*

a. Left *A needlemade rug worked on to a linen foundation. The shape is derived from the rectangular rugs used to cover chests and tables. 1800–20.*
0.72m × 1.7m, 2'4" × 5'7".
The American Museum in Britain, Bath

b. Left *The design of this embroidered hearth rug is based directly on a poster advertising a travelling "Grand Menagerie" that went through New England in 1835.*
0.58m × 1.24m, 1'11" × 4'1".
Old Sturbridge Village, Massachusetts

Although the Caswell carpet is perhaps the only surviving example of this kind of work, we have documentary references to other embroidered room-size carpets in nineteenth-century America. Some women received prizes at county fairs for their efforts, as did Miss Esther Williams of Northampton, Massachusetts, who received an award for "a cloth floor carpet wrought in colors with the needle" when she was sixty-nine years old. Other descriptions are more extensive. The author of *The Lancaster (N.H.) Sketchbook* wrote in 1887:

We had lots of sheep and plenty of wool, so mother took forty pounds and had it carded into rolls. Then she got Nancy Greenleaf and Lucy White to come and spin it. It was spun into good strong yarn, four skeins to the pound. . . . Then Mother had the yarn carried up to Eunice Stockwell's to be woven, and before long it was sent home – a great roll of white flannel. Then it had to be carried to Haverhill, to be fulled and colored. . . . In the meantime, Mother had been coloring yarn – red, yellow, green and blue. She had to make all the dyes herself, but she had some bright, handsome colors. I remember how pretty they looked, hanging out on the line drying. After a while the cloth came home – three great rolls of dark brown, heavy cloth. Then it was cut into breadths, the length of the

room, and Mother and Aunt Betsy marked them off into squares, about a foot each way, so they would match when it was sewn together. In each square was a large star. It was worked in what you call Kensington stitch. That's nothing but just the old fashioned marking stitch. The squares were worked in green, the stars in yellow, and at each point of the stars were little stars, worked in different colors; and so the whole carpet was made by hand. It was real handsome when it was done. Folks came from all around to see it.

Other room-size carpets were made at home in techniques adapted from quiltmaking. Both appliqué and patchwork carpets have survived and there are a few examples in overlapping cloth circles like those of a penny quilt design.

Hearth rugs

In 1828, Noah Webster, in his *Dictionary*, stated that a rug was used "in modern times, particularly for covering the carpet before the fireplace", a sharp contrast to his earlier definition of the term rug as "a woolen cloth used as a bedcover". Many early nineteenth-century hearth-rugs were simply small pieces of leftover carpeting, sometimes with an ornamental fringe or border added around the edges. However, carpet manufacturers soon began to

a. Above *A hooked hearth rug designed by Edward Sands Frost. The reclining dog was a favourite motif in hearth rugs at this period. 1875–90.*
0.64m × 1.08m, 2'1" × 3'8".
New Hampshire Historical Society

b. Above *The design, by Edward Sands Frost, of this hooked rug is based on an oriental carpet. 1870s.*
0.92m,× 1.83m 3'. × 5'10"
New Hampshire Historical Society

produce small rugs with well-composed pictorial designs, using colours and borders that would match or complement the design of room-sized carpets. The appeal of these small rugs must have been irresistible to people having many rooms with totally bare floors. Soon the small hearth rugs were used to protect carpets at the foot of flights of stairs and in doorways, or to provide warmth beside beds, or in front of chairs. Later such rugs were called scatter rugs because of the informal way in which they were used.

Hearth rugs must have offered attractive opportunities for those who enjoyed artistic expression through the means of the loom or the needle, for this type of rug soon became one of the most popular forms of textile art. Because they were used in high traffic areas or to protect more valuable carpets from flying sparks and cinders, hearth rugs are rare today. At the peak of their popularity, in the years from 1830 to 1890, hearth rugs were one of the largest categories of textiles submitted to the judges of rural agricultural fairs. At the fairs they were praised for "their beauty and appearance of durability", the "attention paid in the selection of figures and colors", their "brilliancy of color and their tasteful arrangement", or "their substantial fabric". As early as 1824, the editor of the *New England Farmer*, reporting on the Worcester Agricultural Show in Massachusetts, remarked that he hoped the competition encouraged by exhibition at the fairs would "render this useful article fashionable in every respectable family". In fact, the use of small rugs continued to be a prominent feature of many American homes well into the twentieth century.

Many early hearth rugs were embroidered in cross-stitch like that exhibited at the 1830 Plymouth County (Massachusetts) Cattle Show. This was made "by the widow of the late Samuel Shaw. She is 80 years old, yet we have never seen so successful an effort of the needle; it was wrought with worsted, by the marking stitch . . . beautifully arranged of various colors. It was a rich Rug, more valuable than is usually seen in carpet warehouses."

Actually, the rugs seen in carpet warehouses must have served as design inspiration for many early rug embroiderers. Small dogs and cats, or terrifying lions (see 226b) were popular, along with baskets or vases of flowers, cornucopia, and arrangements of shells. Although Mrs Shaw and some others worked their rugs in cross or marking stitch, other needlewomen used a random running stitch with short surface loops, a technique which is now known as 'yarn sewn'. Rugs worked in this way have often been confused with hooked rugs, although the technique of manufacture is entirely different.

Hooked rugs

Hooked rugs are not made with a needle carrying the pattern yarns on the surface, but with a small hook that pulls the colour from the back into individual loops on the surface of the rug. The colourful pile in hooked rugs is usually made from small strips of coloured woollen cloth, while the pile in an embroidered rug is made of several strands of yarn. Although pile-embroidered and cross-stitched rugs seem to have been made from at least the late

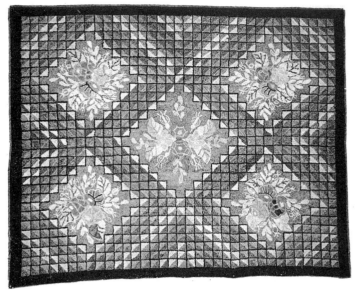

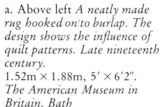

a. Above left *A neatly made rug hooked onto burlap. The design shows the influence of quilt patterns. Late nineteenth century.*
1.52m × 1.88m, 5′ × 6′2″.
The American Museum in Britain, Bath

b. Above right *This rug, to be used as a door mat, is also hooked onto a burlap foundation. Second half of the nineteenth century.*
0.65m × 1.04m, 2′3″ × 3′5″.
The American Museum in Britain, Bath

c. Right *A hooked rug in which the rather primitive pattern was probably drawn at home and may have been adapted from a weathervane. Second half of the nineteenth century.*
0.81m × 1.3m, 2′8″ × 4′3″.
The American Museum in Britain, Bath

eighteenth century, hooked rugs do not seem to predate the mid-1830s. The technique seems to have developed first in Maine and the Maritime Provinces of Canada from which it spread slowly down the eastern seaboard. Hooked rug making always continued to be popular in New England and eastern Canada, particularly in the early twentieth century. It has recently enjoyed a nationwide revival. Many rugs made in fairly recent times employ traditional designs, while others are breathtakingly original in both their composition and their use of colour.

The earliest hooked rugs were made on a linen or cotton backing, with strips of fabric coloured with natural dyes. Those with jute burlap (coarse canvas) backing and harsh synthetic colours date from the years after 1850. During periods of craft revival in the late nineteenth century, the 1920s, and in our own day, many hooked rugs have been made with naturally dyed fabrics. Some of these are deliberate fakes, intended to deceive those who collect antique rugs, while others are the sincere products of purists who wish to recreate the old handcraft traditions.

Since designs for hooked rugs are not common in the sewing manuals or ladies' magazines of the last half of the nineteenth century, nor are they an obvious adaptation of commercially produced carpet designs, the impetus for their great popularity at this period must be found elsewhere. It must certainly derive from the commercial production of pre-stamped patterns on burlap which were

produced and distributed by a number of Maine entrepreneurs, most notably Edward Sands Frost of Biddeford, Maine. The published catalogues of his designs show floral and geometric rugs, along with domestic or ferocious animals (see 227a), masonic motifs, and patterns which are clearly based on oriental (see 227b) or Aubusson carpets.

The appeal of hooked rugs to antique collectors in the heyday of the colonial revival was well expressed by Nancy McClelland in her book, *Furnishing the Colonial and Federal Home:*

Nothing seems more suitable for early American rooms than hooked rugs. They have just the naivete and the texture that these rooms need and are 'not too good for nature's daily food.' I have a feeling that every well-brought up family has a few hooked rug heirlooms, just as it owns a few attic hidden samplers. Old ones, of course, are much the most beautiful. Failing these, it is possible to get 'near antiques' that are very satisfactory, in the form of rugs made in Newfoundland or New England hooked from homedyed materials and washed and treated until they become what is commercially called 'semi-antiques'.

What Nancy McClelland and many others of her generation did not recognize was that hooked rugs were of relatively recent origin, not the products of a distant colonial time.

a. Above *A tiny knitted mat made for a child's doll's-house. Larger mats in the same technique were made at this period, but this small example is in particularly good condition. 1840–50.* 7cm × 12cm, 3″ × 5″.

b. Above *This unusual early rug is composed of braided cards and a braided border applied to a linen backing. The interstices are filled with 'yarn sewn' woollen embroidery. 1830–50. Detail.* (1.47m × 2.23m, 4′10″ × 7′4″.) *Old Sturbridge Village, Massachusetts*

Knitted and braided rugs

Less artistically interesting than embroidered or hooked rugs are those made of knitted (see 229a) or braided (see 229b) yarns or rags. These kinds of rugs have no inherent pictorial interest, but depend on subtle texture and sophisticated colour shading for their beauty.

Knitted carpets were exhibited at agricultural fairs at least as early as the 1820s. An example made by Elizabeth Prescott of Boston was shown at the Massachusetts State Fair in Brighton in 1824 and reported as being "deserving of mention, as evidence of very commendable industry" Some knitted rugs were made of yarn which had been previously knitted and then unravelled. Often this was done deliberately to give a crimp to the yarn rather than as a thrifty re-use of worn-out garments. In 1860 Godey's *Lady's Book* published directions for knitted rugs made of strips of woollen cloth which had been sewn together in the same technique that was used to prepare rags for woven rag carpeting. The editor of Godey's stressed that these knitted rugs were especially useful in front of wash-stands and commodes, and in "other exposed places".

It is uncertain when rug braiding began in America, but braided corn-husk doormats and mats made of marsh grasses are described in colonial and late eighteenth-century sources. Braided woollen rugs were exhibited at agricultural fairs at least as early as 1822 when they "were noticed and admired" at Plymouth, Massachusetts. The thrifty recyling of odds and ends of worn-out garments appealed to the American character and more than one author cited the fact that children could be kept out of mischief by making braided mats.

When Miss Lydia Hunt of Cranston, Rhode Island received an award of two dollars for her rag carpet at the 1826 Rhode Island Agricultural Society Fair, the judges noted that since it "was manufactured from bits and odds and ends of every thing that would otherwise have been wholly useless, and from the neatness with which the various colors were braided together, and its substantial fabric as well as economy, (it) was deemed worthy a premium."

Recognizing the subtle and beautiful effects that could be achieved by careful colour selection, and admiring the simple technique and thrifty use of materials in braided rugs, leaders of the aesthetic movement in the late nineteenth century were instrumental in popularizing this type of rug making.

As the nineteenth century progressed and successful commercial carpet making brought factory-produced floor coverings within the economic reach of most Americans, handmade rug making became more and more a deliberate expression of an aesthetic impulse, a satisfying of the urge to make something out of nothing or a fulfillment of women's domestic role. In a time when it was unsuitable for women to be idle, embroidering hearth rugs, hooking strips of wool through a piece of preprinted burlap, or braiding strands of rags together into small rugs was far more satisfying than doing nothing. "With the toil saved from hours of idleness, elegant and almost everlasting carpet was produced."

Navajo Weaving

At the heart of the Navajo world view is the belief that their ancestors came out of the earth. Long ago, according to tradition, they were led up through successive subterranean worlds to the surface of this one by the Holy People of Navajo mythology. This understanding of their origin – that they came directly from the soil and are inexorably part of it – is the touchstone of the Navajo experience. It influences all that they do and all that they are.

The blankets described here are, like the ancestors of the people who made them, drawn out of the earth. The wool came from the backs of Navajo sheep; the looms on which the blankets were woven were made from tree-trunks and set in place with rocks. The blankets were woven from bottom to top on vertical looms, and so seemed to have taken shape and grown directly out of the earth as if by some process of nature.

Like everything of significance in the Navajo scheme, the art of weaving is firmly grounded in religious tradition. Legend has it that Spider Woman, one of the Holy People, taught them how to weave. Such a strong link between their own origins and the origins of blanket-making served to connect the material world with the spiritual world, identifying blankets as a rendering in physical terms of the mystical universe. When the Navajo wrapped blankets around themselves, they were surrounding their bodies with the totality of their being, gathering about themselves the four corners of a world at once beautiful and familiar. The blankets are not symbolic in any direct sense; efforts have been made to interpret their design symbolically, but these interpretations are imposed by the commentator.

The Navajo saw the blanket differently. Each is individual in design, and each represents both the woman who made it – through the expression and control of its design – and the person who wears it – through the alteration of his appearance. One of the best ways to understand the design of a Navajo wearing blanket is, very simply, to wear it (see 230a). Draped like a cape, brought forward, and pulled together across the arms, the blanket reveals its essential design concept as half units meet to form whole units. Elements break at just the right place, often following the lines of the arms. A central radiating point in the back is very typical, and this same form is often echoed in the front. The strong verticals reinforce the line of the spinal column.

Today the Navajo is the largest Indian tribe in the United States, numbering 145,000 members – an impressive statistic for a people who a century ago, after the defeat by the Americans, and after incarceration in a desolate area of

a. Left *A Navajo wrestler, about 1879. Obviously a posed photograph with a Third Phase Chief blanket hung as a background and a Serape wrapped around him.*

b. Opposite above *The narrowness of the blue and red lines is typical of First Phase Chief Blankets, which were woven throughout the nineteenth century. 1800–60. Maxwell Collection, Maxwell Museum of Anthropology, Albuquerque*

c. Opposite below *A woman's Chief Blanket, Second Phase. The similarity of colours and proportions in the design of these blankets suggests that they were a conventionalized ideal. 1850–65.*
1.44m × 1.80m, 4'9" × 5'11". Natural History Museum of Los Angeles County

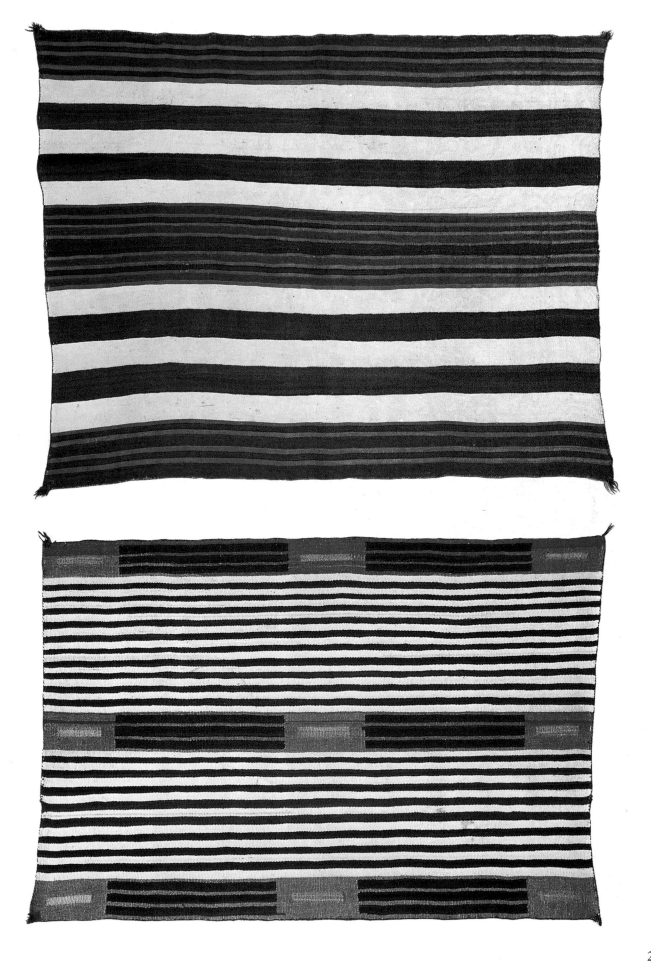

southern New Mexico known as Bosque Redondo, numbered roughly sixteen thousand members. Tribal identity is based for the most part on a common language, the language of their Athapascan ancestors, with modifications out of the Pueblo language and Spanish. Their language both unifies them and sets them apart: they still refer to themselves as the People.

In the sixteenth century, when Spanish conquistadors began to explore the New World, the Navajo had been living in the ruggedly beautiful area around what is now northern New Mexico for some five hundred years. Descended from Athapascan-speaking Indian tribes of Alaska and western Canada, their ancestors migrated south in search of new homes. The Navajo's turbulent history is punctuated with long periods of suffering and deprivation, and the land itself – though sublime and enchanting – presented a challenge to their ingenuity and survival skills. By about 1700, the restless Navajo, having assimilated much of the neighbouring Pueblo culture, including the art of weaving, were tilling the sandy bottoms of canyons, becoming an agrarian people. They still hunted, moved from place to place, and lived in semi-permanent homes; but they also cultivated corn and cotton.

The majority of blankets woven by the Navajo were made entirely or partly of yarns produced from their own animals, the large flocks of sheep which were a source of great pride to their owners. Another yarn used by the Navajo was bayeta. The term 'bayeta' derives from 'baize', a light woollen fabric of a brownish-red or bay colour – hence the name – that was manufactured in England and other European countries from the sixteenth century. 'Bayeta' is now generally used to mean the unravelled yarns rather than the cloth. Bayeta cloth had smooth, hand-twisted threads which the Navajo unravelled to use in their blankets – this use of bayeta did much to spread their fame as weavers. The weaving technique involved was always that of tapestry weave, slanting or stepping the edges of the motifs to avoid making slits.

Although we encounter Navajo blankets as isolated artefacts illustrated in books or hung on walls, they were originally an integral part of a greater context, that of the Navajo and the vast landscape of the Southwest. A gathering of Navajo would bring out Stripe, Chief, and Serape blankets – some old and worn, others newly woven – along with examples of Pueblo and Spanish weaving. Such a scene would have demonstrated the evolving history of Navajo weaving.

Stripe, Chief, Serape – these are the classic blanket styles. The earliest surviving examples date from about 1800 and the designs continue until the mid-1860s – that is, until the coming of the Americans to Navajo country. The term

a. Opposite *This Third Phase Chief Blanket shows the characteristic diamond motifs, which had developed out of rectangular blocks. 1860–80.* 1.53m × 1.89m, 5′ × 6′2″. *The Nelson-Atkins Museum of Art, Kansas City, Gift of Mrs R. Nelson*

b. Above left *A early Classic Serape. The many variations on diamonds and stripes become the cohesive force in the design. 1840–60.* 1.74m × 1.27m, 5′8″ × 4′2″. *Southwest Museum, Los Angeles*

c. Above right *The open format and dominant vertical orientation seen in this late Serape are both changes that occurred in the 1870s.* 2.03m × 1.32m, 6′8″ × 4′4″. *Natural History Museum of Los Angeles County*

'classic' however does not imply the absence of foreign influence. Early textiles were influenced by Pueblo examples and then, in the classic blankets of the nineteenth century, Spanish influence was great, both in the use of trade materials and in design concepts. These blankets made a geometric statement about a world that is distinct and eternal; they reflect a confidence and sense of power and restraint that sets them apart from later weavings. They are classics in the sense that they reflect the Navajo worldview before the arrival of the Americans.

The traditional term 'Chief Blanket' is something of a misnomer. The Navajo had no chiefs in the strictest sense, and any member of the tribe might have worn a Chief Blanket draped over his shoulders. Perhaps the term resulted from the widespread trading of these blankets to other tribes, where they were worn by men of prominence. (Many of the Chief Blankets now in collections were acquired from Plains Indians.) Whatever the origin of their name, the finely woven Chief Blankets were highly prized as items of trade and as a source of prestige to the Navajo.

Worked with the stripes parallel to the weft, wider than high, the Chief Blanket was probably modelled after the Pueblo cape, also woven with the weft running with the wider dimension of the blanket. These capes were designed with wide end-bands at top and bottom. In adapting this

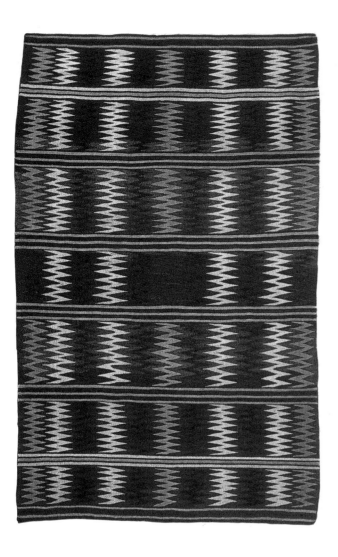

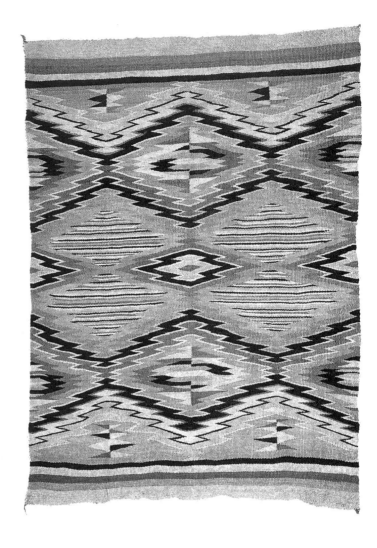

Pueblo style, the Navajo added at the centre an additional band, the same width as the end-bands; narrow brown and white stripes were then placed between the bands.

The development of the Chief Blanket separates into three phases, with distinct variations found in each. A First Phase design consists only of stripes (see 230b). In the Second Phase, rectangular blocks are inserted within the stripes, creating a grid at the top, centre, and bottom (see 230c). The Third Phase Chief Blanket is distinguished by a characteristic diamond motif (see 233a). The development of diamonds out of the Second Phase rectangular blocks was a steady one: instead of red blocks placed within a field of stripes, small stepped blocks in a diamond shape began to appear in the same position. By the 1870s, the Chief blanket had developed into a balanced combination of stripes and diamonds, representing a successful blending of the diamond motifs of the early Serape style with the traditional basic stripe. In this Third Phase style, a central diamond is surrounded by eight triangular elements at the edges. The strong image produced by this configuration has a dramatic and distinctive impact that has made the Third Phase examples the best-known Navajo blankets.

Of all the classic blanket types, the 'Serape' is the only one that is not an adaptation from a Pueblo model. In the Serape blankets alone one finds the Navajo developing a style based on Spanish-Mexican precedents rather than on those developed among the other Indians in the Southwest.

Indian weaving done in Mexico had an important influence in the Southwest of the United States. In fact, even the changes that occurred after the arrival of the Spanish in Mexico were brought north for further change and development. In the early nineteenth century, the Spanish colonists in New Mexico wore a garment generally referred to as the 'Saltillo Serape', after the town in northern Mexico where the elegant and finely woven serape was principally made.

The Navajo 'Classic Serape' (see 233b), having started as a Navajo interpretation of a Spanish-Mexican model, provided the means for the expression of qualities that were central to the tribe. It is possible to follow the general stylistic progression of the Classic Serape, decade by decade, during the period when the majority of those surviving were made, from about 1830 to the mid-1870s. Finally it evolved into the 'Eye-Dazzler', the last stage in the development of the Navajo blanket.

The arrival of the Americans in Navajo territory in the 1860s brought about great political and social upheaval, and radically altered the way in which the Navajo saw themselves and their world. This upheaval was reflected in rapid changes in the style and materials of their blankets:

a. Opposite left *A late Classic Banded Child's Serape. Though smaller in size, children's blankets were woven with particular care. 1865–70. 1.25m × 0.84m, 4'1" × 2'11".*

b. Opposite right *A more loosely-spun Eye-Dazzler in which the design is simplified and enlarged. 1880–90. 2m × 1.43m, 6'6" × 4'8".*

c. Above left *A Germantown Eye-Dazzler Blanket. The patterns of these blankets are full of movement and create strong optical effects. 1885–90. 2.35m × 1.56m, 7'8" × 5'.*

d. Above right *A Transitional piece, possibly conceived for a rug rather than a blanket. 1880–90. 2.07m × 1.35m, 6'8" × 4'9". BankAmerica Art Corporation, San Francisco*

a. Above *A Germantown Transitional rug. Instead of enlarging a single design element, the weaver has compiled a number of designs in different sections. 1880–95. 3.46m × 3.53m, 11' × 11'6".*

Stripe, Chief, and Serape styles were altered; new types evolved, including the trader-controlled rug and the Eye-Dazzler; there was strong American influence on the use of dyes and materials, and on designs. The traders found a broader market for Navajo products, and on the newly completed railroad the blankets left the territory in quantity. Just as Navajo history and American history blend together after this time, Navajo influence and American influence blend in the Navajo blanket.

Between the middle and late 1860s, one can see a shift in the approach to the Serape. They become characterized by backgrounds of one colour in various tones, a delicate yet expansive drawing, and new and unexpected colour combinations using both natural and synthetic dyes. They are often strikingly beautiful.

With the invention of synthetic dyes, a whole new range of colours quickly spread around the world. Navajo weavers, too, responded to the introduction of these dyes. While some synthetic dyes had probably been in use during internment at Bosque Redondo in the late 1860s, traders introduced the new dyes in bulk for the first time in the mid-1870s and instructed the Indians in their use. Within a few years, the Navajo were employing the synthetic-dye colour range to its full potential. Synthetics were less expensive than bayeta, and more quickly prepared than natural dyes. The colours produced were bright and saturated.

During the first half of the 1870s, in the aftermath of their ordeal at Bosque Redondo, the Navajo tried to re-establish their shattered culture. In keeping with this effort, traditional blanket styles continued to be woven, but there was, however, a gradual break with traditional attitudes that contributed to the development of the old styles and allowed the creation of many new ones. Moreover, it has been suggested that the Navajo's exposure at Bosque Redondo to some four thousand old Mexican and New Mexican (Rio Grande) blankets, given to them by the American authorities, played a crucial role in the quickened evolution of a dramatic new style, the Eye-Dazzler, and influenced other blanket styles. The largest number of these Rio Grande blankets were undoubtedly striped. Others were in the 'Banded' style, and some in the Serape style with concentric diamonds. Some possibly may have been in the prized Saltillo Serape style, with its finely detailed background and central diamond, though this is unlikely. All of these styles appear to have influenced Navajo blankets in the next two decades.

After Bosque Redondo, the Banded style largely replaced the Stripe style. Motifs were arranged in rows and alternating bands in a manner remarkably similar to Rio Grande blankets. By the late 1870s, the use of enlarged designs and the greatly expanded colour range resulting from the introduction of synthetic dyes led to the creation of an explosively expressionistic style representing a dramatic shift in aesthetic tone (see 233c, 235a). The best blankets in this new style have an urgency that, in different visual terms, is just as exciting as the classical control of earlier blanket styles. This was a period of new freedom in colour, design, and approach, often resulting in a jazz-like quality of relaxed improvisation. The early traders called these blankets 'Eye-Dazzlers', a name that was by no means an exaggeration. In these, particularly in the loosely woven handspun versions of the Eye-Dazzler, there was a tendency to simplify and enlarge on designs. The colour could then function, freed of the extensive 'drawing' that was integral to the fine Serape-style blankets (see 235b).

While the handspun Eye-Dazzlers moved towards simplification, another group of blankets, woven with machine-spun and plyed yarn, became more complex. The yarn, referred to generally as Germantown, after the town in Pennsylvania where some of it was manufactured, was used to produce very finely woven blankets, much as bayeta and 3-ply vegetable-dyed yarns had previously been used in the classic period. Large diamonds composed of small diamonds and triangles with serrated edges are typical of this style (see 235c).

The most dramatic stylistic changes encouraged by the traders were the introduction of the border, as a framing device, and the limitation of colour. Although borders had appeared in a few early blankets, they were never commonly used and when they did occur, they were an integral part of the design. Occasionally, in blankets made after the mid-1870s, one sees bands placed like a border but only on the two vertical sides, not on the horizontal edges.

The Navajo lived in small isolated family units, and one can imagine the role of the blanket at larger gatherings. The blankets were a form of communication, of direct exchange between members of the tribe, since knowledge and expertise in weaving were shared by all.

There are constants in the Navajo experience which underlie the tradition of these blankets. Foremost of these is a feeling of energy. It is as if each blanket were a diagram of the spiritual presence of an individual.

Decorative carpets

a. Left *These carpets were made for export but the designs are exceptionally fine. Each shape is beautifully drawn and the wide range of colours are enhanced by the ivory field. Persia (Heriz), around 1900.*
3.30m × 2.70m, 10'10" × 8'9".
Vojtech Blau

b. Right *This carpet has a garden design adapted from early floral patterns into a geometric format. The cypress and willow trees on a golden ground are superb and the design evokes the romantic beauty of a Persian garden. Persia (Heriz), around 1880.*
3.35m × 2.64m, 11' × 8'8".
Vojtech Blau

A great force in the carpet trade in recent years has been the emergence of the 'decorative' carpet. Modern interiors require carpets that are not only sturdy and large but also have bold uncluttered designs. Such carpets are not associated with any particular style, country, or technique but may include Eastern and European kilims, dhurries, and needlework carpets, as well as pile weaves. In the late nineteenth and early twentieth centuries, Persian weavers in villages and town workshops produced large carpets specifically for the European and American markets, and many of these are now sought after as decorative carpets. Among the most effective are the Heriz and Serape styles with their powerful geometric motifs and rich colours.

Vojtech Blau in New York is considered by many to be one of the world's leading dealers. He was also one of the first to recognize the value of decorative carpets and since then has handled pieces of quite exceptional quality.

Buying carpets

For the past twenty years I have studied oriental carpets and, as a gallery owner, have also studied the people who buy them. Seeing the innocence of many potential buyers, unsure what they are looking for, and even less sure what they are looking at, I have realized how necessary it is for them to seek honest, reliable advice and to be clear about their needs. As the range of oriental carpets is vast, inexperienced buyers cannot do better than admit their ignorance and then trust in the advice of a reliable gallery.

In establishing a relationship with a gallery, it is just as important for the buyer to charm the seller as it is vice versa. Such a buyer places the seller in an open frame of mind – as well as commanding his respect – and definitely receives preferential treatment. A special kind of loyalty then develops and the sale becomes not a battle of wills, but a clear acceptance of the rules of trading.

Buying for the home

Before searching for a carpet it is important to define your needs: do you want antique or new carpets; should they be pale or brightly coloured; in perfect condition, or worn but beautiful; an investment or something utilitarian; a fine detailed design, or a grand bold one; a floral design or a geometric one? Does the room the carpet will go in raise special problems: is it light or dark; will the carpet receive heavy traffic; are there curtains and furniture with which it should match; what size of carpet is most suitable? Finally, how much can you afford?

In sorting out all these considerations, remember to discuss them with your partner – many hopeful buyers have come to grief because their partners have been brought into the project too late.

The next stage is to track down a gallery that can fulfil your requirements. Ask around – anyone who has been trading for some time will have built up a certain reputation. Avoid anywhere which has a – 'closing down', or 'bankrupt stock' notice. These may be ploys to catch the naïve buyer and many shops display such notices all year round. Instead, find a good gallery in which you like the stock and feel confidence in the owner. When you have found two or three carpets which might be suitable, ask if you can take them home on approval for a few days. This will give you time to discuss them with your partner, if necessary, and to see how they look in daylight and at night. Most galleries are insured and should be happy to let their customers take goods on approval.

At home it will soon be obvious which, if any, of the carpets you really like, but there are still a few more points to consider before making a final decision. The condition of the carpet is important. The price will be affected if it has been painted, repaired, or reduced in size, or if it has a very worn pile. A reliable dealer should always point out such faults early on and if hc fails to do so you have every right to take the carpet back later and ask for a refund. Also, find out if the carpet needs cleaning or an underlay, and make sure that it is strong enough for the location you have chosen, particularly if it is to go in a dining-room or entrance-hall.

The price is also important: is it good value; will it hold its value; and will it be an investment? Any intelligent and far-sighted dealer will want you to be happy about the price, hoping you will come back again and recommend him to your friends. If you buy a number of carpets you should expect a healthy discount. After all, you are showing great faith in the gallery. Only when you are entirely happy with the deal and the carpet is correctly described on the invoice should you conclude the purchase.

Collecting

Collecting carpets can easily become an expensive passion and if you discover you have the collecting bug, you should first gain confidence by working closely with a trustworthy gallery owner. This relationship will develop over the years until you become so knowledgeable that you can fly from the nest, able to rely on your own judgement of pieces and prices. Meanwhile you should study every type of carpet within range of your pocket – and those beyond it. This can be done in museums, galleries, and auction houses. Certain types of carpet will attract you strongly, but you must then discover what makes a 'great' carpet. In every city, village, or tribal grouping, certain weavers have particular artistic flair and dedication. The way they select, spin, and dye the wool, the care with which they set up the loom, their skill in weaving and design – all these affect the look of the carpet.

The industrious collector educates his, or her, eye, building up a library of visual memories and instantly comparing one carpet with another. He also studies prices in auctions and galleries to develop a feel for the market place. Gradually, the buyer's specialized knowledge becomes greater than that of the dealer, although the two may continue to work together, and their joint desire to make a great collection can produce a fruitful partnership. This phenomenon lies behind many magnificent collections, not only of oriental carpets.

Interior decorating

Many art collectors, leading busy lives or with homes in different countries, employ interior decorators to design and furnish their houses. These decorators, if truly professional, usually have close links with dealers in each discipline – furniture, carpets, and paintings. Through these the right object can be found, and when the final presentation is made the client benefits from the taste of two experts. Some projects are on a huge scale and the coordination of the scheme can only be made by a decorator who has contacts in every field in all the major art centres, particularly New York, Paris, London, and Rome.

This method of buying only works if the decorator really is given *carte blanche*. In cases where client, decorator, and dealer are all chasing around the same city looking for the same carpet, the system breaks down totally.

Buying a carpet at auction

The great auction houses play an important role in the world of carpets. Twenty years ago they were relatively ignorant about what they were selling, but over the years

a. Left *The carpet bazaar in Teheran.*

both their expertise and their publicity machines have grown. Now prices at auction are often higher than those in galleries and there is considerable rivalry between dealers and auctioneers. This competition is very beneficial to the buyer, as dealers often woo customers away from the auctions by undercutting their prices.

If you are interested in a carpet coming up for auction and have any doubts about your knowledge, do seek advice – not just from the carpet department of the auction house, but independent advice as well. Careful viewing is a great art and can prevent you from making an irretrievable mistake. Auction rooms rarely buy things back and will only offer them for sale again, which takes a long time and even then the carpet may not reach the price you paid. As bidding at auction requires experience and a cool head it may be better to leave a modest bid with the auction house or use a reputable dealer to bid for you.

Beware of auctions in a hurry: they are just as misleading as shops with 'special offers'. This less reputable end of the trade takes place in quiet hotels and viewing may be only one and a half hours before the sale. The auctioneer is a poet and his glowing words will often convince people to snap up unrepeatable bargains. Often, however, these 'bargains' have been borrowed from a wholesaler over the weekend, and those unsold will be returned on Monday.

In conclusion, many of the pitfalls in buying carpets can be avoided if you are clear about your needs and how much money you can spend; and if you check the reputation of the galleries or auction rooms that you approach. This done, you should be able to buy wisely and will never regret your purchases. But take care of your carpets. You are only their temporary guardians, with a responsibility to hand them over to future generations so they, too, may enjoy them.

Care of Carpets

Like all organic objects, rugs and carpets will inevitably deteriorate in time. It is, however, our responsibility to care for them as well as possible, so future generations and subsequent owners may gain as much pleasure from them as we do. This applies not only to textiles in museums, but particularly to those carpets which adorn our homes and are the special pride of individuals. Rugs which have been bought at considerable expense tend to be treated with care, but those which have been inherited are often overlooked – all are expensive to replace, and some are irreplaceable. If neglected they will deteriorate at an alarming speed, yet proper care is a simple matter, based on an understanding of carpet structure.

Cleaning

Carpets should be kept as clean as possible and never stored while damp or dirty, which could lead to mildew and moth-attack. They should be regularly checked and carefully vacuumed, making sure that grit is removed from the base of the knots. Before vacuuming, the rug should be turned upside down onto paper or sheeting and the back tapped all over. This, repeated several times, will remove an enormous amount of loose dirt. Fragile rugs should be vacuumed with a small dustette hoover through nylon-mesh screening.

Washing and dry-cleaning are both potentially damaging processes which should only be done in consultation with an expert. If well looked after and kept in a relatively unpolluted atmosphere, carpets only need to be washed every twenty years; but more frequent washing is essential if they suffer heavy domestic wear. Silk rugs are best dry-cleaned, by expert oriental carpet cleaners not the local cleaners. Wool carpets, however, should never be dry-cleaned as the process removes too much of the natural oils from the fibres. Instead, they should be washed in cool, de-ionized or softened water with a mild liquid detergent, and then allowed to dry naturally to prevent felting. (Surface cleaning with a damp cloth or commercial carpet cleaner is not recommended, as the dirt can simply be pushed into the base of the knot where it will form a mud pack and be impossible to remove later.) Wool has a natural elasticity and it is a common, though mistaken, practice, to stretch some wool carpets when wet to straighten them. But an irregular shape is often characteristic of tribal weavings and adds to their charm. In attempting to make them square, undue strain may be imposed on certain areas of the rug. It is quite impossible to stretch a silk carpet, and is rarely necessary as most are woven in established workshops where equipment is more sophisticated and the weavers more proficient.

The safest way of dealing with accidental spillages of liquids, such as tea or coffee, is to place a thick, white towel under the wet area and sponge liberally with cold water, providing of course that the dyes appear to be fast. Again, the carpet should dry naturally. More specific advice on stain removal should be sought from an expert within twenty-four hours.

Repairs

If neglected carpets suffer from wear and tear over the years, so repairs, both to strengthen them and to make them more attractive, become necessary. These repairs may take two forms: 'restoration', which will involve re-weaving and re-knotting; or 'conservation', which will avoid such drastic measures, making the carpet safe instead by simple sewing.

The restorer will repair holes and tears by building up a foundation weave of warp and weft with a needle, then inserting the correct number and colour of knots to complete the pattern. If skilfully done, this may restore both the back and the front of the carpet to its original appearance, at the same time making it stronger and more valuable. It is particularly beneficial in re-defining the dark outlines of the motifs, which may have almost disappeared due to the corrosive effects of the iron mordants used to dye these dark shades. The restoration will re-emphasize the fine drawing of the design and the rug will appear brighter, due to the clearer separation of the colours.

However, restoration will do little to improve the carpet if it is not carried out by the most skilled professional. A careless or insensitive restorer may remove quite a few of the original knots in an attempt to neaten the holes before repair, and may also interpret the design inaccurately when re-knotting. Also, the wool used in re-knotting may have unstable dyes which will fade or run, making the originally invisible repair very obtrusive.

When deciding how to treat a carpet, its value should also be considered. Any form of repair tends to be very expensive and it is a good idea to have the carpet valued independently before accepting any estimate. Restoration, while it usually increases the value of a carpet, may actually decrease it if the piece in question is exceptionally rare or fragile; in this case it is better to use a conservation treatment.

Certain carpets are impossible to restore, particularly the very fine, pure silk rugs which have become so fragile that even the insertion of the new warps and wefts would break up the surrounding weave, thereby causing more damage than a simple conservation treatment. In fact, carpets made entirely of silk, or having a silk foundation, present very serious problems. It is common for splits to occur in the foundation, either along the warp or horizontally across the weft, sometimes resulting in a loss of pile. The weaving is often too fine for restoration so it is very tempting, though unwise, to apply some sort of glue to the reverse side to hold the structure together. Once such splits occur the rug becomes extremely vulnerable, so it should be handled very carefully and only repaired by professionals.

It is difficult to ascertain the cause of such splitting. Perhaps it is due to the carpets being soaked in polluted water containing dilute solutions of chloride or other salts, for which silk has considerable affinity. These salts will then weaken the silk fibres, which may be further damaged by drying in hot air. Another possibility is that the silk is deteriorating naturally due to the fineness of its fibres, its vulnerability to light, and the tension under which it was held during the long weaving process.

First-aid treatments

It may be useful to carry out some simple repair to protect the edges of the carpet before it is used or displayed. The warp ends, when cut from the loom, provide the fringes of the rug, and whether plaited, knotted or simply straight, they suffer from wear. Sometimes they are unscrupulously cut off to make the rug look neater and less worn. When the fringes are damaged there is a danger that the weft will eventually begin to unravel. If this is allowed to continue the knots too will loosen and fall out, and whole borders have been lost in this way. A simple method of preventing this is to blanket-stitch the ends but a professional restorer may be able to reinforce the ends with invisible stitching.

The selvedges, too, can suffer from wear, also leading to a loss of pile. This should be dealt with quickly. If the warps remain intact, the selvedges can simply be oversewn with wool or silk of the correct colour, but some coarsely-knotted carpets may be better protected by cotton webbing sewn under the selvedges and ends. Sticky tapes and glue should never be used even for small areas of damage. Instead, small holes should be oversewn until proper repairs are made.

Display

The best way of using and displaying a carpet will depend largely on its size, condition, and value. Although it is tempting to give priority to aesthetic considerations, there are also environmental factors to be taken into account.

Light can affect dyes drastically. It is fatal to place textiles in direct sunlight or close to any bright, uncontrolled lighting, as the fading will occur slowly and gradually before it is discerned, and then cannot be reversed.

Avoid hanging a textile directly over radiators or near convection heating, as the resulting dust and hot, dry air will contribute towards its deterioration. Never use a valuable rug as a floor covering, unless you have a very disciplined family or the rug can be kept in a room which is only used occasionally. I know a collector who keeps some beautiful rugs on the floor, but his family and friends have learnt either to remove their shoes before entering the room or to walk around each carpet.

Never place heavy furniture on carpets, or drag chairs over them. If this is unavoidable the legs of the furniture, especially those with metal castors, should rest on small, wooden discs which can be painted to blend into the colours of the carpet. Furniture can make holes right through the foundation of a carpet if these precautions are not taken.

A good quality underlay, the exact size of the carpet, can reduce wear by taking up the unevenness of the floor, as does wall-to-wall carpeting. To quote from the British National Trust *Manual of Housekeeping*: "The International Wool Secretariat recommends the use of hairfelt underlay of contract quality. Some other types deteriorate so badly that the underlay sticks to the wooden floor. Do not use foam rubber or composition-backed underlays which deteriorate unevenly or those with a dimpled surface which

could cause uneven wear. On stone floors where underfelt could absorb damp, carpet paper should be laid under the felt."

Sometimes carpets will 'creep' across the floor. An underlay will prevent this movement on bare floors, and small pieces of the hooked side of velcro-mesh can be sewn underneath the edges of rugs to keep them in place on fitted carpeting. The curling of selvedges and corners of rugs is due to the extra tension placed on the outer warps during the weaving; it can be prevented by sewing cotton or jute webbing under the selvedges.

When carpets cannot be placed on the floor, various other methods of display are suitable:

For fine silk carpets, and any others not strong enough to hang by their own weight, a flat table provides an excellent support. The surface should first be covered with a blanket or similar padding. Unlike those which are often seen draping to the floor in fifteenth and sixteenth-century paintings, the carpets should not be allowed to hang over the edge, as distortions and holes can result in the corners.

Flat weaves and pile rugs whose structure is reasonably sound can be hung by attaching velcro-mesh to one end of the carpet. It should hang with the warp vertical and the pile lying downwards, so that you can run your hand smoothly from top to bottom. The pile direction may be from side to side, but a rug should not be hung from the selvedge unless its size dictates it. As the warp is continuous from one end to another, it is the strongest yarn of the foundation so it, rather than the selvedge, should take the weight. The hooked side of the velcro is simply tacked to a flat length of wood which is then fixed to the wall, and the soft side, sewn to the carpet, is pressed firmly against it. Two-inch (5 centimetres) wide velcro can easily support the weight of a large and heavy carpet.

Fragments, or carpets which are very weak, should be given some form of full support. This may be provided by a board or, in the case of a large carpet, a stretcher frame. Both board and frame are first covered with fabric which is stretched as much as possible so it will not sag once vertical. The rug is then sewn to this fabric all around the edge and, if necessary, within the field or along the fringes. The fabric should be of a type and colour that will enhance the rug and show it off to its best advantage. This is especially true of a fragment, where the backing material may visually complete a missing portion of the design. Invisible thread or a very fine but strong yarn should be used so the piece seems to float on the wall.

It may be convenient to use a collapsible support. In this case, the hooked side of velcro-mesh is stapled to the wrong side of a stretcher frame. The carpet is sewn to heavyweight canvas or duck. The soft side of the velcro is sewn to the wrong side of the canvas, which is then stretched over and around the frame until the velcro comes together and the canvas is taut. The carpet can be easily removed from the frame while remaining supported on the canvas.

Storage

Firstly, a carpet should never be stored dirty. Secondly, it is a mistaken belief that by rolling a knotted rug with the pile inside it will be protected. This puts considerable strain on the foundation weave; also the pile, if long, will be crushed during long-term storage. Basically, a carpet should be rolled in the way of least resistance, which can be felt during handling. Silk rugs and those with a compact, rigid weave are usually best rolled from selvedge to selvedge, rather than from fringe to fringe. Large carpets may have to be folded if space is limited.

If the carpet is to be rolled for long-term storage, it should be done as follows:

Place the carpet upside down on a flat surface. Use a cardboard roller covered with acid-free tissue and, starting from one warp-end, roll the carpet up, interleaving tissue as you roll. A knotted carpet should be rolled so the pile can be stroked downwards. Finally, cover the rolled carpet with tissue and a white dust-sheet, securing it with wide tapes tied firmly but not tightly. (String can cut the foundation and permanently mark the pile.)

The dust-sheet will allow the textile to 'breathe'. Polythene should never be used as it attracts dust, and condensation may build up inside giving rise to mildew.

Glossary

Abrash Variations of colour tone, usually seen as horizontal delineations in the pile, due to subtle differences in dye strength and composition in different batches of wool.

Afshan Design All-over design of flower stems with stepped polygons superimposed and set down the field like medallions. Seen particularly in Caucasian Chila rugs.

Akstafa Large stylized bird, possibly derived from Persian peacock, originating in the Shirvan district of the Caucasus and found in many variations and sizes over a wide region.

Amaranth An azo dye, similar to cochineal and fast to washing, which is often mistaken for a natural dye.

Anatolia The entire area of Turkey to the east of the Bosphorus.

Aniline Dye A basic direct dye made from coaltar derivatives, first used in carpets around 1860 and prevalent in the Middle East by 1880. Pink, violet, blue, and green were among the first colours in widespread use. The dyes are fugitive and fade to unattractive shades. They were banned by the Persian government from 1903, although they continued to be used with deleterious results in other countries.

Animal Combat Pattern Based on fighting animals and derived from the ancient motif of the combat of the dragon and phoenix. First seen in classical Persian and Mughal rugs, more formalized versions seen in Anatolian and Caucasian designs.

Animal Pelt Pattern See Sinekli.

Arabesque Repetitive interlaced and intricate pattern derived from Arab designs based on stem and plant motifs.

Ardebil Carpet Famous Persian carpet made in the 1530s for the Great Mosque of Ardebil in northern Persia, now exhibited at the Victoria & Albert Museum, London.

Asmalyk A Turkoman five-sided camel flank trapping, used to decorate the bride's camel during a wedding.

Asymmetrical Knot Also known as the Persian or Senneh knot. The yarn only encircles one warp of the pair and is described as being open to the left or the right.

Azo Dye A synthetic dye, classified as acid direct, introduced from 1875 to 1890. Usually yellow, orange, red, or violet red. Tends to run easily in water.

Badge of Tamberlaine See Chintamani.

Barbers' Pole Border pattern of multi-coloured diagonal stripes.

Berlin Rug See Marby Rug.

Boktche Turkoman bags made with envelope flaps.

Boteh A design motif, leaf-shaped with a crest or curving top, or shaped rather like a pine-cone or pear. Developed in the seventeenth century out of Persian and Indian flowering plant motifs; later used in a more angular form in Persian, Caucasian, and sometimes Turkish carpets. Recognizable in its most fluid form as the Paisley pattern.

Cairene 1) Carpets with Mamluk (q.v.) designs made in Cairo in the fifteenth and sixteenth centuries. 2) Carpets in the Ottoman (q.v.) style but with Mamluk technique, made either in Cairo, Istanbul, or Bursa in the sixteenth and seventeenth centuries.

Carpet of Roses Pattern of large cabbage roses originating in Karabagh, Caucasus, as a result of demand for carpets 'in the French manner' by Russian officers from the 1850s to the 1880s. The design has persisted ever since.

Cartouche Oval, occasionally rectangular, decorative shape enclosing a design motif.

Cemetery Rug Anatolian prayer rug for burial rituals, with pattern of mausoleum or mosque and cypress trees. *Mazarlik* in Turkish.

Chemical Dye Synthetic dye.

Chemical Wash A trade technique of washing rugs in chemical compounds which gives newly-made rugs a lustrous silky finish similar to a genuine patina acquired only with age and wear. The process also causes rugs to shrink a little, therefore making them denser and firmer, often disguising loose knotting.

Chi'lin A fabulous beast of Chinese origin, roughly resembling a stag.

Chintamani Three circles arranged as a triangle over two wave-lines, of Buddhist origin, symbolizing the three magic wish-granting pearls cast into the sea. Also known as the 'badge of Tamberlaine' or 'Timur's badge' since it later became the emblem of the Timurid state in Central Asia.

Chrome Dye Improved azo dyes, fast and mordanted, introduced in this century. The uniform dyeing of the wool may result in a dead appearance compared with natural dyes.

Chufti See Jufti.

Chuval See Juval.

Cloud Band One of many variations of Chinese origin based on the shape of clouds. In some versions it resembles a ram's horn.

Cloud Collar A flower-like shape derived from the necks of Chinese porcelain vases decorated with four cloud bands. When seen from above the resulting pattern is known as the cloud collar.

Cloud Pattern A repeating shape also derived from Chinese models based on clouds, resembling a trefoil open on one side. Usually found in the main or subsidiary border.

Cochineal Red dye obtained from the crushed and pulverized bodies of insects (*Coccus cacti*).

Compartment Design Term mainly used of Anatolian kilims where the panels of design are framed in individual compartments, often with borders of their own.

Crow's Foot Arrow pattern like the imprint of a bird's foot.

Density See Knot Count.

Depressed Warp Technique of weaving when alternate warps or groups of warps lie on different levels, increasing the thickness and giving the back a ribbed texture.

Djidjim A refined soumak weave, native to the Caucasus, with the back like a knotted carpet.

Djufti See Jufti.

Dosar A Persian term for a large, relatively narrow carpet.

Elephant's Foot Uninformed trade description of Turkoman *gul* pattern.

Engsi A knotted pile rug woven by the Turkoman to cover the entrance to the tent. The cross shape on the

245

four panel design of the field is known as a *hatchli*.

Ertman Gul Large *gul* of the Chodor Turkoman tribe.

Farsh Persian for knotted carpet.

Field The main part of a carpet contained within the borders.

Flea Pattern Tiny boteh (q.v.) repeated in an all-over pattern.

Foundation See Groundweave.

Gabbeh Persian for 'fringe'. Also means unclipped or shaggy-piled carpets in Persian.

Gelim Persian for kilim (q.v.).

Ghali See Khali.

Ghiordes Knot See Symmetrical Knot.

Glaoua Lustrous black-piled rugs made by the High Atlas Berbers, Morocco.

Graveyard Rug See Cemetery Rug, Mazarlik.

Groundweave Foundation of carpet comprising warp and weft.

Gtifa Traditional red-piled rugs woven by the Tennsift River Arabs, Morocco.

Guard Stripe A narrow stripe between borders, or between border and field.

Gul An angular, usually octagonal, motif found primarily in Turkoman carpets. The different designs of these motifs can often be related to specific tribes and they appear to be heraldic emblems.

Hali Turkish for carpet. See Khali.

Hatchli See Engsi.

Hejira (Hijra) 622 AD was the date of the Hejira, the flight of the Prophet Mahomet from Mecca, and is the start of the Muslim calendar. Dates knotted in the pile of carpets give the number of years after the Hejira, but it must be remembered that the Mus-

lim calendar is based on the lunar year which is eleven days longer than the solar year on which the Christian calendar is based. For a rough dating, add 583 (the number of solar years in 622 lunar years) to the woven date.

Herati Named after the town of Herat, now in Afghanistan, where the design is supposed to have originated. The Herati pattern consists of a lozenge of stems terminating in flower-heads surrounding a central rosette, with four lanceolate leaves curving symmetrically between the flower-heads. Found in many variations – angular, geometric, naturalistic, and formalized in carpets from almost every area.

Heybeh Turkish for saddlebag.

Holbein Name given to fifteenth-century Turkish rugs with geometric designs which appear in paintings by Hans Holbein (1497/8–1543). 'Small-pattern Holbein' carpets have rows of lozenges and octagons, while 'large-pattern Holbeins' frequently have large octagons within squares. Holbein pattern rugs mainly have kufesque borders (q.v.) and also appear in paintings by Bellini, Ghirlandaio, Crivelli, and Pintoricchio.

In-and-Out Palmette Pattern A design in which two pairs of leaf palmettes face alternatively inwards and outwards at the intersections of scrolling arabesques. Secondary palmettes, or blossoms and cloud bands, fill the lozenge-shaped area formed by the latter. It was first used in sixteenth-century Indo-Persian rugs and later developed into the Herati (q.v.) and Afshan (q.v.) designs.

Indigo A blue vat dye obtained from the crushed

leaves of the indigo plant. Made synthetically from about 1890. Natural indigo was prepared in India and exported to Persia and other countries.

Indo-Isfahan Also Indo-Persian or Herat. Sixteenth-century carpets with an in-and-out palmette design (q.v.) made in both India and Persia.

Islamic Calendar See Hejira.

Iznik Town in north-west Anatolia where pottery vessels and tiles were made for the Ottoman court from the end of the fifteenth century.

Jufti Also chufti, djufti. 'False knot' tied over four or more warps. Used in parts of Persia, Spain, and more recently in Pakistan.

Juval A large Turkoman tent bag.

Kapunuk A Turkoman camel trapping forming part of the bride's canopy during marriage rituals. Probably used afterwards as a lintel cover for a tent entrance.

Karamani, karamanli Obsolete generic term for Anatolian kilims, the name being taken from a town near Konya where fine flat weaves were made.

Kazak One of two main groups of Caucasian carpets, distinguished by the fact that they have a fringe at one end only, the top end being finished by turning over and stitching down to the back.

Kellegi A Persian rug measuring approximately 3.5 by 1.5 metres (11½ by 5 feet).

Kenareh A Persian runner carpet measuring approximately 5 by 1 metres (16½ by 3 feet).

Kermes An insect which breeds on the kermes oak, the female producing a red dye similar to lac and cochineal (q.v.).

Khali Persian for a large

knotted pile rug.

Khalyk A camel trapping covering the chest of the animal during Turkoman marriage rituals.

Khilin See Chi'lin.

Kilim A pileless carpet woven in the slit-tapestry technique.

Kis Kilim Anatolian kilim woven as part of a bride's dowry, often interwoven with silver thread.

Knot Count The number of knots per square decimetre or inch, which determines the density or gauge of a carpet. As a rough guide the following table may be useful:

Very coarse:
up to 500 per dm²
(33 per square inch)
Coarse:
500–1000 per dm²
(33–66 per square inch)
Medium:
900–1800 per dm²
(60–120 per square inch)
Fine:
1800–2500 per dm²
(120–166 per square inch)
Very fine:
2500–4500 per dm²
(166–300 per square inch)
Fine silk carpets have a knot count of 15,000 or more per dm² (1000 per square inch).

Kufesque Stylized use of the Arabic Kufic script, particularly in the borders of carpets. Many Islamic artefacts embody some decorative use of this script.

Kuba One of two main groups of Caucasian carpets, distinguished by having cut fringes at both ends of the carpet.

Kurds These tribes are both settled and nomadic. They live in northern and western Anatolia on the borders of Iran and Turkey, and in Kurdistan in north-west Iran. Their weavings are usually of sombre colouring and limited palette, and some nomad work which is not attributable with any greater accuracy is often described as Kurdish.

Lac A deep crimson-red dye obtained from the extract of the female *Tachardia lacca*, an insect indigenous to India.

Lotto Carpets Lorenzo Lotto (c.1480–c.1556) twice included distinctively patterned carpets from Anatolia, possibly from the region of Ushak, in his paintings. These have a design of a yellow lattice on a red ground, contained within either a kufesque or a cartouche border (q.v.).

Madder Dye made from the roots of the madder plant (*Rubia tinctorium*) which is native throughout the Middle East. The colours include reds, oranges, pinks, browns, and purples.

Mafrash A small Turkoman tent bag.

Mamluk Period of Egyptian government by a military regime from the mid-thirteenth century until the early sixteenth century, giving its name to a unique group of oriental carpets. Two of the most famous examples are the silk Mamluk carpet in Vienna and the Medici carpet in the Pitti Palace, Florence.

Marby Rug One of the earliest surviving Turkish pilewoven carpets, dating from the fifteenth century, with a design of birds flanking a tree. Found in Marby church, Jämtland, Sweden and exhibited in the Historiska Museum, Stockholm. The Berlin rug, of similar date and design, was discovered by Wilhelm von Bode in a central Italian church in 1886 and is now in the Berlin Museum, of which von Bode was director.

Mazarlik See Cemetery rug.

Meander A continuous wave-like border pattern.

Memling Motif This is seen in the earliest group of carpets to be depicted in European paintings, namely those by the artist Hans Memling (1430/5–94). The motif comprises *gul*-like octagons containing stepped lozenges with hooked outlines. These octagons may be arranged in straight or offset rows. The motif is found in Anatolian, Caucasian, and north-west Persian rugs down to the present day.

Met-Haneh A particular pattern of Caucasian Talish runner with stars or rosettes in the borders, but with a plain field.

Mian Farsh Persian main carpet approximately 5 by 2.25 metres (16½ by 7½ feet).

Mihrab The prayer niche of a mosque, orientated towards the holy city of Mecca. Often represented on prayer rugs.

Mina Khani A repeating pattern of large flower heads each with small white flowers set in a diamond round it and joined in a lattice pattern.

Mordant Metal hydroxides used with mordant dyes to fix the dye in the yarn. Iron mordants can corrode the wool.

Mordant Dye Dye, made from acidic compounds, that has to be fixed to the yarn with a mordant.

Mughal This dynasty was established in India by Babur, a Turk from Uzbekistan, in 1526 and lasted until 1858. The finest Mughal carpets were woven in the sixteenth and seventeenth centuries.

Namazlyk A Turkoman prayer rug.

Odshalyk Double-ended mihrab (q.v.), in appearance often more like an elongated hexagon with gable ends, found in some Anatolian prayer mats and carpet designs.

Osmalyk See Asmalyk.

Osmanli See Ottoman.

Ottoman The dynasty founded in north-western Anatolia by Osman 1 (reigned 1281–1324). At its height, in the sixteenth century, it extended from Algeria, through Egypt to the shores of the Caspian Sea, north as far as Bessarabia, and westwards to Hungary. It finally disintegrated after the First World War.

Palas Caucasian name for kilim.

Palmette A floral form which probably takes its name from the palm frond which it resembled in Assyrian times. It may resemble a sliced artichoke, a vine leaf, or a stiffly drawn lotus blossom.

Pashm Fine, soft goat wool to be found in Mughal (q.v.) carpets.

Pazyryk Rug Believed to have been made in the fourth or fifth century BC, this famous rug with animal and warrior motifs was found in 1947 in the Altai Mountains of southern Siberia in a Scythian gravemound. It is exhibited in the Hermitage Museum, Leningrad.

Persian Knot See Asymmetrical knot.

Pine Cone Pattern See Boteh.

Plain Weave A simple weave pattern in which the weft passes alternatively over and under each warp. Often used to finish the ends of carpets.

Polonaise Fine silk rugs with gold and silver brocade, usually on a cotton foundation, made in the first half of the seventeenth century, possibly in Isfahan. Frequently exported to Europe, some incorporated Polish arms and armorials – hence the name. A small number of similar rugs were made in Kashan at the beginning of this century, using metallic thread instead of real gold and silver thread, and occasionally one of these turns up in the West.

Portuguese This term is used in carpet terminology to describe a group of carpets which feature marine scenes in the corners with figures in European dress. They date from the sixteenth century and were woven either in India or Persia.

Running Dog Hooked border motif common in Caucasian carpets and rugs and some Anatolian pile rugs and flat weaves.

Saf A prayer rug, wider than long, with a horizontal row of prayer niches, flat or pile woven. Also known as a *saph*.

Safavid The Safavid dynasty was established in 1501 by Shah Ismail 1, then aged 14, after the defeat of the Timurids (q.v.). At its peak it stretched from the Euphrates to Khorasan. It came to an end in 1721.

Salachak A Turkoman child's rug.

Salting Carpet A carpet, now in the Victoria and Albert Museum, London, which was probably woven in Istanbul in the nineteenth century. It was once thought to be a sixteenth-century Persian piece.

Sanguzsko This term describes a group of sixteenth-century Persian carpets, possibly woven in Kashan, with a design of a central medallion combined with animals. The group is named after the medallion carpet now in the possession of Prince Sanguzsko in Paris.

Sassanian Ancient dynasty which ruled the Persian Empire from 211–651 AD.

Saz The Ottoman court style, to be seen in all the decorative arts, featuring feathery curved leaves, rosettes, lotus palmettes, and stylized flowers. It first developed in the middle of the sixteenth century.

Sejjade A prayer rug, approximately 1 by 1.5 metres (3 by 5 feet), suitable for one person's exercise of the Islamic prayer ritual.

Seljuk Turkic-speaking conquerors from Turkestan and Central Asia who over-ran Asia Minor in the eleventh and twelfth centuries. They made Konya their capital city and ruled until overthrown by the Ottoman Turks in the fifteenth century.

Selvedge The finished side edges of a rug or carpet.

Senneh Knot See Asymmetrical knot.

Shaddah See Verneh.

Shah Abbas Ruler of the Persian Safavid Empire from 1587–1629.

Shobakli Anatolian border design consisting of a series of narrow stripes with small ornament.

Sileh A form of Caucasian soumak weaving. The term usually refers to narrow strips with giant S-motifs, possibly derived from the dragon shape, sewn together into larger widths.

Sinekli Small scatter pattern resembling tiny flower-heads, often no more than little circles, found in Turkish carpets as a field pattern and in some Caucasian rugs e.g. Kula. Literally means 'fly specks' and occasionally called 'animal pelt' pattern.

Smyrna The old name for Izmir, a port on the west coast of Turkey. A wide range of inferior carpets in derivative designs were exported to the West through this port in the eighteenth and nineteenth centuries. They are therefore known as Smyrna carpets.

Soumak A flat-weave technique employing a floating weft and giving a thick matted back.

S-Plied Two or more strands of wool plied together in a clockwise direction.

S-Spun Yarn spun in a clockwise direction. See also Z-plied and Z-spun.

Stem, Stem Scroll Curling motif bracketing flowerheads or by itself, either repeated or continuous, found in borders of carpets from almost every area in one variation or another. In its ultimate reduction it becomes the Caucasian 'running dog' border.

Stepped Warp See Depressed Warp.

Sufi, Sufism The ancient Islamic mystic sect, largely Saracenic in origin, whose principal disseminators were poets and artists, notably Mohammed El-Ghazali 'The Spinner' (1058–1111), Ibn El-Arabi, a Spanish Arab (1165–1240), and Jalaluddin Rumi, the Persian Sufi poet (d. 1273). Constantly under threat of persecution from orthodox religions, the Sufis had an elaborate secret language of symbols which were woven into many textiles and carpets, including the palm tree containing the nine elements, the magic square of fifteen, a tiger dragging down a camel, and the pillars of Sufi knowledge. Even wool itself, in which the Sufis clothed themselves, had a mystic meaning.

Suzaneh Large embroidered hangings or curtains from East Turkestan and Central Asia.

Symmetrical Knot Also known as the Turkish or Ghiordes knot. The cut ends of the warp emerge in the middle of the two warps around which it has been tied.

Synthetic Dye See Aniline, Chrome, and Azo.

Tauk Nosha Gul A Turkoman *gul* (q.v.), with eight little stylized animals, used by the Yomut, Arabatchi, Kizil Ayak, Chodor, and Ersari.

Temirchen Gul A Turkoman *gul* (q.v.), used by the Saryk and the Ersari, which incorporates a motif of overlapping arrow heads.

Timurid The dynasty established by Timur (or Tamberlaine) between 1380 and 1405. The Timurids were of mixed Mongol and Turkic stock and their empire extended from Tashkent to Mesopotamia. Though renowned for their cruelty, the Timurids were great patrons of the arts and their curvilinear decorative style was influential in carpet designs. They were defeated in 1501 by the Safavids (q.v.).

Torba A shallow Turkoman wall bag, to be suspended from the trellis of the tent.

Transylvanian Carpets Prayer carpets of the *sejjade* format (q.v.), generally incorporating a centralized design with corner spandrels. So-named since many of them have been found in Rumania and Hungary.

Turkic Refers to peoples and cultures from all over west and central Asia, bound together by the use of Turkic languages (Khirgiz, Kipchak, Yakut, Cumanic, Uzbek, Turkmen etc).

Turkish Refers to peoples of a specific Turkic group, those living mainly in what is today the Republic of Turkey, but also in the Balkans and other regions adjoining Turkey.

Turkish Knot See Symmetrical Knot.

Turkmen Properly spelt with an umlaut (Türkmen) refers to nomadic Turkic peoples from any part of west and central Asia. Also known as Turkoman.

Vase Carpet Technique A weaving technique, employed in sixteenth-century Persian Vase carpets, which gives a depressed warp (q.v.).

Verneh A Caucasian term usually used for a flatwoven rug made of narrow strips sewn together and brocaded.

Warp The vertical threads of a carpet. The warp is strung on the empty loom and provides the framework for weaving.

Wave Scroll A fluid, flattened scroll, otherwise similar to a stem scroll. Turkoman carpets feature an extremely angular version of the wave scroll.

Weft The horizontal continuous thread woven into the warp. One or more shoots of weft thread usually separates the rows of knots which are tied to the warp.

Weld A yellow dye extracted from the *Reselda lutuola* plant.

Yastik Turkish for small rugs or the faces of cushion and bolster covers.

Yolami A Turkoman tent band.

Yuruk A Turkish word meaning pastoral nomad.

Ziegler The Manchester firm established in 1883 in Arak, Persia. It was Zieglers who discovered the Ardebil carpet and sold it to the Victoria & Albert Museum.

Z-Plied Two or more strands of yarn plied together in an anti-clockwise direction.

Z-Spun Yarn spun in an anti-clockwise direction. See also S-plied and S-spun.

Select Bibliography

ARTS COUNCIL OF GREAT BRITAIN, *The Arts of Islam*, (exhibition catalogue), London, 1976

ARTS COUNCIL OF GREAT BRITAIN, *The Eastern Carpet in the Western World*, (exhibition catalogue), London, 1983

ARTS COUNCIL OF GREAT BRITAIN, *Islamic Carpets from the Joseph V. McMullan Collection*, (exhibition catalogue), London, 1972

AZADI, SIAWOSCH, *Turkoman Carpets*, Fishguard, 1975

BALPINAR, BELKIS and HIRSCH, UDO, *Flatweaves of the Vakiflar Museum, Istanbul*, Wesel, 1982

BEATTIE, MAY, *The Thyssen-Bornemisza Collection of Oriental Rugs*, Castagnola, 1972

BEATTIE, MAY, *Carpets of Central Persia*, (exhibition catalogue), Sheffield, 1976

BIDDER, HANS, *Carpets from Eastern Turkestan*, London, 1964

BODE, W. VON and KÜHNEL, ERNST, *Antique Rugs from the Near East*, (trans. Charles Grant Ellis), London, 1970

BOGOLYUBOV, A.A., *Carpets of Central Asia*, (ed. Jon Thompson), Ramsdell, 1973

DENWOOD, P., *The Tibetan Carpet*, London, 1974

DILLEY, A.H., *Oriental Rugs and Carpets*, (revised by M.S. Dimand), New York, 1959

DIMAND, MAURICE S. and MAILEY, JEAN, *Oriental Rugs in the Metropolitan Museum of Art*, New York, 1973

EDWARDS, A.C., *The Persian Carpet*, (revised edition), London, 1975

EILAND, MURRAY L., *Oriental Rugs*, (2nd edition), New York, 1976

EILAND, MURRAY L., *Chinese and Exotic Rugs*, London and Boston, 1979

ELLIS, CHARLES GRANT, *Early Caucasian Rugs*, Textile Museum, Washington, 1976

EMERY, IRENE, *The Primary Structure of Fabrics*, Textile Museum, Washington, 1965

ERDMANN, KURT, *Seven Hundred Years of Oriental Carpets*, (trans. May Beattie and Hildegard Herzog), London, 1970

ERDMANN, KURT, *Oriental Carpets, an Account of their History*. (trans. Charles Grant Ellis), Fishguard, 1976

ERDMANN, KURT, *The History of the Early Turkish Carpet*, London, 1977

HOUSEGO, J., *Tribal Rugs*, London, 1978

ITEN-MARITZ, J., *Turkish Carpets*, New York, 1975

JARRY, M., *The Carpets of the Manufacture de la Savonnerie*, Leigh-on-Sea, 1966

JARRY, M., *Carpets of Aubusson*, Leigh-on-Sea, 1966

KENDRICK, A.F. and TATTERSALL, C.E.C., *Handwoven Carpets, Oriental and European*, New York, 1973

KONIECZNY, M.G., *Textiles of Baluchistan*, London, 1979

KÜHNEL, ERNST and BELLINGER, L., *The Textile Museum Catalogue Raisonné: Cairene Rugs and others technically related, 15th–17th centuries*, Washington, 1957

LOGES, WERNER, *Turkoman Tribal Rugs*, London, 1980

LORENTZ, H.A., *A View of Chinese Rugs from the Seventeenth to the Twentieth Century*, London, 1972

MACKIE, LOUISE W. and THOMPSON, JON, *Turkmen–Tribal Carpets and Traditions*, Textile Museum, Washington, 1980

MARTIN, F.R., *A History of Oriental Carpets before 1800*, Vienna, 1908

MCMULLAN, JOSEPH V., *Islamic Carpets*, New York, 1965

NEFF, IVAN C. *Dictionary of Oriental Rugs*, London, 1977

OPIE, JAMES, *Tribal Rugs of Southern Persia*, Portland, 1981

PETSOPOULOS, Y., *Kilims – The Art of Tapestry Weaving in Anatolia, the Caucasus and Persia*, London, 1979

PONTING, K.G., *A Dictionary of Dyes and Dyeing*, London, 1980

POPE, A.U., *Introduction to Persian Art*, London, 1930

RUDENKO, SERGEI, *Frozen Tombs of Siberia*, (trans. Dr M.W. Thompson), London, 1970

SCHÜRMANN, ULRICH, *Central Asian Rugs*, London, 1969

SCHÜRMAN, ULRICH, *Caucasian Rugs*, London, 1974

TATTERSALL, C.E.C., *A History of British Carpets*, Leigh-on-Sea, 1966

THOMPSON, JON, *Carpet Magic*, London, 1983

TSCHEBULL, RAOUL, *Kazak, Carpets of the Caucasus*, New York, 1971

YETKIN, SERARE, *Historical Turkish Carpets*, Istanbul, 1981

Index

INDEX

Acknowledgements

The copyright owners, consultant editor, and publishers would like to thank the private collectors who have given permission for their carpets to be reproduced. They also gratefully acknowledge the following for their kind assistance:

Chris Farr

Michael Franses

P. G. Gates

William Robinson

Yasin Safadi

Jackie Stanger

Annette Valeo

Dave Ward

The extract on page 243 from the *National Trust Manual of Housekeeping* by Hermione Sandwith and Sheila Stainton (Allen Lane in association with the National Trust, 1984, © The National Trust, 1984, p.200) is reprinted by permission of Penguin Books Ltd.

Picture credits:

Academy of Sciences of U.S.S.R.: 44b, 47ab (adapted from *Kultura Nasaleniya Gornogo Altaya v Skilfskoe Vremya*, Moscow, 1953)
Felicity Ashbee: 111a
Anthony Berlant: 235abc, 236a
David Black: 11a, 109b, 113c, 155b

David Black and Clive Loveless: 86a, 91b, 93ab, 95b, 97c, 99b, 101b, 103b, 105b, 107ab, 113ab, 115ab, 117bc, 119ab, 121abc, 123abc, 125abc, 127c, 129abc, 133abc, 135c, 137abc, 139abc, 145c, 149abc, 151abc, 153c, 155ac, 157abc, 159abc, 162a, 165a, 169a, 171a, 173a, 201a
Vojtech Blau: 8a, 143c
British Museum: 25a (add. 25900 Folio 3 verso), 67a (add. 18113 Folio 45 verso)
Christie's: 91a, 95a, 97ab, 99a, 101a, 103a, 105a, 117a, 135ab, 141abc, 143ab, 145ab, 147ab, 153ab, 197abc
Steven Cohen: 201b
Douglas Dickins: 12a
Yusuf Durul: 45ab
John Eskenazi: 179b, 181abc, 187a, 189abc, 191bc, 193bc
Michael Franses: 119c, 127ab, 161a, 163a, 167ab, 169b, 171b, 173b, 175b, 183a
Gabinetto Fotografico SBAS Firenze: 62b, 63a
Sonia Halliday Photographs: 6a, 22a, 26b, 244a
Robert Harding Picture Library: 10a, 24a, 88a
John McCarthy: 220b
Jane Nylander: 229a
Oxford University Press: 32abc (adapted from *A Survey of Persian Art* by A. U. Pope and P. Ackerman, second edition 1965)
Josephine Powell: 14ab, 15ab
Smithsonian Institution: 230a (photo no. 2422-a)
Tolga Tollu: 109a
Vigo Carpet Gallery: 198b
Mark Whiting: 24b
Roger Wood: 130a, 163c, 241a
World of Islam Festival Trust and May Beattie: 29b (adapted from *The Carpets of Central Asia*, Sheffield, 1976)